Programming Distributed Systems

Programming Distributed Systems

Henri Bal

SILICON PRESS

PRENTICE HALL
New York   London   Toronto   Sydney   Tokyo   Singapore

Library of Congress Cataloging in Publication Data

is available from the publisher

British Library Cataloguing in Publication Data

Bal, Henri E.
  Programming distributed systems.
  I. Title
  005.13

  ISBN 0–13–722083–9

1 2 3 4 5 95 94 93 92 91

This book is a revision of the author's Ph.D. thesis. Parts of Chapters 1, 3, and 4 have been
previously published in the *ACM Computing Surveys*. Parts of Chapter 2 have been previously
published in the *Proceedings of the AFIPS National Computer Conference 1987*. Parts of
Chapters 5 and 6 have been previously published in the *Proceedings of the IEEE Computer
Society 1988 International Conference on Computer Languages*. Parts of Chapter 7 have been
previously published in the *Proceedings of the USENIX Workshop on Experiences with Building
Distributed and Multiprocessor Systems*. This research was supported in part by the Netherlands
organization for scientific research (N.W.O.) under grant 125-30-10.

Contents

3   Language Support for Programming Distributed Systems

4   Languages for Programming Distributed Systems

5   The Shared Data-object Model

Preface

Distributed systems consisting of multiple autonomous computers connected through a network are becoming commonplace. Frequently, such systems are used for running different jobs or services on different machines. This book, however, is concerned with how multiple computers can cooperate in executing single jobs. In particular, the book discusses how the turnaround time of a job can be reduced by running different pieces of a job in parallel on multiple machines.

The book discusses a new model for implementing user applications on distributed systems. The proposed model, called the *shared data-object model*, is intended to ease distributed programming by providing a communication mechanism that hides the physical distribution of the underlying system. In this way, it combines the advantages of distributed systems (good price/performance ratio and extensibility) and shared-memory multiprocessors (relative ease of programming). Also, the book describes a new language based on this model and it discusses the implementation, usage, and performance of this language.

The book first defines the term 'distributed system', to avoid confusion on this controversial point. The systems covered by the definition include message-passing multicomputers and collections of workstations connected through a network. Distributed systems can be used for a broad spectrum of applications, for example high-performance parallel applications and fault-tolerant applications. The book is mainly concerned with parallel applications.

Three issues distinguish programming these systems from programming uniprocessors: the use of multiple processors, the cooperation among the processors, and the potential for partial failure. Programming support for these three issues may either be given by the operating system or by a programming language.

In the first case, the distributed system is programmed in an existing sequential language extended with library routines that invoke operating system primitives. In Chapter 2, this option is considered. Two parallel applications are implemented in C on top of the Amoeba distributed operating system, using remote procedure call for interprocess communication. The performance of these two programs is described and several important problems with this approach are identified.

In the remaining chapters, the second approach, using a language designed for distributed programming, is studied. Chapter 3 gives a survey of the state of the art in research on language support for distributed programming. Chapter 4 describes several important languages in some detail. These two chapters cover a broad spectrum of language primitives, including synchronous message-passing, asynchronous message-passing, rendezvous, remote procedure call, objects, atomic transactions, functional parallelism, shared logical variables, and distributed data structures. A critical evaluation of these primitives shows they have many shortcomings when used for distributed application programming.

The shared data-object model is introduced in Chapter 5. In this model, shared data are encapsulated in data objects, which are instances of user-defined abstract data types. A data object may be shared between the process that created the object and its descendants. Each process sharing the object can apply the operations defined by the object's abstract data type. All these operations are executed indivisibly, so mutual exclusion synchronization is done implicitly. Condition synchronization is expressed by allowing operations to block.

A simple, type-secure, procedural language based on this model is also described in Chapter 5. The language, called Orca, supports dynamic process creation, abstract data types, a variety of data structures, and also generic types and modules. It is designed especially for distributed programming and integrates the sequential and distributed constructs in a clean way.

The implementation of the language is discussed in Chapter 6. The most important issue in a distributed implementation is efficient management of shared data-objects. The key idea is to replicate each object on those processors that frequently use it, to reduce interprocess communication. An operation that only reads (but does not modify) its object can then be applied to the local copy of the object, without doing any communication.

Different replication strategies are discussed and protocols are described for updating the replicas of an object in a consistent way. Two of these protocols have been implemented in two prototype run time systems, using an Ethernet-based distributed system. For comparison, a third RTS has been written that runs on a nondistributed system (a shared-memory multiprocessor). All three RTSs use the same compiler, which has been built with the Amsterdam Compiler Kit.

The three RTSs have been used for developing several parallel applications in Orca. In Chapter 7, five of these applications are described in detail. Also, performance measurements for these programs are given. The measurements show that significant speedups can be obtained on all three RTSs. A larger application, a parallel chess problem solver is also described briefly.

In the last chapter, some conclusions and ideas for future research are presented. The appendices of the book show the source code of the programs discussed in Chapter 7 and give detailed information on the performance measurements described in Chapters 2 and 7. Finally, an extensive bibliography with more than 300 references is given.

Acknowledgements

The book is based on research being done at the Vrije Universiteit in Amsterdam. The research studies how to program applications for distributed systems, such as the Amoeba system, which also originated at the Vrije Universiteit. The book describes the results obtained during the first five years of the project.

The first step in the research was to implement several parallel distributed applications on Amoeba, using a sequential language extended with library routines for invoking Amoeba's communication primitives. This part of the research was carried out by Robbert van Renesse and me. Although we managed to get some interesting applications up and running, the exercise showed us that distributed programming is far from easy, especially when using a language that is not intended for implementing distributed applications.

From then on, the research focused on language support for distributed programming. I followed two different directions: the study of existing languages for distributed programming and the development of a new language.

The study of programming languages for distributed systems was a joint effort with Jennifer Steiner and Andy Tanenbaum. It resulted in an extensive survey paper, which has been published in *ACM Computing Surveys*. (Most of the paper is also contained in Chapters 1, 3, and 4 of the book.) Here, I wish to express my gratitude to Jennifer for her enormous efforts invested in the paper.

The second research direction was the development of a new language for distributed application programming. This language was eventually called *Orca*, out of displeasure with acronyms and in awe of killer whales. During the design of Orca, I received useful feedback from many people, especially Andy Tanenbaum, Dick Grune, and, at an earlier stage, Nick Carriero.

The implementation of Orca has been worked on in parallel by several people. Frans Kaashoek did a splendid job implementing an Orca run-time system on top of an Ethernet-based distributed system. Owing to his fast, reliable, broadcast protocol, the performance of this implementation is very good. Since Orca is intended for speeding up distributed applications, it is crucial to have such an implementation.

Frans' work was thus of great value to me. I would also like to thank Frans for the many discussions we had on language and implementation issues.

Jack Jansen implemented a heuristic run-time system, using Amoeba RPC for inter-process communication. For most programs, this implementation achieves somewhat lower performance than the broadcast system. Still, Jack's work is very useful, as it allows us to compare the performance of Orca on broadcast and point-to-point networks.

I was also very fortunate to have the help of Wim van Leersum, who implemented the compiler front end for Orca. In addition, Wim helped debug the run-time systems and made various improvements to the language definition.

Also, I would like to thank Ceriel Jacobs for his help on the compiler, Hans van Staveren and Greg Sharp for their assistance on Amoeba and for allowing me to use 'their' pool processors, and Leo van Moergestel for keeping the hardware in good shape as much as possible.

Creating a new language is pointless without also having someone use it. Fortunately, several people were interested in using Orca. Robert-Jan Elias wrote a parallel chess problem solver, the largest application implemented so far. Rien van Veldhuizen implemented several numerical applications. Arnold Geels has worked on an implementation of a distributed backtracking package. I would like to thank them for their interest in the language.

A number of people, including Frans Kaashoek, Arnold Geels, Erik Baalbergen, Dick Grune, and Susan Flynn-Hummel have read the draft of the book and provided useful comments on it. I am also very grateful to Nick Carriero, who has suggested many important improvements. About thirty people provided comments on the Computing Surveys paper, so they have contributed indirectly to this book. Here, I will confine myself to thanking Peter Wegner, the guest editor of the special issue in which the paper has been published.

The book has been written using troff and most of its preprocessors. It would not have looked the way it does now, however, without Robbert van Renesse's macro package, which takes care of running headers, the table of contents, the index, references, figures, page balancing, and much more.

I would also like to thank the Netherlands Organization for Scientific Research (NWO) for supporting the project, Ed Keizer for his help with troff, and Maarten van der Meulen for his work on parallel chess.

Finally and most importantly, I would like to thank Andy Tanenbaum. Andy has contributed many inspiring ideas. Also, he has made numerous important improvements to this book. I am very grateful to him for his support and encouragements.

CHAPTER 1

Introduction

Distributed computing systems are gradually evolving from laboratory curiosities into production systems that can be used for real applications. Research on architectures and interconnection networks has resulted in low-cost distributed systems with large numbers of powerful processors that can communicate at high speeds. Research on distributed operating systems has produced ways for employing this high computing potential by dividing the total workload among the available processors. By executing different programs on different processors, the system will have a high throughput. Some system programs (e.g. a file server) may also be distributed among multiple processors, to achieve higher speed and higher reliability. Many user applications can also benefit from such distribution, for the same reasons. The task of distributing a single user program among multiple processors, however, clearly falls outside the scope of an operating system. Thus, to achieve this distribution, extra effort is required from the applications programmers. In this book, we will look at ways of minimizing this effort.

In general, there are several different approaches for facilitating the implementation of distributed applications. One way is to take an existing sequential language and to extend it with library routines that invoke operating system primitives for creating processes and sending messages. Such a library is easy to implement. This method is frequently used by commercial systems. As we will see, however, this approach also has severe disadvantages and still leaves most of the real problems to the applications programmer.

At the other extreme, one can envision a clever compiler that takes a sequential program as input and automatically generates output code that runs on multiple processors. This time, the applications programmer is relieved of all worries related to distribution. Unfortunately, the implementation of such a compiler is difficult, if not impossible. In any event, it is far beyond the current state of the art in compiler technology.

The approach taken in this book is to provide the applications programmer with suitable language support for distributed programming. The intent in using a new language for distributed programming is to hide as much of the underlying distributed hardware as is practical, without requiring miracles of the compiler. Put in a nutshell, we have designed a new language based on a computational model with explicit parallelism but implicit communication. Parallel execution is under the control of the programmer, but the physical distribution of the hardware is hidden from the programmer, by providing a communication model based on shared data. In other words, programmers have to deal with parallelism, but not with the physical (message passing) communication between processors. This approach is new, and we believe, highly promising.

Below, we first give our view of what a distributed system is, illustrating it with examples to avoid confusion on this important and controversial point. We elaborate this definition by giving four classes of application that might be executed on distributed systems. Then we describe the three main characteristics that distinguish distributed programming languages from ordinary sequential languages, namely, how they deal with parallelism, communication, and partial failures. After that we give a brief, initial overview of the different language models used for distributed programming. (A much more detailed discussion will be given in Chapter 3.) Finally, we present an overview of our research, including the goals we are trying to achieve, the relation with other research projects, and the organization of the rest of this book.

1.1   Distributed computing systems

There is considerable disagreement in the literature as to what a distributed computing system is. Among the many definitions that we have seen, there is only one point of agreement: they all require the presence of multiple processors. The confusion may be due to the large number of different architectural models one finds in multiple processor systems. *Vector computers*, for example, use many processors that simultaneously apply the same arithmetic operations to different data [Russell, 1978]. They are best suited to computation-intensive numerical applications. *Dataflow* and *reduction machines* apply different operations to different data [Treleaven *et al.*, 1982]. *Multiprocessors* consist of several autonomous processors sharing a common primary memory [Jones and Schwarz, 1980]. These are well suited for running different subtasks of the same program simultaneously. *Multicomputers* are similar to multiprocessors, except that the processors do not share memory, but rather communicate by sending messages over a communications network [Athas and Seitz, 1988]. As a final example, there are systems comprised of workstations or minicomputers connected by a local- or wide-area network. This type of system is frequently the target for distributed operating systems [Tanenbaum and Van Renesse, 1985]. (We will refer to these latter two systems as *workstation LANs* and *workstation WANs*.)

Experts strongly disagree as to which architectures are to be considered distributed systems. Some people claim all of the configurations mentioned above fall under this category. Others include only geographically distributed computers connected by a wide area network. Every combination between these two extremes also has its defenders. The meaning we intend to convey by our use of the term *distributed computing system* is the following:

Definition: A distributed computing system consists of multiple autonomous processors that do not share primary memory, but cooperate by sending messages over a communications network.

We will sometimes also use the term 'distributed system' as a shorthand notation for 'distributed computing system.'

Each processor in such a system executes its own instruction stream(s) and uses its own local data, both stored in its local memory. Occasionally, processors may need to exchange data; they do so by sending messages to each other over a network. Many different types of network exist (e.g. a hypercube, a local area network, a wide area network), as will be discussed below. Although these networks have very different physical properties, they all fit into the same model: they are a medium for transferring messages among processors (see Figure 1.1a). Distributed systems can be contrasted with multiprocessors, in which processors communicate through a shared memory (see Figure 1.1b). Both distributed systems and multiprocessors belong in the MIMD (multiple instruction multiple data streams) of Flynn's classification [Flynn, 1972].

Of the architectures mentioned in the list of examples above, multicomputers, workstation LANs, and workstation WANs qualify as distributed computing systems; vector computers, dataflow and reduction machines, and multiprocessors do not. We do not intend to claim, however, that programming support for distributed systems always is different from that for nondistributed systems. For example, several researchers have looked at unified models for programming many different parallel architectures [Chandy and Misra, 1988; Browne *et al.*, 1989]. The definition given above merely delimits the kinds of system studied in this book.

Distributed systems can be characterized by their interconnection networks. The network determines the speed and reliability of interprocessor communication, and the spatial distribution of the processors. Traditionally, a distributed architecture in which communication is fast and reliable and where processors are physically close to one another is said to be *closely coupled* (or tightly coupled); systems with slow and unreliable communication between processors that are physically dispersed are termed *loosely coupled*.

Closely coupled distributed systems use a communications network consisting of fast, reliable, point-to-point links, which connect each processor to some subset of the other processors. Examples of such systems are: the Cosmic Cube [Seitz, 1985], hypercubes [Ranka *et al.*, 1988], and Transputer® networks [May and Shepherd, 1984]. Communication times for this type of system used to be in the order of a millisecond, but are expected to drop to less than a microsecond in the near future [Athas and Seitz, 1988].

A more loosely coupled type of distributed system is a workstation LAN. The local area network allows direct communication between any two processors. Communica-

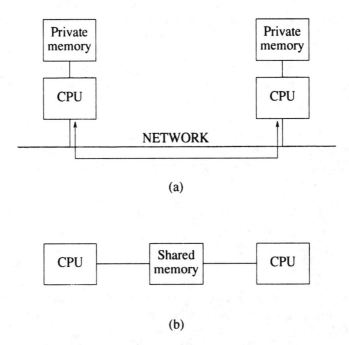

(a)

(b)

Figure 1.1 *(a) Communication in distributed systems versus (b) shared-memory multiprocessors.*

tion cost is typically in the order of a millisecond. In many LANs, communication is not totally reliable. Occasionally, a message may be damaged, arrive out of order, or not arrive at its destination at all. Software protocols must be used to implement reliable communication.

A LAN limits the physical distance between processors to a few kilometres. To interconnect processors that are farther apart, a wide area network is needed. A workstation WAN can be seen as a very loosely coupled distributed system. Communication in a WAN is slower and less reliable than in a LAN; communication cost may be in the order of seconds. On the other hand, the increased availability of wide area lines at speeds above 1 Mbit/s (e.g. T1 lines in the USA), will blur the distinction between LANs and WANs in the future.

In summary, there is a *spectrum* of distributed computing systems, ranging from closely coupled to very loosely coupled. Although communication speed and reliability decrease from one end of the spectrum to the other, all systems fit into the same model: autonomous processors connected by some kind of network that communicate by sending messages.

Below, we will first look at several classes of application that have been written for distributed computing systems. Then we will consider what kind of support is required for these applications and how it can be provided by a programming language.

1.2   Classes of distributed applications

Distributed computing systems are now available to many potential users. These systems are used for many different types of application. We will look at the reasons (besides availability) why a distributed system might be favoured over other architectures, such as uniprocessors or shared-memory multiprocessors, and we will classify the distributed applications accordingly. The reasons for programming applications on distributed systems fall into four general categories:

1. Decreasing turnaround time for a single computation.
2. Increasing reliability and availability.
3. Using parts of the systems to provide special functionality.
4. Inherent distribution of the application.

We will now look at each of these in turn.

1.2.1   Parallel, high-performance applications

Achieving speedup through parallelism is a common reason for running an application on a distributed computing system (e.g. a hypercube). By executing different parts of a program on different processors at the same time, some programs will finish faster. In principle, these parallel applications can be run just as well on shared-memory multiprocessors. Shared-memory systems, however, do not scale to large numbers (thousands) of processors, which explains the considerable interest in implementing parallel programs on distributed systems.

Parallel applications can be classified by the *grain* of parallelism they use. The grain is the amount of computation time between communications. *Large-grain parallel programs* spend most of their time doing computations and communicate infrequently; *fine-grain parallel programs* communicate more frequently; *medium-grain parallel programs* are in between. Note that grain size refers to the nature of the application, whereas coupling describes the architecture.

Fine-grain and medium-grain parallelism are most suited for closely coupled distributed systems; on loosely coupled systems, the communication overhead is usually prohibitively expensive. The literature contains numerous papers discussing applications that can benefit from large-grain parallelism. Recent introductory papers on this subject are [Athas and Seitz, 1988] and [Ranka *et al.*, 1988].

Large-grain parallelism is suitable for both closely and loosely coupled distributed systems.* Most of the research in this area has focused on implementing large-grain parallel applications on top of existing distributed operating systems. Example applications are: compiling modules of a given program in parallel on different machines [Baalbergen, 1988] and implementing heuristic search algorithms [Finkel and Manber, 1987]. Also, some of the world's best chess programs run on loosely coupled distributed systems. ParaPhoenix, for example, runs on a collection of SUNs connected by an Ethernet [Schaeffer, 1989].

1.2.2   Fault-tolerant applications

For critical applications like controlling an aircraft or an automated factory, a uniprocessor may not be reliable enough. Distributed computing systems are potentially more reliable, because they have the so-called *partial failure* property: as the processors are autonomous, a failure in one processor does not affect the correct functioning of the other processors. Reliability can therefore be increased by replicating the functions or data of the application on several processors. If some of the processors crash, the others can continue the job.

Some fault-tolerant applications may also be run on other multiple-processor architectures that can survive partial failures (e.g. shared-memory multiprocessors). However, if the system must survive natural disasters like fires, earthquakes, and tornados, one might want the processors to be geographically distributed. To implement a highly reliable banking system, for example, a loosely coupled or very loosely coupled distributed system might be the obvious choice.

Research in this area has mainly focused on software techniques for realizing the potential increase in reliability and availability. Example projects are: Circus [Cooper, 1985], Clouds [LeBlanc and Wilkes, 1985], Argus [Liskov, 1988], Camelot [Spector *et al.*, 1986], and ISIS [Joseph and Birman, 1986].

1.2.3   Applications using functional specialization

Some applications are best structured as a collection of specialized services. A distributed operating system like Amoeba, for example, may provide a file service, a print service, a process service, a terminal service, a time service, a boot service, and a gateway service [Tanenbaum and Van Renesse, 1985]. It is most natural to implement such an application on distributed hardware. Each service can use one or more dedicated processors, as this will give good performance and high reliability. The ser-

---

* If the grain of parallelism is large enough, even very loosely coupled distributed systems might be considered for running parallel applications. Recently, an international project was undertaken to find the prime factors of a 100-digit number. The problem was solved in parallel using 400 computers located at research institutes on three continents (New York Times, Oct. 12, 1988).

vices can send requests to each other across the network. If new functions are to be added or if existing functions need extra computing power, it is easy to add new processors. As all processors can communicate through the network, it is easy to share special resources like printers and tape drives.

1.2.4 Inherently distributed applications

Finally, there are applications that are inherently distributed. One example is sending electronic mail between user's workstations. The collection of workstations can be regarded as a distributed computing system, so the application (email) has to run on distributed hardware. Similarly, a company with multiple offices and factories may need to set up a distributed system so that people and machines at different sites can communicate.

1.3 Requirements for distributed programming support

We have described a spectrum of distributed architectures and several kinds of application that may be run on such hardware. We now address the issue of how these applications are to be implemented on these architectures. We will refer to this activity as *distributed programming*.

There are basically three issues that distinguish distributed programming from sequential programming:

1. The use of multiple processors.
2. The cooperation among the processors.
3. The potential for partial failure.

We will look at these three issues in turn.

Distributed programs execute pieces of their code in parallel on different processors. High-performance applications use this parallelism for achieving speedups. Here, the goal is to make optimal use of the available processors; the decision as to which computations to run in parallel is of great importance. In fault-tolerant applications, decisions to perform functions on different processors are based on increasing reliability or availability. For special-function and inherently distributed applications, functions may be performed on a given processor because it has certain capabilities or contains needed data. The first requirement for distributed programming support is therefore the ability to assign different parts of a program to be run on different processors.

The processors of a distributed system need to cooperate while executing a distributed application. With parallel applications, processors sometimes have to exchange intermediate results and synchronize their actions. In a system that controls an automated factory, for example, processors have to keep an eye on each other to detect failing processors. The services of a distributed operating system will need each other's assistance: a process service, for example, may need the help of a file service to obtain the binary image file of a process. With distributed electronic mail, messages have to be forwarded between processors. In all these examples, processors must be able to *communicate* and *synchronize* with each other, a second requirement for distributed programming support.

In a uniprocessor system, if the CPU fails, all work ceases instantly. But in a distributed system, some CPUs may fail while others continue. This property can be used to write programs that can tolerate hardware failures. This is particularly important for fault-tolerant applications, but it is desirable for other applications as well. For a distributed computer chess program participating in a tournament, for example, the ability to survive processor failures is highly useful. The third and final requirement for distributed programming support, therefore, is the ability to detect and recover from partial failure of the system.

Ideally, programming support for implementing distributed applications must fulfil all three of these requirements. The support may either be provided by the (distributed) operating system or by a language especially designed for distributed programming. In the first case, applications are programmed in a sequential language extended with library routines that invoke operating system primitives. As a disadvantage of this approach, the control structures and data types of the sequential language frequently are inadequate for distributed programming. We consider two examples of tension between sequential and distributed programming.

Simple actions, like forking off a subprocess or receiving a message from a specific sender, can be expressed relatively easily through library calls. But problems arise, for example, if a process wants to receive a message selectively from one of a number of other processes, where the selection criteria depend on, say, the state of the receiver and the contents of the message. While concise language notations exist for such cases (e.g. the select statement discussed in Section 3.2.3), the library method would probably need a number of complicated calls.

Problems with data types arise if one tries to pass a complex data structure as part of a message to a remote process. As the operating system does not know how data structures are represented, it is unable to pack the data structure into a network packet (i.e. a sequence of bytes). Instead, the programmer has to write explicit code that flattens the data structure into a sequence of bytes on the sending end, and reconstructs the original data structure on the receiving end. A language designed for distributed programming, on the other hand, can do the conversion automatically.

Language-level support for distributed programming also gives other advantages, such as improved readability, portability, and static type checking. Finally, and most important, a language may present a programming model that is higher level and more abstract than the message-passing model supported by most operating systems. Several such models will be discussed in this book. Below, we will first give a rough overview of the most important language models.

1.4   Languages for distributed programming

A central question encountered by developers of distributed software is: 'Given a certain application that has to be implemented on a particular distributed computing system, which programming language should be used?' A language can be considered as a candidate if:

1. The language is suitable for the application.
2. The language can be implemented with reasonable efficiency on the given hardware.

Many languages for distributed programming have evolved during the past decade, making the choice of the most suitable language a difficult one. More important, the underlying *models* of the languages differ widely. Below, we will look at several models. We begin by describing 'the basic model,' which is characterized by processes, message passing, and explicit failure detection. Next, we will look at alternative ways of dealing with parallelism, communication, and processor failures.

The most basic model is that of a group of sequential processes running in parallel and communicating through message passing. This model directly reflects the distributed architecture, consisting of processors connected through a communications network. Languages based on this model include CSP and occam.* The language may ease the programming task in many ways, for example by supporting different kinds of message passing (as discussed in Chapter 3), by masking communication errors, and by type checking the contents of messages. Such languages usually provide a simple mechanism for detecting failures in processors (e.g. an exception is generated or an error returned on attempt to communicate with a faulty processor). An example of a language supporting such features is SR.

For many applications, this basic model of processes and message passing may be just what is needed. The model can be mapped efficiently onto the distributed architecture and it gives the programmer full control over the hardware resources (processors and network). For other applications, however, the basic model may be too low-level and inflexible. Therefore, several alternative models have been designed for parallelism, communication, and partial failures, which provide higher level abstractions. Below, we will give some examples of alternative models.

Several researchers have come to believe that imperative (algorithmic) languages are not the best ones for dealing with parallelism. Because of the 'one-word-at-a-time' von Neumann bottleneck [Backus, 1978], imperative languages are claimed to be inherently sequential. This has led to research on parallelism in languages with inherent parallelism, like functional, logic, and object-oriented languages. The lack of side-effects in functional languages (like ParAlfl) allows expressions to be evaluated

---

* All languages mentioned in this section are described in more detail in Chapter 4 and references are provided there.

in any order, including in parallel. In logic languages, different parts of a proof procedure can be worked on in parallel, as exemplified by Concurrent Prolog and PARLOG.

Parallelism can also be introduced into object-oriented (or object-based) languages, by making objects active; this approach is taken in Emerald. As a result, models for expressing parallelism that are quite different from the process model have been developed. The parallelism in these models is usually much more fine-grain than in the process model, however. These languages can be made suitable for large-grain distributed architectures by supplementing them with mapping notations, which will be discussed in Chapter 3.

Likewise, some people are dissatisfied with message passing as the basic communication primitive, and have developed communication models that do not directly reflect the hardware communication model. One step in this direction is to have processors communicate through a (generalized form of) procedure call. This approach is used in Distributed Processes. A more fundamental break with message passing is achieved through communication models based on shared data. Although implemented on a physically distributed system, such shared data systems are logically nondistributed.

Let us make this distinction between *logical* and *physical* distribution. As discussed above, distributed computing systems do not have shared memory; the hardware of such systems is *physically distributed*. Distributed systems can be contrasted with multiprocessors or uniprocessors, which have a single system-wide primary memory; these systems are *physically nondistributed*.

A similar distinction can be used for classifying software systems, only here the distinction concerns the logical distribution of the data used by the software, rather than the physical distribution of the memories. For software systems the distinction is *logical* rather than physical. We define a logically distributed system as follows:

Definition: A logically distributed software system consists of multiple software processes that communicate by explicit message-passing.

This is in contrast with a logically nondistributed software system, in which software processes communicate through shared data.

There are four different combinations of logical and physical distribution, each of which is viable:

1. Logically distributed software running on physically distributed hardware.
2. Logically distributed software running on physically nondistributed hardware.
3. Logically nondistributed software running on physically distributed hardware.
4. Logically nondistributed software running on physically nondistributed hardware.

Let us briefly examine each of these. The first class is simple. A typical example is a collection of processes, each running on a separate processor and communicating using SEND and RECEIVE primitives that send messages over a network (e.g. a hypercube network, LAN, or WAN). The second class has the same logical multiple-process structure, only now the physical message-passing is simulated by implementing message passing using shared memory. The third class tries to hide the physical distribution by making the system look like a shared memory multiprocessor to the programmer. Finally, the fourth class also uses communication through shared data, only the existence of physical shared memory makes the implementation much easier.

In this book we only discuss languages that can be implemented (with reasonable efficiency) on physically distributed systems (categories 1 and 3). Most of these languages are based on logical distribution. Several others, however, are logically nondistributed and allow processes to communicate through some form of shared data. In such languages, the implementation rather than the programmer deals with the physical distribution of data over several processors. One example in this class is Linda, which supports an abstract global memory called the tuple space. Other examples are parallel logic languages (e.g. Concurrent Prolog and PARLOG) and parallel functional languages (e.g. ParAlfl).

The third important issue in the design of a model for distributed programming – besides parallelism and communication – is handling of processor failures. The basic method for dealing with such failures is to provide a mechanism for failure detection. With this approach, the programmer is responsible for cleaning up the mess that results after a processor crash. The major problem is to bring the system back into a consistent state. This usually can only be done if processor crashes are anticipated and precautions are taken during normal computations (e.g. each process makes checkpoints on secondary storage at regular intervals). To shield the programmer from all these details, models have been suggested to make recovery from failures easier. Ideally, the system should hide all processor failures from the programmer. Such models have, in fact, been implemented [Borg *et al.*, 1983]. Alternatively, the programmer can be given high-level mechanisms for expressing which processes and data are important and how they should be recovered after a crash. Languages that use this approach are Argus and Aeolus.

Which model of parallelism, interprocess cooperation, and fault tolerance is most appropriate for a certain application depends very much on the application itself. A distributed system that controls an aircraft may be able to do without fancy constructs for parallelism. In a distributed banking system the programmer may want to 'see' the distribution of the hardware, so a language that hides this distribution would be most inappropriate. Finally, it makes no sense to apply expensive techniques for fault tolerance to a parallel matrix-multiplication batch-program that takes only a few seconds to execute. On the other hand, there also are numerous cases where these models are useful.

1.5   Overview of our research

Above, we have given a general description of distributed computing systems, together with their applications and languages. We will now turn our attention to our own research.

Our goal is to facilitate the implementation of user applications on distributed computing systems. In the past, a large amount of research has been done on the construction of distributed *system software*, such as operating system kernels and various kinds of servers. In addition, many languages have been proposed for easing the implementation of such software. In our research, however, we specifically focus on *user applications* running on distributed systems.

Although the distinction between distributed system software and application software is not always clear cut, there are several characteristic differences between them. Systems programs are usually designed for serving other programs. A file server, for example, repeatedly accepts requests from other programs for opening, reading, writing, closing, and deleting files. User applications, on the other hand, aim at solving specific problems. A distributed chess program, for example, will interact with a user, but will probably not be called by other programs.

The applications we have in mind are typically implemented as monolithic programs, running on multiple processors and communicating with end-users. We do not consider critical, real-time applications used for controlling, say, aircraft or factories. We will mainly focus on parallel, high-performance applications, although other applications (e.g. those based on functional or inherent distribution) may benefit from our work as well.

Below, we will first describe the general approach taken for achieving our research goal. Next, we will discuss the relation between our research and other projects undertaken at the Vrije Universiteit. Finally, we will outline the structure of the rest of this book.

1.5.1   Research approach

As we have already discussed above, there are several redundant approaches for implementing distributed applications. The simplest one is to build the application on top of a distributed operating system. In this case, we can use a sequential language and access the operating system primitives through calls to library routines. Alternatively, we can use a language especially designed for distributed programming. In our research, we have looked at both options.

We started out by implementing two applications, parallel branch-and-bound and parallel alpha-beta search, on top of an existing distributed operating system, Amoeba. During this experiment we discovered many disadvantages of this approach and felt that a suitable language for distributed programming could ease the implementation of such applications.

The next step in our research was to study languages for distributed programming, together with their underlying constructs and models. This study deliberately spanned a wide spectrum of languages and was not restricted to the classical imperative message-passing languages. In particular, we paid attention to functional, logic, and object-oriented languages. In addition, we studied languages intended for fault-tolerant applications, despite the fact that fault tolerance is not a major goal for most of the applications we are interested in.

Our study showed many shortcomings in existing languages, when used for implementing user applications. We therefore felt it justifiable to work on a new language for distributed applications programming. The goals we tried to achieve with this new language are the following:

Expressiveness
> The language should provide a high-level computational model, easing the expression of parallelism, communication, and synchronization.

Simple semantics
> The language should have simple and clean semantics. In particular, the sequential and distributed constructs of the language should integrate smoothly.

Type security
> The language should be type-secure. Incorrect use of structured variables (e.g. an array reference with a too low or high bound) should be detected by the implementation.

Efficiency
> Programs written in the language should execute with reasonable efficiency on distributed systems.

Readability
> The language should encourage readability of programs, as this greatly affects the maintainability of programs.

Portability
> The language should be implementable on a range of distributed configurations, target processors, and operating systems.

With these objectives in mind, we have designed a new model for distributed programming, the *shared data-object model*, and a new language based on this model. The shared data-object model hides the physical distribution of the underlying system. It allows processes on different processors to share data encapsulated in objects, which are instances of abstract data types. The intention is that the language run-time system takes care of the distribution of objects among the processors. In particular, it may replicate frequently used objects on multiple processors.

The language based on this model is called *Orca*. Orca is an imperative language, but deliberately lacks features present in most imperative languages, such as global variables and pointers. Parallelism in Orca is expressed through the explicit creation of sequential processes. Processes communicate implicitly through shared data-objects, as described above.

The model and the language are *logically* nondistributed, but are designed to allow an efficient implementation on a *physically* distributed system. To show the feasibility of the latter claim, we have implemented working prototypes of the compiler and of several run-time systems. We have worked on multiple run-time systems in order to illustrate various design choices in implementing Orca. The distributed run-time systems are all based on replication of shared data, but differ in their strategy for replicating shared data and in the way they update these replicas.

The compiler and the run-time systems are prototypes in the sense that they do not aim at achieving maximum efficiency. We have only paid attention to optimizations that are essential for showing that an efficient distributed implementation is feasible. Also, the prototype run-time systems do not address the issue of handling processor failures, so the implementations are not fault tolerant.

We have also used these prototype implementations for testing both several example applications written in Orca and measuring their performance. The applications we have used are relatively small and all fall into the category of parallel, high-performance applications.

1.5.2   Relation with other projects

Our research is related to two other ongoing research projects at the Vrije Unversiteit: the *Amoeba* project and the *Amsterdam Compiler Kit* project. We will briefly describe the relations among these projects.

Amoeba [Tanenbaum and Mullender, 1981; Mullender and Tanenbaum, 1986] is a capability-based distributed operating system, developed at the Vrije Universiteit and now being further developed there and at the Centrum voor Wiskunde en Informatica (CWI). We have used the Amoeba system for two different purposes during our research. First, we used Amoeba as a test bed for implementing distributed applications (i.e. without using a distributed language). Second, we used Amoeba for two of the prototype implementations of our language.

Basically, the availability of the Amoeba system has allowed us to carry out the experiments needed for our research. As a minor consequence, part of the discussion in the following chapters is slightly biased towards Amoeba. We note, however, that the design – as opposed to the current implementation – of Orca is not affected in any way by Amoeba. Orca is a portable language, whose compiler can be ported to any distributed operating system.

Our research also benefits from the Amsterdam Compiler Kit (ACK) project [Tanenbaum *et al.*, 1983]. ACK is a toolkit for building portable compilers. The prototype compiler for Orca has been implemented using ACK technology. The Orca compiler generates code for a 'virtual Orca machine', which is an extension of the EM intermediate code used by ACK.

1.5.3 Organization of the book

The book is structured as follows. In Chapter 2 we will report on our experiences in implementing distributed applications directly on top of an operating system, without using special language support for distributed programming. As stated above, we have used the Amoeba system as a test bed for this work. Our conclusions hold for many other systems as well, however, since the communication primitive provided by Amoeba (remote procedure call) is also used by most other distributed operating systems.

In Chapter 3 we will give a general survey of the language constructs found in distributed programming languages. We discuss how parallelism and interprocess communication are expressed in distributed languages and how partial failures can be dealt with by such languages or their implementation.

In Chapter 4 we will present short descriptions of several representative distributed languages, to give the flavour of each. The examples include languages based on message passing, rendezvous, remote procedure call, objects, and atomic transactions, as well as functional languages, logic languages, and distributed data structure languages. We evaluate these languages and discuss several of their shortcomings. It was these shortcomings that led us to conclude that a new model and language were needed.

In Chapter 5 we will introduce the shared data-object model and Orca. We focus on the major design issues behind the model and the language, rather than giving a complete definition of the language. We also compare the shared data-object model with related models, such as objects (in object-oriented languages), monitors, and Linda's tuple space.

In Chapter 6 we will discuss the implementation of Orca. The most important topic of this chapter is how to implement shared data-objects without using physical shared memory. We first present several design alternatives and then describe the actual (prototype) implementations.

In Chapter 7 we will describe several example applications implemented in Orca. We will also discuss their performance on the prototype implementations of Orca. The complete sources of these programs are given in the appendices. In this chapter, we also note various opportunities for improving the implementations.

In Chapter 8 we will present our conclusions and discuss issues that need more attention in the future. We conclude with a comprehensive bibliography listing over 300 relevant papers.

The book contains material that has been published earlier by the author. Parts of Chapter 2 were published in the *Proceedings of the AFIPS National Computer Conference 1987* [Bal *et al.*, 1987]. Parts of Chapters 1, 3, and 4 have been published in a special issue of *ACM Computing Surveys* on programming language paradigms, edited by Peter Wegner [Bal *et al.*, 1989c]. Parts of Chapters 5 and 6 have been published in the *Proceedings of the IEEE Computer Society 1988 International Conference on Computer Languages* [Bal and Tanenbaum, 1988]. Some of the performance measurements of Chapter 7 have been published in the *Proceedings of the USENIX Workshop on Experiences with Building Distributed and Multiprocessor Systems* [Bal et al., 1989a].

## CHAPTER 2

Distributed Programming Without Language Support

Distributed applications can be built directly on top of the hardware, on top of an operating system, or in a special language for distributed programming. The first method provides total control over all primitives provided by the hardware, such as interrupt vectors and interfaces to communication devices. Although this method may be flexible and allows efficient utilization of the available hardware resources, it has the severe disadvantages of being highly hardware-dependent and labour intensive. We will not discuss this approach to building distributed applications in this book.

The second approach uses an existing sequential language plus a collection of operating system primitives accessed through library routines. The operating system can be a nucleus (providing only processes and interprocess communication), a network operating system, or a full-blown distributed operating system. Applications implemented this way are described in [Berglund and Cheriton, 1984; Finkel and Manber, 1987]. Such applications can be made hardware independent, but they always will be operating system dependent.

The third method employs a programming language containing all the necessary constructs for expressing distributed programs. This shields the applications programmer from both the operating system and the hardware. As a second major advantage, a programming language can ease the programming task by presenting a higher level, more abstract model of a distributed system.

Many languages for distributed programming have already been developed and implemented. These languages and their properties are the main subject of the following chapters. Before examining these languages in detail, however, we will take a look at how distributed systems can be programmed without special language support. We will give examples of how parallelism, interprocess communication and synchronization, and partial failures are handled when programming directly on top of a distributed operating system. This will later be contrasted with the expression of these phenomena with programming language support.

Most distributed operating systems are designed primarily for controlling the resources of a distributed system in a convenient and preferably *transparent* way.

Communication primitives are frequently designed for handling remote file accesses efficiently, as these are highly important in distributed applications like file servers, directory servers, and database servers. The applications we are interested in, however, use much more complex distributed algorithms than the above applications and need different programming support. The purpose of this chapter is to determine to what extent existing distributed operating systems are suitable for the implementation of complex distributed algorithms. The discussion in this chapter will be used to determine areas in which more programming support is desirable, in the form of a language for distributed programming.

We first briefly review operating system support for distributed programming. It turns out that many distributed operating systems provide remote procedure calls (RPC) for communication. We take a closer look at one representative RPC-based system, Amoeba. Next, we report on our experiences with the implementation of two parallel algorithms (for branch-and-bound and alpha-beta) using Amoeba's RPC primitives. Finally, we evaluate the implementations and draw some conclusions.

2.1 Operating system support for distributed programming

A wide variety of mechanisms for dealing with parallelism, interprocess communication and synchronization, and partial failures is provided by existing distributed operating systems. To illustrate this diversity, we will briefly survey some frequently used mechanisms.

2.1.1 Parallelism

The unit of parallelism in most distributed operating systems is the *process*. A process has its own state, code, and data. It executes instructions sequentially. Such processes usually are *heavyweight*: they carry a lot of status information (like open files, signal handlers, accounting information, and status of child processes) and are expensive to create. Some systems allow processes to be split up into smaller, less expensive, *lightweight* processes (or *threads of control*) that execute in quasi-parallel. Lightweight processes share a common address space and can communicate through shared variables.

Processes are created by calling a library routine that sends a request either to the operating system kernel or to a *process server*. The code to be executed by the new process is usually stored in a file, whose name is passed as an argument to the library routine. A process can terminate itself by calling some kind of *exit* library routine. Mechanisms to terminate remote child processes are often provided too.

The choice of a strategy for scheduling processes on processors is an important issue in the design of a distributed system. Schedulers try to spread the load of the system evenly over the available processors. They give each process a fair share of the processor cycles. The scheduling problem can be divided into two subproblems:

choosing *local* and *global* scheduling strategies. Global scheduling determines which processes are to be run on which processors. Local scheduling of a single processor determines which of the competing processes is to be run at a given point in time. Both problems have been studied extensively [Wang and Morris, 1985]. Some systems try to balance the load of the system dynamically, by supporting *process migration*, the ability to move a process from one processor to another [Powell and Miller, 1983; Theimer *et al.*, 1985; Douglis and Ousterhout, 1987].

Most operating systems treat each process as an isolated entity and hardly consider the possibility that several processes may actually be cooperating in a single program. (A notable exception is Medusa [Ousterhout, 1982].) The scheduling strategy may be inappropriate if processes cooperate rather than compete (e.g. fairness need not be an issue). Support may be missing for cooperative termination of all (or part of) the processes of a single program.

2.1.2 Interprocess communication and synchronization

A distributed operating system should provide primitives that allow processes to exchange information and to synchronize their actions. The designers of these systems generally choose mechanisms based on *message passing*. Still, there are many important design decisions to be made. We will briefly discuss these issues.

In general, the underlying hardware does not provide reliable delivery of messages. Message passing can be made more reliable by adding software protocols. These protocols can be placed at different levels of the system, as discussed in [Saltzer *et al.*, 1984]. Most distributed operating systems include the protocols in the kernel.

Message passing can be *synchronous* or *asynchronous*. With asynchronous message-passing, the sender immediately proceeds after sending the message. If the sender expects a reply message, it can later wait explicitly for the arrival of this message. With synchronous communication, the sender is blocked until the receiver has accepted the message. Synchronous message-passing is often claimed to be easier to use, but it has the potential disadvantage of reducing parallelism.

One important form of synchronous communication is remote procedure call (RPC) [Nelson, 1981; Birrell and Nelson, 1984]. With RPC, one process sends a message to another process, which accepts the message, does some processing, and then sends back a result message. RPC is a two-way communication mechanism, resembling a normal procedure call. Many distributed operating systems use some form of RPC as the primary communication primitive (e.g. Amoeba, the Cambridge system [Needham and Herbert, 1982], and Eden [Almes *et al.*, 1985].)

Whatever form of message passing may be chosen, the operating system usually knows little or nothing about the *contents* of the messages. Messages are typically regarded simply as sequences of bytes. This means that the sender and receiver of a message must agree on the form and contents of the message, because inconsistencies will probably go undetected.

The communication primitives should allow a certain degree of nondeterminism. A receiving process should be able to wait for a message from any of a set of processes. In the client/server model, most server processes want to provide services to many clients. Such a server should be able to accept requests from any of its clients. One way of achieving nondeterminism is by sending and receiving messages indirectly through a *communication port*. A more sophisticated message-passing mechanism would allow the server to accept messages *conditionally*, or to *sort* incoming messages in some order, both depending on the sender of the message and the contents of the message. Most distributed operating systems give only rudimentary support in this area. Other features that may be supported are *multicast* (i.e. the ability to send a message to several processes) and *forwarding* of messages to other processes.

2.1.3   Partial failure

Existing distributed operating systems differ significantly in their ability to deal with partial failures. At one end of the spectrum, there are systems without any special provisions for dealing with such failures. At the other end, there are systems specifically designed to support fault-tolerant applications.

The approach taken in the V system is to let the programmer deal with all exceptional situations. If an exception (e.g. an addressing error) occurs, the kernel sends a message to an *exception server* [Berglund, 1986]. The programmer can instruct the exception server what to do in such cases, by letting some process register itself to the server.

Amoeba uses a *boot service* for guarding important services. If a service S registers itself with the boot server, the latter will periodically poll S to see if it is still alive. If S fails to respond within a certain time, the boot server assumes S has crashed and it will start up a new version of S.

In the Eden system a process can permanently save its own internal state via a single atomic *checkpoint* operation. Periodic checkpointing can be used to build robust applications.

The Clouds system supports fault-tolerant distributed applications. Clouds allows data to be encapsulated in *objects*. Objects can be made resilient by using stable storage for recording the object's state. Operations on objects can be grouped into *atomic transactions*. Atomic transactions have 'all-or-nothing' semantics: they either fail or complete. Until completion, they have no effect on their environment. A failing transaction has no effect at all. Resilient objects and atomic transactions together facilitate the implementation of fault-tolerant applications.

2.2   A case study: the Amoeba distributed operating system

The Amoeba system runs on a collection of (possibly different) processors, each with its own local memory, which communicate over a local network. The hardware consists of four basic components. First, each user has a personal workstation, to be used for editing on a bitmap graphics terminal and other activities that require dedicated computing power for interactive work. Second, there is a pool of processors that can be dynamically allocated to users as needed. For example, a user who wants to run a five-pass compiler might be allocated five pool processors for the duration of the compilation, to allow the passes to run largely in parallel. Third, there are specialized servers: file servers, directory servers, process servers, bank servers (for accounting), etc. Fourth, there are gateways that connect the system to similar systems elsewhere.

The Amoeba distributed operating system is based on the client/server model [Tanenbaum and Van Renesse, 1985]. Amoeba uses a simple form of RPC for inter-process communication: the client sends a request to any server that is willing to offer a certain service and some server sends a response back. The primitive provided for clients is called a *remote operation* in Amoeba:

```
do-operation(request-header, request-buffer, request-size,
             reply-header, reply-buffer, reply-size)
```

(Remote operations were previously called 'transactions' in Amoeba; we will not use the latter term, however, to avoid confusion with 'atomic transactions'.) The first three parameters specify the request. The header contains a *capability* for the requested service and may contain a few parameters. Additional parameters can be supplied through a buffer, whose size is also specified. If the size is zero, no buffer is supplied, yielding a somewhat more efficient remote operation.

For servers, Amoeba provides two primitives: *get-request* to accept a request, and *put-reply* to send the results of the request back to the client:

```
get-request(request-header, request-buffer, request-size)
put-reply(reply-header, reply-buffer, reply-size)
```

All these messages are delivered reliably. During remote operations, the Amoeba kernel of the client sends 'are-you-still-there?' messages to the kernel of the server at regular intervals. If the kernel of the server does not respond within a certain time interval, the remote operation is aborted and returns an error status. This allows the client to detect that the server has crashed.

One problem with the RPC model is the fact that the caller (client) is blocked during the call, so a separate mechanism is needed to obtain parallelism. In Amoeba, a process (or *cluster*) consists of one or more lightweight processes called *tasks*.* Tasks share a common address space and run in parallel on the same processor. While a task is blocked in an RPC other tasks in its cluster may run if they have work to do. Tasks in the same cluster may communicate through shared data; they are synchronized implicitly, as the Amoeba kernel schedules tasks nonpre-emptively. Alternatively, any two tasks (whether in the same cluster or not) may communicate through RPCs.

---

* This is the terminology used in most research papers on Amoeba. The current terminology uses 'threads' instead of tasks and 'processes' instead of clusters.

We have used the Amoeba system for the implementation of two parallel algorithms in C, branch-and-bound and alpha-beta search. We found these two problems highly useful as test cases, because they are fairly complex. Moreover, they are interesting applications, as indicated by the large number of research papers on parallel branch-and-bound [El-Dessouki and Huen, 1980; Lai and Sahni, 1983; Wah *et al.*, 1985; Lai and Sprague, 1985; Lai and Miller, 1986; Finkel and Manber, 1987] and parallel alpha-beta search [Akl *et al.*, 1980; Marsland and Campbell, 1982; Finkel and Fishburn, 1982, 1983; El-Dessouki and Darwish, 1984; Wah *et al.*, 1985]. A survey of parallel alpha-beta algorithms is given in [Bal and Van Renesse, 1986]. Finally, the parallelism employed in the algorithms is sufficiently large-grained for distributed systems.

Below, we will discuss the C/Amoeba implementation of parallel branch-and-bound and alpha-beta search. We will also give performance measurements for these two programs on an Ethernet-based distributed system. In Chapter 7, we will compare the performance of these programs with similar programs written in Orca, running on the same hardware configuration.

2.3   Parallel branch-and-bound on Amoeba

The branch-and-bound method is a technique for solving a large class of combinatorial optimization problems. It has been applied to integer programming, machine scheduling problems, the travelling salesman problem, and many others [Lawler and Wood, 1966]. We have chosen to implement the travelling salesman problem (TSP), in which it is desired to find the shortest route for a salesman to visit each of the *n* cities in his territory exactly once.

Abstractly, the branch-and-bound method uses a *tree* to structure the space of possible solutions. A *branching rule* tells how the tree is built. For the TSP, a node of the tree represents a partial tour. Each node has a branch for every city that is not on this partial tour. Figure 2.1 shows a tree for a four-city problem. Note that a leaf represents a full tour (a solution). For example, the leftmost branch represents the tour New York – Chicago – St. Louis – Miami.

A *bounding rule* avoids searching the whole tree. For TSP, the bounding rule is simple. If the length of a partial tour exceeds the length of any already known solution, the partial tour will never lead to a solution better than that already known. In Figure 2.1, for example, the leftmost full route has length 6, so the partial route starting with New York – Miami – Chicago (of length 7) cannot lead to an optimal solution.

2.3.1   A parallel branch-and-bound algorithm

Parallelism in a branch-and-bound algorithm is obtained by searching parts of the tree in parallel. If enough processors were available, a new processor could be allocated to

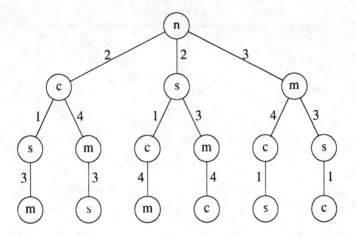

Figure 2.1 *Search tree for four-city TSP (New York, Chicago, St. Louis, Miami).*

every node of the tree. Every processor would select the best partial path from its children and report the result back to its parent. If there are N cities, this approach would require O(N!) processors. More realistically, the work has to be divided among the available processors. In our model, each processor starts at the node given to it and generates the complete partial tree reachable from that node down to *depth* levels. Each time the processor generates a node at level *depth* it hands out this node to a sub-contractor for further evaluation. These evaluations and the generation of the partial tree occur in parallel. Figure 2.2 shows how the tree of Figure 2.1 can be searched, using a two-level processor hierarchy (i.e. a subcontractor has no subcontractors itself).

In Figure 2.2, the processor that traverses the top part of the tree (the root processor) searches one level. It splits off three subtrees, each of depth two, which are traversed in parallel by the subcontractors. This algorithm is shown in Figure 2.3. The algorithm sets the global variable minimum to the length of the shortest path. This variable is initialized to a very high value.

Both the root processor and subcontractors traverse the tree in *nearest-city-first* order. Given an initial route T_1, T_2,... , T_i, the algorithm first considers the city closest to T_i that is not on the initial route.

A processor only blocks if it tries to hand out a subtree while there are no free sub-contractors. Each subcontractor executes the same traversal process, with a different initial node and probably with a different initial depth. In general, a subcontractor may split up the work over even more processors, so a subcontractor may also play the role of a root processor.

Root processor

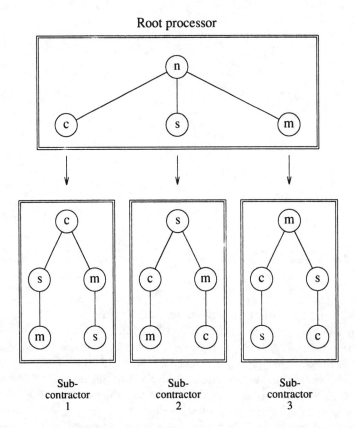

Figure 2.2 *Example of a distributed search tree.*

2.3.2   Implementation of parallel TSP on Amoeba

The travelling salesman problem has been implemented under Amoeba using the algorithm described above. A processor playing the role of a subcontractor can be viewed as an Amoeba *server*. The service it offers is the evaluation of a TSP subtree. Each server repeatedly waits for some work, performs the work, and returns the result. A processor playing the role of a root processor is a *client*.

The 'handing out of work' is implemented using remote procedure calls (Amoeba remote operations). As stated before, a problem with RPC is the fact that the caller (client) is blocked during the call. Therefore, the client cluster is split up into several tasks, as shown in Figure 2.4. A cluster C_p running on processor p contains one *manager* task M_p that performs the tree traversal. If the cluster has N subcontractors, it also contains N *agent* tasks $A_{p,1}$ .. $A_{p,N}$. An agent $A_{p,j}$ controls the communication with subcontractor j.

After the manager task M_p receives a subtree T to evaluate, it starts the tree traversal of Figure 2.3. When it finds a subtree that has to be subcontracted out, it tries to

```
procedure traverse(node,depth,length);
begin
    { 'node' is a node of the search tree. It contains
      a list of the cities on the current partial tour.
      'length' is the length of the partial path so far.
      'depth' is the number of levels to be searched
      before the rest of the tree should be handed
      out to a subcontractor }
    if length < minimum then
    begin  { if length >= minimum skip this node }
        if 'node' is a leaf then
            minimum := length;
        else if depth = 0 then
            hand out subtree rooted at 'node'
            to a subcontractor;
        else
            for each child c of 'node' in nearest-city-first order do
                traverse(c, depth–1, length+distance(node,c));
    end
end
```

Figure 2.3 *Tree traversal algorithm.*

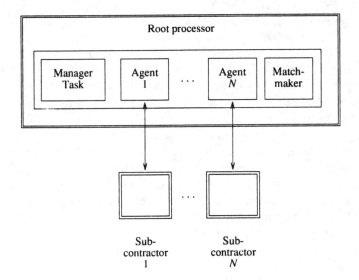

Figure 2.4 *Process structure of the TSP program.*

find a free agent, say $A_{p,j}$. The agent $A_{p,j}$ sends the work to be done to the manager M_j of subcontractor j, using an RPC with a partial path and the current best solution as parameters. This manager M_j starts executing the process we describe here on processor j. When M_j finishes the evaluation of the subtree, it returns the result to $A_{p,j}$. This agent checks if the current best solution has to be updated, and then becomes available again for the next request from M_p. In the mean time, the manager M_p continues its tree traversal and eagerly tries to find new work to distribute. The entire client cluster only blocks if the manager tries to deal out work while all agents (and thus all subcontractors) are busy.

Of special importance is the way subcontractors join and leave the system. Whenever a new server is started, it reports itself to a special *matchmaker* task that is also part of the client cluster. This matchmaker task creates an agent task for the server and from then on the server can participate in the game. So, extra processors can be added at any time to speed up the program.

This matchmaker mechanism is also used to achieve fault tolerance. If an agent task notes that its RPC has failed (timed out), it concludes that its server processor has crashed. It then hands out its work to any other agent task. Once this work has been accepted, the first agent stops executing. The crashed server processor no longer participates in the game. When it is brought back up, it reports itself to the matchmaker as described above, to register its availability for doing work, at which time a new agent task is created to handle it.

2.3.3   Discussion

The algorithm described in Section 2.3.1 uses a global variable `minimum`, shared by all processes. In a distributed system, processes on different processors have disjunct address spaces, so they cannot share variables. In principle, the variable could be stored on one processor and accessed by others through remote calls, but this is prohibitively expensive, as the variable is used very frequently (see Figure 2.3). Our implementation therefore keeps a local copy of the variable on every processor.

When an agent task sends a new subtree to its server, it also supplies the current value of `minimum`. The server uses this value to initialize its local copy. Ideally, whenever a subcontractor finds a better route, the length of the new route should be made known to all other processes in the system. In the RPC model this is hard to express, however, because a server (subcontractor) cannot return any 'intermediate' results. Therefore, improvements to the current best solution are not made known to the outside world immediately. Instead, the subcontractor first completes the analysis of its entire subtree and then sends its best solution to its agent. If this solution is better than the current best solution known by the client, it will from then on be used when handing out new work.

As a disadvantage of this implementation, servers sometimes do not have up-to-date information on the current best solution. Suppose two servers (S_1 and S_2) are each given a subtree to evaluate. Both servers are also given the length of the current best route (say M). If server S_1 finds a new route of length M_1 ($M_1 < M$), then S_2 will not know about this new route. If S_2 analyses a partial route P with length L such that $M_1 \le L < M$, then S_2 will wrongly assume that P is still worthwhile searching. This will not cause the program to return the wrong answer, but it will cause servers to do useless work. This extra work is called the *search overhead*. In summary, the implementation is correct but somewhat inefficient.

The speedup of the TSP program on a distributed system consisting of ten MC68020 processors connected by an Ethernet is shown in Figure 2.5. The program

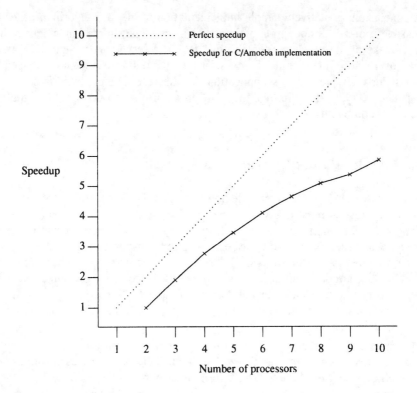

Figure 2.5 *Measured speedup for C/Amoeba implementation of the travelling sales-man problem, averaged over three randomly generated graphs with 12 cities each. The program uses one client processor, searching two levels, and a varying number of server processors.*

has been run with a number of server processors varying from one to nine. The speedup is taken relative to the single-server case. We have used three randomly generated input graphs with 12 cities each and determined the average speedups over these three problems. In each case, the root processor generates partial routes containing three cities. The actual execution times for each problem are shown in Appendix G.

Because of the search overhead, the speedup obtained is less than linear. One way to attack this problem is to use extra tasks in both the client and the servers and to return intermediate results through these tasks. The client then knows the new solution before the server has finished analyzing its entire subtree. There still is a problem in informing other servers about the new solution, however. One could extend each server with yet another task, which waits for messages from the client to update its local copy of minimum. In Amoeba, this is not as easy as it sounds, because tasks are scheduled nonpre-emptively. The extra task will not be scheduled until the task doing the TSP search does a remote operation. An alternative is to interrupt the TSP task, but this makes the implementation even more complex.

In conclusion, a relatively simple implementation of the TSP algorithm on Amoeba is possible if one does not aim at optimal efficiency. The simple implementation uses several tasks in the client cluster and one task per server. Although there is some mental overhead in using multiple tasks for the client, synchronization between these tasks is fairly simple for this application, so the resulting program is still easy to understand. Trying to improve the efficiency of the program will significantly increase its complexity.

2.4   Parallel alpha-beta search on Amoeba

Alpha-beta search is an efficient method for searching game trees for two-person, zero-sum games. A node in such a game tree corresponds to a position (e.g. a board) in the game. Each node has one branch for every possible move in that position. A value associated with the node indicates how good that position is for the player who is about to move. At even levels of the tree, this value is the *maximum* of the values of its children; at odd levels it is the *minimum*, as the search algorithm assumes each player will choose the move that is least profitable for his or her opponent. Most implementations negate the values of the odd-level nodes, so the values are maximized at all levels.

The alpha-beta algorithm finds the best move in the current position, searching only part of the tree. It uses a *search window* (alpha,beta) and prunes positions whose values fall outside this window. The algorithm is shown in Figure 2.6.

2.4.1   A parallel alpha-beta search algorithm

Alpha-beta search differs significantly from branch-and-bound in the way the best solution is constructed. A branch-and-bound program potentially updates its solution every time a processor visits a leaf node (see Figure 2.3). That processor only needs to know the current best solution and the value associated with the leaf. An alpha-beta program, on the other hand, has to *combine* the values of the leaves and the interior nodes, using the structure of the tree.

One way to implement this is to assign a processor to each node of the tree, up to a certain level [Finkel and Fishburn, 1982]. A processor assigned to a given node waits for the results from the processors assigned to the children of its node. Next, it computes the value for its own node and sends this value to its parent processor. As a disadvantage of this approach, processors associated with high-level interior nodes spend most of their time waiting for their children to finish.

Our solution avoids this problem by working the other way round. The child processors compute the values for their parent nodes, so there is no need for their parent processors to wait. To do this, an *explicit* tree structure is built, containing the alpha and beta bounds at each node. The search tree is no longer just a concept, but it is actually built as a data structure.

```
function AlphaBeta(node, depth, alpha, beta): integer;
begin
    if depth = 0 then  { leaf node? }
        alpha := evaluation(node)  { do static evaluation }
    else  { interior node }
      for each child c of 'node' do
      begin
          r := -AlphaBeta(c, depth-1, -beta, -alpha)
          if r > alpha then
          begin  { improved alpha ? }
              alpha := r;
              if alpha >= beta then
                  exit loop;  { pruning }
          end
      end
      AlphaBeta := alpha {result value }
end
```

Figure 2.6 *Sequential alpha-beta algorithm.*

2.4.2   Implementation of parallel alpha-beta on Amoeba

Alpha-beta search can be implemented on Amoeba in as similar a way as TSP. The process structure of alpha-beta is somewhat simpler than that of TSP, because the shared tree can be used for synchronization within the client cluster. Hence there is no need for a manager task. The implementation can be made fault tolerant using a similar mechanism as for TSP (i.e. through the matchmaker task). This will not be discussed any further. The client cluster contains as many tasks as there are subcontractors (see Figure 2.7).

Each task essentially executes the sequential alpha-beta algorithm of Figure 2.6. To keep other tasks from evaluating the same positions, each task leaves a trace of what it has done already by building the tree. Each task does a depth-first search in the tree until it either finds an unvisited node or it decides that the subtree rooted at the current node should be evaluated by another processor. In the first case it generates all children of the unvisited node and continues with the first child node. In the second case it sends the node to a subcontractor using RPC and waits for the result.

After a subtree has been evaluated (whether local or remote) its result should be used to update the alpha and beta values of other nodes in the tree. This is illustrated in Figure 2.8. In Figure 2.8(a), the subtrees rooted at nodes 3, 4, 6, and 7 have been evaluated. After the subtree rooted at node 8 has been evaluated the value of the parent of node 8 (node 5) is updated (as 20 > 15). This is shown in Figure 2.8(b). Furthermore, the evaluation of the subtree rooted at 5 has now been completed. As its final value (−20) is the highest value of level 1, the value of node 1 is updated too.

After the value of a node has been improved this new value can be used as a tighter alpha bound for its children. Each child can use this new alpha value as a tighter beta bound for its own children, and so on. So new values are propagated down the tree, to ensure each node uses the smallest possible alpha-beta window.

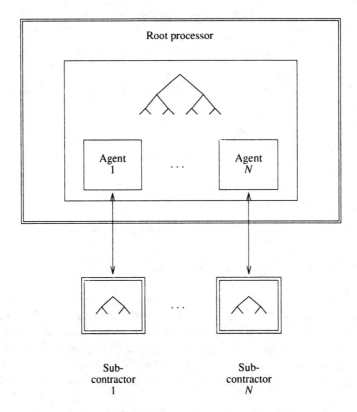

Figure 2.7 *Process structure of the alpha-beta program.*

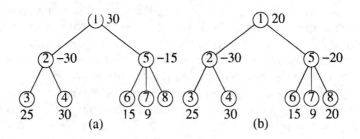

Figure 2.8 *Example of alpha-beta search.*

2.4.3 Discussion

In the TSP program of Section 2.3, processes share a single variable, which is replicated on all processors. In alpha-beta search, processes share the search tree. Replicating this data structure on every processor is not a sensible thing to do, as the tree changes very frequently and each processor is only interested in part of the tree. Our implementation stores the top part of the tree on the root processor. Each server searches a number of subtrees. For efficiency, the subtrees need not actually be built as data structures in memory, since they are not shared.

The most difficult aspect of the implementation is the synchronization of the agent tasks. The agents share the top part of the tree, so they can all read and modify this data structure. There are three occasions when an agent needs to change the tree:

1. While an agent is searching for work, it adds new nodes to the tree.
2. If an agent receives the result from its server, it updates the values of some nodes.
3. As a result of updating these values, some nodes should be removed from the tree. A node is no longer needed if either all its children have been evaluated, or its alpha value is greater than or equal to its beta value.

The agents must be synchronized to prevent multiple interleaving updates. Amoeba uses nonpre-emptive scheduling for mutual exclusion synchronization. Although this scheme looks simple, it must be used with utmost care. For example, if a process prints a message or allocates a new block of memory, it will do a remote operation (with the terminal server and process server, respectively), so it will be rescheduled. Nonpre-emptive scheduling is convenient for synchronizing simple actions only. In the TSP implementation this is no problem, as an action consists of updating a single variable. For alpha-beta search, actions are more complicated: they may affect several nodes of the tree and they may allocate or deallocate nodes. We therefore use per-node lock variables to synchronize the agents.

The speedup for the C/Amoeba implementation of alpha-beta search is depicted in Figure 2.9. The speedup shown in Figure 2.9 is averaged over three randomly generated game trees with fanout 38 (which is a typical value for chess) and depth 6. The nodes of the tree contain integer values, rather than real board positions of an actual game. The trees differ in the value of the leaf nodes, since we have used different static evaluation functions in all three cases.

The search depth of the root processor is an important parameter that influences the performance. In general, increasing this search depth decreases the search overhead but increases communication overhead [Bal *et al.*, 1987]. We found that, for the trees of Figure 2.9, the best results are obtained by letting the root processor search only one level of the tree. The subcontractors search the remaining five levels.

As for TSP, the speedup is computed relative to the single-server case. The actual execution times are shown in Appendix G. Again, the speedup is far less than linear, due to the large number of extra nodes searched by the parallel algorithm.

2.5 Evaluation

In Section 2.1 we reviewed operating system support for distributed programming. In Sections 2.2 through 2.4 we discussed the mechanisms provided by one specific system, Amoeba, and described how they can be used to implement distributed algo-

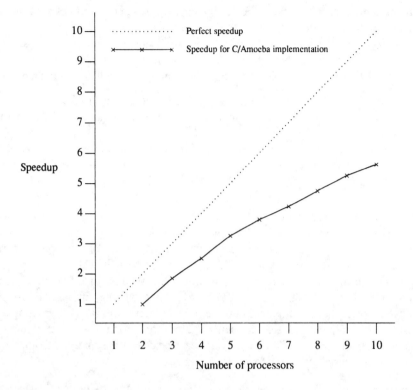

Figure 2.9 *Measured speedup for the C/Amoeba implementation of alpha-beta, averaged over three randomly generated game trees with fanout 38 and depth 6. The program uses one client processor, searching one level, and a varying number of server processors.*

rithms. In this section we will evaluate the suitability of Amoeba's primitives for distributed applications programming. We will also extend our discussion to other operating systems.

2.5.1   Parallelism

Support for parallelism in Amoeba comes in the form of processes, which consist of one or more lightweight tasks. Both applications we have studied use a single process per processor, so they make little demand on the operating system's scheduling policy. They just require the operating system to allocate a free processor to run a specific process. For the performance of both applications, it is essential that the operating system scheduler does not get in the way by letting different slave processes of one program timeshare the same physical processor. The order in which the trees are searched has great impact on the performance of the programs, so the operating system should not change this order behind the back of the programmer.

The prototype version of Amoeba we have used allows allocation of pool processors dedicated to a specific application, so it is well suited for our experiments. Many other distributed operating systems do not have a processor pool, but allow workstations that are currently not used by their owners to be allocated temporarily to other applications. The V system, for example, provides a remote execution facility to execute a job on any idle workstation. This facility can also be used to run parallel programs structured as master/slave processes [Berglund, 1986].

2.5.2 Interprocess communication and synchronization

IPC in Amoeba is based on remote procedure call. The Amoeba message primitives (*do-operation*, *get-request*, and *put-reply*) guarantee reliable delivery, provided the receiver can be contacted and has not crashed. Reliability is a highly desirable feature for applications programming, as it frees the programmer from dealing with lost messages, retransmissions, and so on.

RPC is a synchronous communication model and by itself does not support parallelism. If a client and a server communicate through RPCs, either the client or the server is running at any instant, so there is only one active process. In Amoeba, there are several ways to get around this problem. The server can reactivate the client by doing a *put-reply* and then continue executing the procedure. This clearly violates the RPC paradigm and it makes it awkward to return any other results, as a server can send only one reply. A better solution, used in our programs, is to make the client multithreaded and to let only certain threads be blocked in an RPC, rather than the whole process. Communication between threads of different processes uses strict RPC. Threads within the same process may violate the RPC model, for example by reactivating clients before the procedure is finished or by communicating through shared data. This approach is reasonable, although a variety of threads may be needed to make optimal use of parallelism.

Many of the problems discussed above are caused by the synchronous nature of RPC. Although most distributed operating systems use RPC, there also are systems based on asynchronous message-passing. Accent [Rashid and Robertson, 1981], for example, provides asynchronous communication through ports, which are protected kernel objects that can contain a limited number of messages. With asynchronous message-passing, the implementations of branch-and-bound and alpha-beta search would be significantly different. The client process can be single-threaded and sends its 'work-to-do' messages directly to the servers, rather than through an intermediate agent, without being blocked. Each server returns its result in a separate message, which is also sent asynchronously. These result messages may arrive on the client's processor at any time. In the Amoeba implementation, separate threads are used for handling result messages; in a single-threaded implementation, a different mechanism is needed. Accent provides a special 'software interrupt', which interrupts a process when a message comes in. It seems that such a feature would be helpful here. An alternative avoiding interrupt handlers would be to let the client periodically check for incoming messages.

Although the asynchronous implementation would use only one thread for the client, this thread would be more complicated than the threads in the Amoeba implementation. The structure of the client would still be far from trivial. A distinct advantage of the asynchronous model is the possibility of a server returning several messages to the client, so sending intermediate results to the client would be a straightforward extension.

The basic problem with the implementations of the two algorithms is the fact that they need *logically shared data*. In TSP, the global variable minimum is shared; in alpha-beta search, the search tree is shared. This is not to say the applications need physical shared memory for their implementations. On the contrary, many distributed implementations exist for both problems, including our own implementations. The availability of conceptually shared data, however, would significantly ease their implementations. Our implementations on Amoeba essentially simulate shared data.

2.5.3   Handling partial failures

The primary reason for running applications like heuristic search on a distributed system is to decrease their execution times. A secondary reason might be to make the implementations more tolerant of hardware failures. Distributed systems survive partial failures, so a program running on such a system can, at least in principle, be made fault tolerant. Whether or not a programmer is going to realize this potential depends primarily on the kind of application being dealt with. For air traffic control systems, fault tolerance clearly is sacred; for distributed chess programs, it is of less vital interest. We are dealing mainly with applications of the latter kind. Our main concern is to reduce the effort needed by the programmer to achieve fault tolerance.

It was straightforward to implement the applications studied in this chapter in a fault-tolerant way using the RPC model. The implementations are structured as a client process interacting with several server processes through remote procedures. The servers just accept requests for work from the client and send back the results; they do not have any side-effects. The latter property greatly simplifies the problem of making them fault tolerant: if a server crashes, its work is redone by another server. The only thing the programmer has to do is to write code that checks the return status of the RPC and retries any failing RPCs on other servers. This model has one Achilles' heel, however. A failure of the client's processor cannot be recovered from easily. To solve this problem, Amoeba's boot service could be used to keep an eye on the client processor, just as the client processor keeps an eye on the server processors.

For applications where RPCs have side-effects, more effort will be needed to achieve fault tolerance. Some distributed operating systems (e.g. Clouds and Camelot) support atomic transactions to ease the implementation of such applications. Other systems [Borg *et al.*, 1983] even try to make failures transparent to the programmer. It depends on the overhead introduced by these mechanisms whether they are useful for general applications.

2.5.4 Other issues

There are several other important issues concerning distributed programming on top of an operating system. We will discuss some of them below.

As should be clear from the above discussions, distributed operating systems use widely different mechanisms for parallelism, communication and synchronization, and fault tolerance. Even the underlying communication models vary considerably from system to system, let alone the exact conventions for calling the system's library routines. Programs written on top of a specific system are therefore difficult to port to other systems.

As an example, one member of the Amoeba group ported Finkel and Manber's Distributed Backtracking package [Finkel and Manber, 1987] to Amoeba. DIB was developed for the Crystal multicomputer [Finkel *et al.*, 1986], but its authors claim that 'DIBs requirements from the distributed operating system are minimal'. Indeed, DIB only requires primitives for creating and terminating processes and for sending and receiving messages. As DIB uses asynchronous message-passing and Amoeba only provides (synchronous) RPC, the effort of porting DIB to Amoeba was still substantial, especially when considering DIB's relatively small size (less than 3000 lines of code).

An area in which distributed operating systems frequently fail to give sufficient support is *strong type checking*. A good example is the way parameters are passed in Amoeba remote operations. Some parameters are passed through the request and reply headers; others are stored in dynamically sized request and reply buffers. In neither case does the system check whether the sender and receiver are interpreting the parameters consistently. If the sender stores ASCII text in the buffer and the receiver tries to extract double-precision floating-point numbers from it, chaos will result.

Another problem with Amoeba's remote operations (and corresponding primitives in other systems) arises when one has to send a complex data structure, such as a tree or a graph, to a remote process. Typically, the programmer has to write code to convert the data structure to a sequence of bytes and back. Not only is this an extra nuisance, it also affects the readability of the program and it increases the risk of making subtle mistakes in passing parameters.

CHAPTER 3

Language Support for Programming Distributed Systems

In the previous chapters, we discussed our definition of the term 'distributed comput-ing system' and described the kinds of task that might profitably be applied to these systems. We outlined the support required for programming such applications. We also studied two specific applications, parallel branch-and-bound and parallel alpha-beta search, and showed how these can be implemented on top of a distributed operat-ing system.

We will now turn our attention to language support – as opposed to operating sys-tem support – for distributed programming. Before describing several distributed languages in detail in Chapter 4, we discuss in a general way the methods which can be used by programming languages to fulfil the requirements set out in the preceding chapters.

As mentioned in Chapter 1, there are three issues that may be addressed in design-ing a language for distributed programming, above and beyond other programming language issues. These are parallel execution, communication and synchronization between parallel parts of the program, and exceptional conditions brought about by partial failure of the system. As we shall see, each of these issues may be addressed to a greater or lesser degree in a given language, and they may be resolved in quite different ways, often depending on the class of distributed application for which the language is intended. Table 3.1 gives an overview of the primitives described in this chapter, together with some examples of languages that use the primitives.

3.1 Parallelism

The first issue which must be dealt with in a language for distributed programming is parallel execution. Since a distributed system has by definition more than one proces-sor, it is possible to have more than one part of a program running at the same time. This is what we mean by parallelism.

We begin by drawing a distinction between true parallelism and what we will term *pseudo-parallelism*. It is sometimes useful to express a program as a collection of

Table 3.1 *Overview of language primitives discussed in Chapter 3*

Primitive	Example languages
PARALLELISM	
Expressing parallelism	
Processes	Ada, Concurrent C, Linda, NIL
Objects	Emerald, ConcurrentSmalltalk
Statements	occam
Expressions	ParAlfl, FX-87
Clauses	Concurrent Prolog, PARLOG
Mapping	
Static	occam, StarMod
Dynamic	Concurrent Prolog, ParAlfl
Migration	Emerald
COMMUNICATION	
Message passing	
Point-to-point messages	CSP, occam, NIL
Rendezvous	Ada, Concurrent C
Remote procedure call	DP, Concurrent CLU, LYNX
One-to-many messages	BSP, StarMod
Data sharing	
Distributed data structures	Linda
Shared logical variables	Concurrent Prolog, PARLOG
Nondeterminism	
Select statement	CSP, occam, Ada, Concurrent C, SR
Guarded Horn clauses	Concurrent Prolog, PARLOG
PARTIAL FAILURES	
Failure detection	Ada, SR
Atomic transactions	Argus, Aeolus, Avalon
Transparent fault tolerance	NIL

processes running in parallel, whether or not these processes actually run at the same time on different processors. For example, a given problem might lend itself well to being expressed as several largely independent processes, running logically in parallel, even though the program may in fact be run on a uniprocessor with only one piece of it running at a given moment. The UNIX® operating system, for example, was built using this approach. We call this *pseudo-parallelism*. (Some authors use the term *concurrency* for denoting pseudo-parallel execution. Other authors use the term as a synonym for real parallelism, however, so we will not use it.) Pseudo-parallelism has been employed in programming languages, especially those intended for writing uniprocessor operating systems, for quite some time.

Pseudo-parallelism is just as useful in distributed programming as it is in uniprocessor programming. But the difference between true parallelism and pseudo-parallelism must be kept in mind, despite the fact that in some languages the distinction is hidden from the programmer. For example, if a program consists of four processes and is running on a distributed system of four or more available processors, the four processes may run in truly parallel fashion – one on each processor. On the other hand, the same program may be running on a system with only two processors, in which case two processes may be assigned to run on each of the two processors. In this case, there are two processes running in pseudo-parallel on each processor. At a given moment, at most two of the program's four processes are running truly in parallel.

In some languages, on the other hand, the distinction between parallelism and pseudo-parallelism is not hidden from the programmer. It may be possible for the programmer explicitly to assign (or *map*) pieces of program to processing units. This delivers more complexity into the hands of the programmer, but also provides more flexibility. For example, given a language in which the programmer controls the mapping of processes onto processors, it is possible to support shared variables among processes known to be running on the same processor, and to disallow the sharing of variables between processes assigned to different processors. This is the case with several languages discussed in Chapter 4 (e.g. SR and Argus).

The granularity of parallelism varies from language to language, as mentioned above. The *unit of parallelism* in the languages we discuss below ranges from the process (in Concurrent C, for example) to the expression (in ParAlfl and others). In general, the higher the cost of communication in a distributed system, the larger the appropriate granularity of parallelism. For example, it may be possible to support fine-grained parallelism efficiently in a distributed system with low communication costs, such as a hypercube; whereas in a system with high communication costs, such as a wide area network, the communication cost of fine-grained parallelism may outweigh the gain in parallel computation.

Note that the *fact* of parallelism is distinct from parallelism as an *objective*. That is, in some applications, a high degree of parallelism is a goal, as it results in shortened computing time for an application. However, not all distributed applications have high parallelism as their main objective. Yet even in these latter applications, the ability to express parallelism may be important, since this reflects what is actually occurring in the distributed system.

Finally, we point out that not all languages support explicit control of parallelism. In some languages, the dividing-up of code into parallel segments is done by the compiler rather than by the programmer. Moreover, in some languages the sending of a message on behalf of one process results in the implicit generation of another, parallel process on the remote host to handle the request.

Below we describe several ways in which parallelism can be expressed in programming languages for distributed systems. We then discuss the mapping of parallel computations to physical processors. For a discussion of the expression of pseudo-parallelism, we refer to [Andrews and Schneider, 1983].

3.1.1   Expressing parallelism

Parallelism can be expressed in a variety of ways. An important factor is the language's unit of parallelism. In a sequential language, the unit of parallelism is the whole program. In a language for distributed programming, however, the unit of parallelism can be a process, an object, a statement, an expression, or a clause (in logic languages). We will discuss each of these in turn, beginning with the process, as it is intuitively the most obvious.

Processes

In most procedural languages for distributed programming, parallelism is based on the notion of a *process*. Different languages have different definitions of this notion, but in general a process is a logical processor that executes code sequentially and has its own state and data. Processes (or process types) are declared, just like procedures (and procedure types).

Processes are created either implicitly by their declaration or explicitly by some **create** construct. With implicit creation, one usually first declares a process type and then creates processes by declaring variables of that type. Often, *arrays* of processes may be declared. In some languages based on implicit process creation, the total number of processes is fixed at compile time. This makes the efficient mapping of processes onto physical processors easier, but it imposes a restriction on the kinds of application that can be implemented in the language, since it requires that the number of processes be known in advance.

Having an explicit construct for creating processes allows more flexibility than implicit process creation. For example, the creation construct may allow parameters to be passed to the newly created process. These are typically used for setting up communication channels between processes. If processes do not take parameters (as in Ada), the parameters have to be passed to the newly created process using explicit communication. A mechanism is needed to set up the communication channel over which the parameters are sent.

Another important issue is *termination* of processes. Processes usually terminate themselves, but some primitive may be provided to abort other processes too. Some precautions may be needed to prevent processes from trying to communicate with a terminated process. In Section 3.2.3 we will discuss mechanisms for cooperative termination of multiple processes.

Objects

The notion 'object-oriented programming' causes as much confusion as the term 'distributed system'. In general, an object is a self-contained unit that encapsulates both *data* and *behaviour*, and that interacts with the outside world (i.e. other objects) exclusively through some form of message passing. The data contained in the object are visible only within the object itself. The behaviour of an object is defined by its *class*, which comprises a list of operations that can be invoked by sending a message to the object. *Inheritance* allows a class to be defined as an extension of another (previously defined) class. Languages that support objects but lack inheritance are usually said to be *object based*.

Objects are primarily intended for structuring programs in a clean and understandable way, reflecting the structure of the problem to be solved as much as possible. At least two different opinions exist on what should be treated as an object. The Smalltalk-80® view is simply to consider everything an object, even integers and Booleans [Goldberg and Robson, 1983]. The second view (taken, for example, in Aeolus) is less pure and lets programmers decide what objects are.

Parallelism in object-oriented languages can be obtained in one of two ways. Smalltalk-80 includes the traditional notion of a process and lets the programmer deal with two kinds of module: objects and processes. A more orthogonal approach is to use the object itself as the unit of parallelism.

Sequential object-oriented languages are based on a model of *passive* objects. An object is activated when it receives a message from another object. While the receiver of the message is active, the sender is waiting for the result, so the sender is passive. After returning the result, the receiver becomes passive again and the sender continues. At any time, only one object in the system is active. Parallelism can be obtained by extending the sequential object model in any of the following ways:

1. Allow an object to be active without having received a message,
2. Allow the receiving object to continue execution after it returns its result,
3. Send messages to several objects at once, or
4. Allow the sender of a message to proceed in parallel with the receiver.

Methods 1 and 2 effectively assign a parallel process to each object, resulting in a model based on *active* objects. Method 4 can be implemented using asynchronous message-passing (instead of synchronous message-passing) or by letting a single object consist of multiple threads of control.

Parallel statements
Another way of expressing parallelism is by grouping together statements that are to be executed in parallel. Occam allows consecutive statements to be executed either sequentially, as in

```
SEQ
    S1
    S2
```

or in parallel, as in

```
PAR
    S1
    S2
```

This method is easy to use and understand. Initiation and termination of parallel computations are well defined. However, this method gives little support for the structuring of large parallel programs.

The parallel statement described above creates only a fixed number of parallel units. Another method is to use a parallel *loop* statement. Occam contains a parallel **for** statement, similar to a traditional **for** statement, except that all iterations of the loop are executed in parallel, as in

```
PAR i = 0 FOR n
    A[i] := A[i] + 1
```

Although this construct is easy to use, it is not as general as other mechanisms.

Functional parallelism

In a pure functional (applicative) language, functions behave like mathematical functions: they compute a result that depends only on the values of their input data. Such functions do not have any *side-effects*. In contrast, procedural (imperative) languages allow functions to affect each other in various ways, for example through global variables or pointer variables. Procedural languages are claimed to be more flexible, while functional languages have a sounder mathematical basis. We will not enter into the holy war between these two schools of thought, but we will concentrate on the way functional languages can be used for programming distributed systems.

If functions do not have any side-effects, it makes no difference (except perhaps for termination) in which order they are executed. For example, in the expression

```
h(f(3,4), g(8))
```

it is irrelevant whether f or g is evaluated first. Consequently, it is possible to evaluate f and g in parallel. In principle, all function calls can be executed in parallel, the only restriction being that a function using the result of another function waits for that result to become available (e.g. h waits for f and g). This implicit parallelism is fine grained and is well suited for architectures supporting such parallelism, such as dataflow computers. Several dataflow languages are based on this principle, for example Id and VAL [Ackerman, 1982].

For distributed systems, and to some extent also for other architectures, the functional approach has some problems that need be resolved. First of all, blindly evaluating all functions in parallel is not a very good idea. If a function does relatively little work, such as adding two integers, the overhead of doing it in parallel and communicating the result back to the caller will far outweigh the savings in elapsed computation time. If a certain function call is selected for remote execution, there still remains the choice between evaluating its arguments either locally (and then sending them to the remote processor) or remotely (by dispatching the unevaluated expressions).

Ideally the compiler should analyze the program and decide which processor should perform each function call. Since current compilers are not yet capable of taking maximum advantage of parallelism in this way, mechanisms have been proposed to put control in the hands of the programmer [Burton, 1984; Hudak, 1986].

AND/OR parallelism

Logic programming offers many opportunities for parallelism [Takeuchi and Furukawa, 1986]. We will describe AND/OR parallelism, as this mechanism is suitable for distributed programming and has been incorporated into many parallel logic programming languages.

Logic programs can be read *declaratively* as well as *procedurally*. In the code below, two *clauses* for the predicate A are given:

```
(1) A :- B, C, D.
(2) A :- E, F.
```

The declarative reading of the clauses is: 'if B, C, and D are true, then A is true' (clause 1) and 'if E and F are true then A is true' (clause 2). Procedurally, the clauses can be interpreted as: 'to prove theorem A, you either have to prove subtheorems (or *goals*) B, C, and D, or you have to prove subtheorems E and F'. From the procedural reading it becomes clear that there are two opportunities for parallelism as follows:

1. The two clauses for A can be worked on in parallel, until one of them succeeds, or both fail.
2. For each of the two clauses, the subtheorems can be worked on in parallel, until they all succeed, or any one of them fails.

The former kind of parallelism is called *OR* parallelism the latter is called *AND* parallelism

The parallel execution of a logic program can also be described in terms of processes, resulting in a third interpretation, the *process reading*, of logic programs. If we associate a separate process with every subtheorem to be proved, then clause 1 simply states that a process trying to prove A can be replaced by three parallel processes that try to prove B, C, and D. In general, a clause like

$$P_0 :- P_1, \ldots, P_N$$

causes a single process to be replaced by N other processes. If $N = 0$, the original process *terminates*. For $N = 1$, the process effectively changes its state, going to work on a different goal. If $N > 1$, then $(N - 1)$ new processes are created. Such processes are very lightweight and similar in granularity to a procedure call in a procedural language.

If the goals of a clause share some variables, they cannot be evaluated independently, because *conflicts* may arise when several goals try to generate a value for a shared variable. For example, in the clause

```
A :- B(X), C(X)
```

the variable X creates a dependency between the goals B and C. Several approaches have been suggested to deal with this problem. One method is to let the programmer restrict the rights of goals to instantiate (or *bind*) shared variables. In Concurrent Prolog, the notation

```
A :- B(X), C(X?)
```

indicates that B is allowed to generate a binding for X, but C is only allowed to read X. This mechanism can be used for interprocess communication and synchronization, as will be discussed later. Another method for dealing with conflicts is to solve dependent goals sequentially. In general, both compile-time analysis and run-time checks are used to determine if two clauses are independent. Both solutions – restricted instantiation and sequential solution of dependent goals – necessarily restrict parallelism.

3.1.2   Mapping parallel computations onto physical processors

In the previous section, we described several ways in which languages for distributed programming can provide support for the expression of parallelism. A related issue is how these parallel computations are distributed over the available physical processors, in other words, which parallel unit is executed on which processor at a given time. We refer to the assignment of computations to processors as *mapping*. Some languages give the programmer control over mapping, and in this subsection we describe some ways in which this can be expressed.

Mapping strategies vary depending on the application to be implemented. The assignment of processes to processors will be quite different between an application whose objective is to obtain maximum speedup through parallelism, and an application whose objective is to obtain high availability through replication, for example.

When the goal of a distributed program is to speed up computation time through parallelism, the mapping of processes to processors is similar to load balancing in distributed operating systems: both attempt to maximize parallelism through efficient use of available computing power. But there are important differences. An operating system tries to distribute the available processing power *fairly* over competing processes from different programs and different users. It may try to reduce communication costs by letting processes that communicate frequently run in pseudo-parallel on the same processor. The goal of mapping, however, is to minimize the execution time of a single distributed program. As all parallel units are part of the same program, they are cooperating rather than competing, so fairness need not be an issue. In addition, the reduction of communication overhead achieved through mapping processes to the same processor must be weighed against the resulting loss of parallelism [Kruatrachue and Lewis, 1988].

If the application's goal is to increase fault tolerance, an entirely different mapping strategy may be taken. Processes may be replicated to increase availability. The mapping strategy should at least assign the replicas of the same logical process to different physical processors.

An important choice in the design of a parallel language is whether mapping will be under user control. If not, mapping is done transparently by the compiler and language run-time system, possibly assisted by the operating system. At first sight, this may ease the programmer's task, but the system generally does not have any knowledge about the problem being implemented, so problem-specific mapping strategies are ruled out. This is a severe restriction for many applications.

Programmable (i.e. user-controlled) mappings usually consist of two steps. In the first step, the parallel units are mapped onto the physical processors. Several parallel units may be mapped onto the same processor. In the second step, the units on the same processor are scheduled by a local mapping, usually based on *priorities* assigned to the parallel units.

There are three approaches for assigning parallel units to processors, whether the assignment is done by the programmer or the system: the processor can either be fixed at compile time, fixed at run time, or not fixed at all. The first method is least flexible, but has the distinct advantage that it is known at compile time which parallel units will run on the same processor, allowing the programmer to take advantage of the fact that these processes will have shared memory available. StarMod uses the notion of a *processor module* that groups together processes located on the same processor [Cook, 1980]. These processes are allowed to communicate through shared variables, whereas communication between processes on different processors is restricted to message passing.

With the run-time approach to mapping computations to processors, a parallel unit is assigned to a processor when that unit is created. An example is the Turtle notation designed by Shapiro for executing Concurrent Prolog programs on an infinite grid of processors, where each processor can communicate with its four neighbours [Shapiro, 1984]. Every process has a *position* and a *heading*, just like a Turtle in the LOGO programming language [Papert, 1981]. By default, the position and heading of a process are those of its parent (creator), but they can be altered using a sequence of Turtle commands. For example, if a process located on processor P and heading northwards uses the rule

```
A :- B, C @ (left,forward), D @ (right,forward).
```

to solve A, then process B is created on processor P, process C is created on the processor to the west of P, and process D is created on the processor to the east of P. B is headed northwards, C westwards, and D eastwards. (This Turtle notation was later generalized into a layered method, using virtual machines [Taylor *et al.*, 1987a]. The layered method is also suitable for architectures other than a processor grid.)

Only a few languages support the third approach to processor allocation, allowing a process to execute on different processors during its lifetime. Emerald, for example, is an object-based language that allows objects to migrate from one processor to another [Jul *et al.*, 1988]. The language has primitives to determine the current location of an object, to fix or unfix an object on a specific processor, and to move an object to a different processor.

3.2   Interprocess communication and synchronization

The second issue which must be addressed in the design of a language for distributed programming is how the pieces of a program which are running in parallel on different processors are going to cooperate. This cooperation involves two types of interaction: communication and synchronization. For example, process A may require some data X which is the result of some computation performed by process B. There must be some way of getting X from B to A. In addition, if process A comes to the point in its execution which requires the information X from process B, but process B has not yet communicated the information to A for whatever reason, A must be able to wait for it. Synchronization and communication mechanisms are closely related and we treat them together.

An issue related to synchronization is nondeterminism. A process may want to wait for information from any of a group of other processes, rather than from one specific process. As it is not known in advance which member (or members) of the group will have its information available first, such behaviour is nondeterministic. In some cases it is useful to control dynamically the group of processes from which to take input. For example, a buffer process may accept a request from a producer process to store an item in the buffer whenever the buffer is not full; it may accept a request from a consumer process to add an item whenever the buffer is not empty. To program such behaviour, a notation is needed to express and control nondeterminism. We will look at such notations in Section 3.2.3.

Expression of interprocess communication (IPC)* in the languages we survey falls into two general categories – shared data and message passing – although this categorization is not always clear cut. Parallel logic languages that provide shared logical variables, for example, are frequently used for programming in a message-passing style. Note that the *model* provided by the language for expressing IPC and the *implementation* of that model may be two entirely different things; in particular, since we restrict our discussion to languages for systems without shared memory, any shared data model must be simulated in the language implementation.

3.2.1   Message passing

We first discuss communication through message passing. Many factors come into play in the sending of a message: who sends it, what is sent, to whom is it sent, is it guaranteed to have arrived at the remote host, is it guaranteed to have been accepted by the remote process, is there a reply (or several replies), and what happens if some-

---

* We adopt the well-known term 'interprocess communication' although it is somewhat misleading, since the unit of parallelism is not always the process, as has been discussed above. In the rest of this section we will use the term 'process' as a shorthand for 'unit of parallelism'.

thing goes wrong. There are also many considerations involved in the receipt of a message: for which process or processes on the host, if any, is the message intended; is a process to be created to handle this message; if the message is intended for an existing process, what happens if the process is busy – is the message queued or discarded; and if a receiving process has more than one outstanding message waiting to be serviced, can it choose the order in which it services messages – be it FIFO, by sender, by some message type or identifier, by the contents of the message, or according to the receiving process's internal state.

We will begin with a general discussion of issues common to all message-passing mechanisms. We then outline four specific message-passing models: point-to-point messages, rendezvous, remote procedure call, and one-to-many messages.

General issues

The most elementary primitive for message-based interaction is the point-to-point message from one process (the sender) to another process (the receiver). Languages usually provide only *reliable* message-passing. The language run-time system (or the underlying operating system) automatically generates acknowledgement messages, transparent at the language level.

Most (but not all) message-based interactions involve two parties, one *sender* and one *receiver*. The sender initiates the interaction *explicitly*, for example by sending a message or invoking a remote procedure. On the other hand, the receipt of a message may either be explicit or *implicit*. With explicit receipt, the receiver is executing some sort of *accept* statement specifying which messages to accept and what actions to undertake when a message arrives. With implicit receipt, code is automatically invoked within the receiver. It usually creates a new thread of control within the receiving process. Whether the message is received implicitly or explicitly is transparent to the sender.

Explicit message receipt gives the receiver more control over the acceptance of messages. The receiver can be in many different *states*, and accept different types of message in each state. More accurate control is possible if the accept statement allows messages to be accepted conditionally, depending on the arguments of the message (as in SR [Andrews, 1981] and Concurrent C [Gehani and Roome, 1989]). A file server, for example, may want to accept a request to open a file only if the file is not locked. In Concurrent C this can be coded as

```
accept open(f) suchthat not_locked(f) {
    ...
    process open request
    ...
}
```

Some languages give the programmer control over the *order* of message acceptance. Usually, messages are accepted in FIFO order, but occasionally it is useful to change this order according to the type, sender, or contents of a message. For example, the file server may want to handle read requests for small amounts of data first:

```
accept read(f,offset,nr_bytes) by nr_bytes {
    ...
    process read request
    ...
}
```

The value given in the **by** expression determines the order of acceptance. If conditional or ordered acceptance is not supported by the language, an application needing these features will have to keep track of requests that have been accepted but not handled yet.

Another major issue in message passing is *naming* (or addressing) of the parties involved in an interaction: to whom does the sender wish to send its message, and, conversely, from whom does the receiver wish to accept a message? These parties can be named *directly* or *indirectly*. Direct-naming is used to denote one specific process. The name can be the static name of the process or an expression evaluated at run time. A communication scheme based on direct naming is *symmetric* if both the sender and the receiver name each other. In an *asymmetric* scheme only the sender names the receiver. In this case, the receiver is willing to interact with any sender. Note that interactions using implicit receipt of messages are always asymmetric with respect to naming. Direct naming schemes, especially the symmetric ones, leave little room for expressing nondeterministic behaviour. Languages using these schemes therefore have a separate mechanism for dealing with nondeterminism (see Section 3.2.3).

Indirect naming involves an intermediate object, usually called a *mailbox*, to which the sender directs its message and to which the receiver listens. In its simplest form a mailbox is just a global name. More advanced schemes treat mailboxes as values that can be passed around, for example, as part of a message. This option allows highly flexible communication patterns to be expressed. Mailing a letter to a post office box rather than a street address illustrates the difference between indirect and direct naming. A letter sent to a post office box can be collected by anyone who has a key to the box. People can be given access to the box by duplicating keys or by transferring existing keys (possibly through another PO box). A street address, on the other hand, does not have this flexibility.

Synchronous and asynchronous point-to-point messages
The major design issue for a point-to-point message-passing system is the choice between *synchronous* and *asynchronous* message-passing. With synchronous message-passing, the sender is blocked until the receiver has accepted the message (explicitly or implicitly). Thus, the sender and receiver not only exchange data, but they also synchronize. With asynchronous message-passing, the sender does not wait for the receiver to be ready to accept its message. Conceptually, the sender continues immediately after sending the message. The implementation of the language may

suspend the sender until the message has at least been copied for transmission, but this delay is not reflected in the semantics.

In the asynchronous model, there are some semantic difficulties to be dealt with. As the sender S does not wait for the receiver R to be ready, there may be several *pending* messages sent by S, but not yet accepted by R. If the message-passing primitive is *order preserving*, R will receive the messages in the order they were sent by S. The pending messages are *buffered* by the language run-time system or the operating system. The problem of a possible buffer overflow can be dealt with in one of two ways. Message transfers can simply fail whenever there is no more buffer space. Unfortunately, this makes message passing less reliable. The second option is to use *flow control*, which means the sender is blocked until the receiver accepts some messages. This introduces a synchronization between the sender and receiver and may result in unexpected deadlocks.

In the synchronous model, however, there can be only one pending message from any process S to a process R. Usually, no ordering relation is assumed between messages sent by different processes. Buffering problems are less severe in the synchronous model, as a receiver need buffer at most one message from each sender, and additional flow control will not change the semantics of the primitive. On the other hand, the synchronous model also has its disadvantages. Most notably, synchronous message-passing is less flexible than asynchronous message-passing, because the sender always has to wait for the receiver to accept the message, even if the receiver does not have to return an answer [Gehani, 1987].

Rendezvous
A point-to-point message establishes one-way communication between two processes. Many interactions between processes, however, are essentially two-way in nature. For example, in the client/server model the client requests a service from a server and then waits for the result returned by the server. This behaviour can be simulated using two point-to-point messages, but a single higher level construct is easier to use and more efficient to implement. We will describe two such constructs: rendezvous and remote procedure call.

The rendezvous model is based on three concepts: the *entry declaration*, the *entry call*, and the *accept statement*.* The entry declaration and accept statement are part of the server code, while the entry call is on the client side. An entry declaration syntactically looks like a procedure declaration. An entry has a name and zero or more formal parameters. An entry call is similar to a procedure call statement. It names the entry and the process containing the entry and it supplies actual parameters. An accept statement for the entry may contain a list of statements, to be executed when the entry is called, as in the following accept statement for the entry `incr`:

---

* We use the terminology introduced by Ada here.

```
accept incr(X: integer; Y: out integer) do
   Y := X + 1;
end;
```

An interaction (called a rendezvous) between two processes S and R takes place when S calls an entry of R, and R executes an **accept** statement for that entry. The interaction is fully synchronous, so the first process that is ready to interact waits for the other. When the two processes are synchronized, R executes the **do** part of the accept statement. While executing these statements, R has access to the input parameters of the entry, supplied by S. R can assign values to the output parameters, which are passed back to S. After R has executed the **do** statements, S and R continue their execution in parallel. R may still continue working on the request of S although S is no longer blocked.

Remote Procedure Call
Remote procedure call (RPC) is another primitive for two-way communication. It resembles a normal procedure call, except that the caller and receiver are different processes. When a process S calls a remote procedure P of a process R, the input parameters of P, supplied by S, are sent to R. When R receives the invocation request, it executes the code of P and then passes any output parameters back to S. During the execution of P, S is blocked. S is reactivated by the arrival of the output parameters. This is in contrast to the rendezvous mechanism, where the caller is unblocked as soon as the accept statement has been executed. Like rendezvous, RPC is a fully synchronous interaction. Acceptance of a remote call is usually (but not always) implicit and creates a new thread of control within the receiver.

A major design choice is between a *transparent* and a *nontransparent* RPC mechanism. Transparent RPC offers semantics close to a normal procedure. This model, advocated by Nelson and Birrell, has significant advantages [Nelson, 1981; Birrell and Nelson, 1984]. Foremost, it gives the programmer a simple, familiar primitive for interprocess communication and synchronization. It also is a sound basis for porting existing sequential software to distributed systems.

Unfortunately, achieving exactly the same semantics for RPC as for normal procedures is close to impossible [Tanenbaum and Van Renesse, 1988]. One source of problems is that, in the absence of shared memory, pointers (address values) are meaningless on a remote processor. This makes pointer-valued parameters and call-by-reference parameters highly unattractive. Dereferencing a pointer passed by the caller has to be done at the caller's side, which implies extra communication. An alternative implementation is to copy the value pointed at to the receiver, but this has subtly different semantics and may be difficult to implement if the pointer points into the middle of a complex data structure, such as a directed graph. In languages lacking strong type checking it may not even be clear what type of object the pointer points to. Similarly, call-by-reference can be replaced by copy-in/copy-out, but also at the cost of slightly different semantics. The issue of passing arguments to a remote procedure is discussed further in [Herlihy and Liskov, 1982].

The possibility of processor crashes makes it even more difficult to obtain the same semantics for RPC as for normal procedures. If S calls a remote procedure P of a process R and the processor of R crashes before S gets the results back, then S clearly is in trouble. First of all, the results S is waiting for will never arrive. Second, it is not known if R died before receiving the call, during the execution of P, or after executing P (but before returning the results). The first problem can be solved using timeouts. The second problem is more serious. If P has no side-effects, the call can be repeated, perhaps on a different processor or after a certain period of time. If P does have side-effects (e.g. incrementing a bank account in a database), executing (part of) P twice may be undesirable.

Because of these difficulties in achieving normal call semantics for remote calls, Hamilton argues that remote procedures should be treated differently from the start, resulting in a nontransparent RPC mechanism [Hamilton, 1984]. Almes describes an RPC implementation in the context of an existing language (Modula-2) and distributed operating system (the V system) [Almes, 1986]. Although the goal of the implementation was to make remote calls as similar to normal calls as possible, special features for remote calls had to be added to obtain an efficient implementation. His RPC system therefore is also nontransparent.

One-to-many message passing

Many networks used for distributed computing systems support a fast *broadcast* or *multicast* facility. A broadcast message is sent to all processors connected to the network. A multicast message is sent to a specific subset of these processors. In some LANs, it takes about the same time to broadcast or multicast a message as to send it to one specific processor. Unfortunately, it is not guaranteed that messages are actually delivered at all destinations. The hardware attempts to send the messages to all processors involved, but messages may be lost because of communication errors or because some receiving processors are not ready to accept a message.

Despite being unreliable, broadcast and multicast are useful for operating system kernels and language run-time systems. For example, to locate a processor providing a specific service, an enquiry message may be broadcast. In this case, it is not necessary to receive an answer from every host: just finding one instance of the service is sufficient. Broadcast and multicast are also useful for implementing distributed algorithms, so some languages provide a *one-to-many* message passing primitive.

One-to-many communication has several advantages over point-to-point message passing. If a process needs to send data to many other processes, a single multicast will be faster than many point-to-point messages. More importantly, a broadcast primitive may guarantee a certain *ordering* of messages that cannot be obtained easily with point-to-point messages [Birman and Joseph, 1987]. A broadcast primitive that delivers messages at all destinations in the same order, for example, is highly useful for consistent updating of replicated data [Joseph and Birman, 1986]. Finally, broadcasting may lead to new programming styles.

Gehani describes a system of broadcasting sequential processes (BSP) based on CSP and the concept of *broadcast programming* [Gehani, 1984b]. In CSP, a message is sent to one specific process. In BSP, a message can also be sent to *all* processes or to a list of processes. Both primitives are reliable (i.e. messages are delivered at all destinations). If the underlying hardware is not reliable, extra software protocols have to be added by the operating system or language run-time system. Broadcast in BSP is asynchronous, because the sender normally does not want to wait until all other processes are ready to receive a message. Two forms of broadcast are defined. An *unbuffered* broadcast message is only received by those processes ready to accept one. *Buffered* broadcast messages are buffered by the receiving processes, so each process will eventually receive the message. A receiver may accept messages from any process, or it may screen out messages based on their contents or on the identity of the sender (passed as part of the message).

3.2.2   Data sharing

In the previous section, we discussed models of interprocess communication based on message passing. In this section, we will describe how parts of a distributed program can communicate and synchronize through the use of shared data. If two processes have access to the same variable, communication can take place by one process setting the variable and the other process reading it. This is true whether the processes are running on the host where the variable is stored and can manipulate it directly, or if the processes are on different hosts and access the variable by sending a message to the host it resides on. The use of shared variables for the communication and synchronization of processes running in pseudo-parallel on a uniprocessor has been studied extensively. We assume a familiarity with this material; the uninitiated reader is referred to [Andrews and Schneider, 1983] for an excellent overview.

As mentioned above, many distributed languages support processes running in pseudo-parallel on the same processor, and these often use traditional methods of communication and synchronization through shared variables. See, for example, the description of **mutex** in Argus and semaphores in SR in Chapter 4. What we are interested in here, however, is the use of shared data for communication and synchronization of processes running on different processors.

At first sight it may seem to be strange to use shared data for communication in a distributed system, as such systems do not have physically shared memory. However, the shared data paradigm has several advantages (as well as disadvantages) over message passing. While a message generally transfers information between two specific processes, shared data are accessible by any process. Assignment to shared data conceptually has immediate effect, but for message passing there is a finite delay between sending a message and its being received. On the other hand, shared data require precautions to prevent multiple processes from simultaneously changing the same data. As neither of the paradigms is universally better than the other one, both paradigms are worth investigating.

Simple shared variables, as used for example in Algol 68 [Van Wijngaarden *et al.*, 1975], are not well suited for distributed systems. In principle, they can be implemented by simulating shared physical memory, using for example a method such as Li's *shared virtual memory* [Li and Hudak, 1986]. None of the languages we know of do this, however, probably because of performance considerations. Several other communication models based on shared data exist, however, that are better suited for distributed systems. These models place certain restrictions on the shared data, making a distributed implementation feasible. Below we describe two methods for providing shared data to distributed processes: distributed data structures and shared logical variables. Both models are used in several languages for distributed programming (see Chapter 4) that have been implemented on different kinds of distributed architecture. These languages are mainly useful for applications where the programmer need not be aware of the physical distribution of main memory, as discussed in Chapter 1.

Note that objects, whose role in expressing parallelism was discussed in Section 3.1.1, may also be thought of as implementing shared data in a distributed program. Just as with the shared data models that will be discussed in this section, two processes may communicate indirectly with one another by invoking operations on a given object. Objects, since they control access to the data they manage, can also implement synchronization of access to those data by other processes, analogously to the synchronization of pseudo-parallel processes accessing data controlled by a monitor.

A different approach to the synchronization of distributed access to shared data is taken by languages that implement atomic transactions. Since this approach also involves dealing with partial failures of the distributed systems, we will treat it later in the section on atomic transactions.

Distributed data structures

Distributed data structures are data structures that can be manipulated simultaneously by several processes [Carriero *et al.*, 1986]. This paradigm was first introduced in the language Linda, which uses the concept of a *tuple space* for implementing distributed data structures [Ahuja *et al.*, 1986]. We will use the tuple space model for discussing the distributed data structures paradigm

The tuple space (TS) is conceptually a shared memory, although its implementation does not require physical shared memory. The TS is one global memory shared by all processes of a program [Gelernter, 1985]. The elements of TS, called *tuples*, are ordered sequences of values, similar to records in Pascal [Wirth, 1971]. For example,

```
["jones", 31, true]
```

is a tuple with three fields: a string, an integer, and a Boolean.

Three atomic operations are defined on TS: **out** adds a tuple to TS, **read** reads a tuple contained in TS, **in** reads a tuple and also deletes it from TS. Unlike normal shared variables, tuples do not have addresses. Rather, tuples are addressed by their contents. A tuple is denoted by specifying either the *value* or the *type* of each field.

This is expressed by supplying an *actual* parameter (a value) or a *formal* parameter (a variable) to an operation. For example, if age is a variable of type integer and married is a variable of type Boolean, then the tuple shown above can be read in the operation

read ("jones", **var** age, **var** married)

or read and removed in the operation

in ("jones", **var** age, **var** married).

In both operations, the variable age is assigned the value of the second field (31) and the variable married gets the value of the last field (true). Both the **in** and the **read** operations try to find a matching tuple in TS. A tuple matches if each field has the value or type passed as parameter to the operation. If several matching tuples exist, one is chosen arbitrarily. If there are no matching tuples, the operation (and the invoking process) *blocks* until another process adds a tuple that does match (using **out**).

There is no operation that modifies a tuple in place. To change a tuple, it must first be removed from TS, then modified, and then put back into TS. Each **read**, **in**, or **out** operation is atomic: the effect of several simultaneous operations on the same tuple is the same as that of executing them in some (undefined) sequential order. In particular, if two processes want to remove the same tuple, only one of them will succeed and the unlucky one will block. These two properties make it possible to build distributed data structures in TS. For example, a distributed array can be built out of tuples of the form [name, index, value]. The value of element i of array A can be read into a local integer variable X with a simple **read** operation:

read ("A", i, **var** X)

To assign a new value Y to element i, the current tuple representing A[i] is removed first, then a tuple with the new value is generated:

in ("A", i, **var** void)
out ("A", i, Y)

To increment element i, the current tuple is removed from TS, its value is stored in a temporary variable, and the new value is computed and stored in a new tuple:

in ("A", i, **var** tmp)
out ("A", i, tmp + 1)

If two processes simultaneously want to increment the same array element, the element will indeed be incremented twice. Only one process will succeed in doing the **in** and the other process will be blocked until the first one has put the new value of A[i] back into TS.

In a distributed implementation of the TS, the run-time system takes care of the distribution of tuples among the processors. Several strategies are possible, such as replicating the entire TS on all processors, *hashing* tuples onto specific processors, or storing a tuple on the processor that did the **out** operation [Gelernter, 1985].

In contrast to interprocess communication accomplished through message passing, communication through distributed data structures is anonymous. A process reading a tuple from TS does not know, or care, which other process inserted the tuple. Neither did the process executing an **out** on a tuple specify which process the tuple was intended to be read by. This information could in principle be included in a distributed data structure, for example by having *sender* and *receiver* fields as part of the structure, but it is not an inherent part of the model.

Shared logical variables

Another shared data model is the shared logical variable. Logical variables have the 'single-assignment' property. Initially, they are unbound, but once they receive a value (by unification) they cannot be changed. In Section 3.1.1 we noted that this property can cause conflicts between parallel processes sharing logical variables. Below, we will show how such variables can be used as communication channels between processes.

As an example, assume the three goals of the conjunction

```
goal_1(X,Y), goal_2(X,Y), goal_3(X)
```

are solved in parallel by processes P1, P2, and P3. The variable X (initially unbound) is a communication channel between these processes. If any of them binds X to a value, the other processes can use this value. Likewise, Y is a channel between P1 and P2.

Processes synchronize by suspending on unbound variables. If Y is to be used to send a message from P1 to P2, then P2 can suspend until Y is bound by P1. There are several ways to realize suspension on shared variables, but the general idea is to restrict the rights of specific processes to generate bindings for variables (i.e. to unify them with anything but an unbound variable). If a process wants to unify two terms, the unification may need to generate a binding for some variables. If the process does not have the right to bind one of these variables, the process suspends until some *other* process that does have this right generates a binding for the variable. The first process can then continue its unification of the two terms. Examples of mechanisms to restrict the rights for binding variables are the *read-only variables* of Concurrent Prolog and the *mode declarations* of PARLOG.

At first sight, shared logical variables seem to be capable of transferring only a single message, as bindings cannot be undone. But in fact, the logical variable allows many communication patterns to be expressed. The key idea is to bind a logical variable to a term containing other (unbound) variables, which can be used as channels for further communication. A logical variable is like a genie from whom you can ask one wish. What would you ask such a genie? To have two more wishes! Then use one of them, and iterate.*

This idea has been used to develop several programming techniques. For example, a *stream* of messages between a producer and a consumer is created by having the producer bind a shared variable to a list cell with two fields, head and tail. The head is bound to the message, and the tail is the new stream variable, used for subsequent communications (wishes). This is illustrated in Figure 3.1.

In Figure 3.1, the first call producer(1,S) will cause S to be bound to [1|S1], where S1 is an unbound variable. The next (recursive) call producer(2,S1) binds S1 to [4|S2], where S2 is unbound. The call consumer(S) will cause the consumer process to be blocked until S is bound by the producer. When S is bound to [1|S1] the consumer wakes up, calls use(1), followed by the recursive call consumer(S1). The latter call blocks until S1 is bound to [4|S2], and so on.

Other techniques implementable with shared logical variables are bounded-buffer streams [Takeuchi and Furukawa, 1985], one-to-many streams, and incomplete messages. An incomplete message contains variables that will be bound by the receiver, thus returning reply values. The sender can wait for replies by suspending on such a variable. Incomplete messages can be used to implement many different message protocols (e.g. remote procedures and rendezvous, discussed above) and to set up communication channels dynamically between processes.

The shared logical variable model also has some disadvantages, as discussed by Gelernter [Gelernter, 1984]. Only a single process can append to a stream implemented through logical variables (e.g. in Figure 3.1, only the producer can append to S). Applications based on the client/server model, however, require multiple clients to send messages to a single server (many-to-one communication). To implement this in a parallel logic language, each client must have its own output stream. There are two alternatives for structuring the server. First, the server may use a separate input stream for each client, and accept messages sent through each of these streams. This requires the server to know the identities of all clients and thus imposes a limit on the number of clients. The second alternative is to *merge* the output streams of all clients and present them as a single input stream to the server. Such merge operations can be expressed in parallel logic languages [Shapiro and Safra, 1986], but Gelernter argues that the resulting programs are less clear and concise than similar programs in languages supporting streams with multiple readers and writers.

3.2.3   Expressing and controlling nondeterminism

As discussed in the introduction of Section 3.2, the interaction patterns between processes are not always deterministic, but sometimes depend on run-time conditions. For this reason, models for expressing and controlling nondeterminism have been introduced. Some communication primitives that we have already seen are nondeterministic. A message received indirectly through a port, for example, may have been

---

* This analogy was contributed by Ehud Shapiro.

```
/* the consumer is not allowed to bind S */
mode producer(N?, S^), consumer(S?).

producer(N, [X|Xs]) :-   /* produce stream of squares */
    X is N*N, N2 is N+1, producer(N2,Xs).

consumer([X|Xs]) :-
    use(X), consumer(Xs).

/* start consumer and producer in parallel */
main :- producer(1,S), consumer(S).
```

Figure 3.1 *Implementation of streams with shared logical variables.*

sent by any process. Such primitives provide a way to *express* nondeterminism, but not to *control* it. Most programming languages use a separate construct for controlling nondeterminism. We will look at two such constructs: the *select statement*, used by many algorithmic languages, and the *guarded Horn clause*, used by most parallel logic programming languages. Both are based on the *guarded command statement*, introduced by Dijkstra as a sequential control structure [Dijkstra, 1975].

The select statement
A select statement consists of a list of guarded commands of the following form:

> *guard* → *statements*

The guard consists of a Boolean expression and some sort of 'communication request'. The Boolean expression must be free of side-effects, as it may be evaluated more than once during the course of the select statement's execution. In CSP [Hoare, 1978], for example, a guard may contain an explicit receipt of a message from a specific process P. Such a request may either *succeed* (if P has sent such a message), *fail* (if P has already terminated), or *suspend* (if P is still alive but has not sent the message yet). The guard itself can either succeed, fail, or suspend: the guard succeeds if the expression is 'true' and the request succeeds; the guard fails if the Boolean expression evaluates to 'false' or if the communication request fails; or the guard suspends if the expression is 'true' and the request suspends. The select statement as a whole blocks until either all of its guards fail or some guards succeed. In the former case, the entire select statement fails and has no effect. In the latter case, one succeeding guard is chosen nondeterministically and the corresponding statement part is executed.

In CSP, the select statement can be used to wait nondeterministically for specific messages from specific processes. The select statement contains a list of input requests and allows individual requests to be enabled or disabled dynamically. For example, the buffer process described above can interact with a consumer and a producer as shown in Figure 3.2.

Communication takes place as soon as either (1) the buffer is not full and the producer sends a message `DepositItem`, or (2) the buffer is not empty and the consumer sends a message `AskForItem`. In the latter case the buffer process responds by sending the item to the consumer.

CSP's select statement is asymmetric in that the guard in CSP can contain only an input operator, not an output operator. Thus, a process P can only wait to receive messages nondeterministically; it cannot wait nondeterministically until some other process is ready to accept a message from P. Output guards are excluded from most languages, because they usually complicate the implementation. Languages that do allow output guards include Joyce and Pascal-m.

Select statements can also be used for controlling nondeterminism other than communication. Some languages allow a guard to contain a *timeout* instead of a communication request. A guard containing a timeout of T seconds succeeds if no other guard succeeds within T seconds. This mechanism sets a limit on the time a process wants to wait for a message. Another use of select statements is to control *termination* of processes. In Concurrent C, a guard may consist of the keyword **terminate**. A process that executes a select statement containing a **terminate** guard is willing to terminate if all other guards fail or suspend. If all processes are willing to terminate, the entire Concurrent C program terminates. Ada uses a similar mechanism to terminate parts of a program. Roughly, if all processes created by the same process are willing to terminate and the process that created them has finished the execution of its statements, all these processes are terminated. This mechanism presumes hierarchical processes.

A final note: select statements in most languages are *unfair*. In the CSP model, for example, if several guards are successful, one of them is selected nondeterministically. No assumptions can be made about which guard is selected. Repeated execution of the select statement may select the same guard over and over again, even if there are other successful guards. An *implementation* may introduce a degree of fairness, by assuring that a successful guard will be selected within a finite number of iterations, or by giving guards equal chances. On the other hand, an implementation may evaluate the guards sequentially and always choose the first one yielding 'true'. The semantics of select statements do not guarantee any degree of fairness, so programmers cannot rely on it.

Proposals have been made for giving programmers explicit control over the selection of succeeding guards. Silberschatz suggests a partial ordering of the guards [Silberschatz, 1984]. Elrad and Maymir-Ducharme propose prefixing every guarded command with a compile-time constant called the *preference control value* [Elrad and Maymir-Ducharme, 1986]. If several guards succeed, the one with the highest preference control value (i.e. priority) is chosen. If there are several guards with this value, one of them is chosen nondeterministically. This feature is useful if some requests are more urgent than others. For example, the buffer process may wish to give consumers a higher priority than producers.

```
[
        not full(buffer); producer?DepositItem(x) →
            add x to end of buffer;

    [] not empty(buffer); consumer?AskForItem() →
            consumer!SendItem(first item of buffer);
            remove first item from buffer;
]
```

Figure 3.2 *A select statement in CSP used by a buffer process. The statement consists of two guarded commands, separated by a '[]'. The '?' is the input (receive) operator. The '!' is the output (send) operator.*

Guarded Horn clauses

Logic programs are inherently nondeterministic. In reducing a goal of a logic program, there are often several clauses to choose from (see Section 3.1.1). Intuitively, the semantics of logic programming prescribes that the underlying execution machinery must simply choose the 'right' clause, the one leading to a proof. This behaviour is called *don't know nondeterminism*. In sequential logic languages (e.g. Prolog), these semantics are implemented using *backtracking*. At each choice point an arbitrary clause is chosen, and if it later turns out to be the wrong one, the system resets itself to the state before the choice point and then tries another clause.

In a parallel execution model, several goals may be tried simultaneously. In this model, backtracking is very complicated to implement. If a binding for a variable has to be undone, all processes that have used this binding must backtrack too. Most parallel logic programming languages therefore avoid backtracking altogether. Rather than trying the clauses for a given predicate one by one and backtracking on failure, parallel logic languages (1) search all these clauses in parallel and (2) do not allow any bindings made during these parallel executions to be visible to the outside until one of the parallel executions is committed to. This is called OR parallelism. Unfortunately, this cannot go on indefinitely, because the number of search paths worked on in parallel will grow exponentially with the length of the proof.

A popular technique to control OR parallelism is *committed-choice nondeterminism* (or *don't care nondeterminism*), which nondeterministically selects one alternative clause and discards the others. It is based on guarded Horn clauses of the form:

$$A :- G_1, ..., G_n \mid B_1, ..., B_m \quad (n \geq 0, m \geq 0)$$

The conjunction of the goals G_i is called the *guard*; the conjunction of the goals B_i is the *body*. Declaratively, the *commit operator* '|' is also a conjunction operator.

Just like the guards of a select statement, the guard of a guarded Horn clause can either succeed, fail, or suspend. A guard suspends if it tries to bind a variable that it is not allowed to bind, as explained in Section 3.2.2. If a goal with a predicate A is to be reduced, the guards of all clauses for A are tried in parallel, until some guards succeed. The reduction process then chooses one of these guards nondeterministically and *commits* to its clause. It aborts execution of the other guards and executes the body of the selected clause.

So far, this all looks much like the select statement, but there are some subtle differences. A guard should not be allowed to affect its environment until it is selected. Guards that are aborted should have no side-effects at all. Precautions must be taken against guards that try to bind variables in their environment. For example, consider the following piece of code:

```
A(X)  :-  G(X)  |  B(X).
A(X)  :-  H(X)  |  C(X).
G(1)  :-  P(1).
H(2)  :-  Q(2).
```

The guard G of the first clause binds X to 1 and then calls P. Guard H of the second clause binds X to 2 and calls Q. These bindings should not be made visible to the caller of A until one of the guards G or H is committed to. PARLOG ensures this by using mode declarations to distinguish between input and output variables of a clause. The compiler checks that guards (or any other goals in the body) do not bind input variables. If a guard binds an output variable, this binding is initially made to a temporary variable. When a clause is committed to, the bindings made by its guard are made permanent and the bindings generated by the other guards (to temporaries) are thrown away. If a guard is ultimately not selected, it has no effect at all.

Concurrent Prolog, on the other hand, allows variables in the environment to be changed before commitment. But the effects only become visible outside the clause if the clause is committed to. The semantics and distributed implementation of commitment in Concurrent Prolog are similar to those of atomic transactions [Taylor *et al.*, 1987b].

For reasons of simplicity and ease of implementation, most of the recent effort in parallel logic programming languages centres on their so-called 'flat' subsets. In a flat guarded Horn clause, guards are restricted to simple predefined test predicates.

3.3   Partial failure

The final issue which must be addressed by languages for programming distributed systems is the potential for partial failure of the system. Distributed computing systems have the potential advantages over centralized systems of higher *reliability* and *availability*. If some of the processors involved in a distributed computation crash, then, in principle, the computation can still continue on the remaining processors, provided that all vital information contained by the failing processors is also stored on some healthy ones. Thus the system as a whole becomes more reliable. This principle of *replication* of information can be used to increase the availability of the system. A system is said to be *fault tolerant* if it still continues functioning properly in the face of processor crashes, allowing distributed programs to continue their execution and allowing users to keep on using the system.

In general, it is not an easy task to write programs that can survive processor crashes and continue as if nothing had happened. The responsibility for achieving reliability can be split up among the operating system, the language run-time system, and the programmer. Numerous research papers have been published about how operating systems can support fault tolerance [LeBlanc and Wilkes, 1985; Powell and Presotto, 1983]. In the following sections we will discuss how programming languages can contribute their part.

3.3.1   Programming fault tolerance

The simplest approach to handling processor failures is to ignore them altogether. This means that a single crash will cause the entire program to fail. Typically, processes trying to interact with a sick processor will either be blocked forever or discover an unexpected communication failure and terminate. A program running in parallel on several processors has a higher chance of failing than its single processor counterpart (although the shorter execution time of the parallel version may compensate a bit). Still, as processor crashes are rare, for many applications this is not a problem.

The next simplest approach to implementing fault tolerance is to let the programmer do it. The operating system or language run-time system can detect processor failures and return an error status to every process that wants to communicate with a crashed processor. The programmer can write code to deal with this contingency. For some programs, this approach is quite adequate.

In the travelling salesman problem discussed in Section 2.3, for example, each processor repeatedly chooses an initial path for the salesman and computes the length of the best full path that starts with the given partial path. If a processor crashes before returning the result, all that need be done is to have another processor analyze the given partial path. This simple scheme only works because the processors have no side-effects except for returning the length of the best full path. No harm is done if a certain partial path is examined twice. In general, a job may be given away multiple times, until the receiver executes it without crashing.

A possible improvement to this scheme is to let the language run-time system take care of repeating requests for work after a processor crash. Nelson has studied this approach in the context of the remote procedure call model [Nelson, 1981]. If the run-time system detects that processor P has crashed, P's processes are restarted, either on P or on another processor. Furthermore, all outstanding RPCs to P are repeated.

As procedures can have side-effects, it is important to specify accurately the semantics of a call that may have been executed (entirely or partially) more than once. Nelson gives a classification of these *call semantics*. The simplest case is a local procedure call (the caller and callee are on the same processor). If the processor does not crash, the call is executed exactly once (*exactly once semantics*). If the processor does crash, the run-time system restarts all processes of the crashed processor, including the caller and the callee of the procedure. The call will eventually be repeated, until it succeeds without crashing. Clearly, the results of the last executed call are used by the caller, although earlier (abandoned) calls may have had side-effects that survived the crash (e.g. changing a file in the processor's local disk). These semantics are called *last-one semantics*.

For remote procedure calls, where the caller and callee are on different processors, the best that can be hoped for is to have the same semantics as for local calls, which are exactly once without crashes and last-one with crashes. The former is not very hard to obtain, but achieving last-one semantics in the presence of crashes turns out to be tricky, especially if more than two processors are involved. Suppose processor P1 calls procedure f on processor P2, which in turn calls procedure g on processor P3. While P3 is working on g, P2 crashes. P2's processes will be restarted and P1's call to f will be repeated. The second invocation will again call procedure g on P3. Unfortunately, P3 does not know that P2 has crashed. P3 executes g twice and may return the results in any order, possibly violating last-one semantics. The problem is that, in a distributed environment, a crashed processor may still have outstanding calls to other processors. Such calls are appropriately called *orphans*, because their parents (callers) have died. To achieve last-one semantics, these orphans must be terminated before restarting the crashed processes. This can be implemented either by waiting for them to finish or by tracking them down and killing them (orphan extermination). As this is not an easy job, other (weaker) semantics have been proposed for RPC. *Last-of-many semantics* is obtained by neglecting orphans. It suffers from the problem described above. An even weaker form is *at-least-once semantics*, which just guarantees that the call is executed one or more times, but does not specify which results are returned to the caller.

One key idea is still missing from our discussion. Procedure calls (local as well as remote) can have side-effects. If a call is executed many times (because of processor crashes), its side-effects also are executed many times. For side-effects like incrementing a bank account stored in a database, this may be highly undesirable (or highly desirable, depending upon one's point of view). A mechanism is needed to specify that a call either runs to completion or has no effects at all. This is where atomic transactions come in.

3.3.2 Atomic transactions

A distributed program can be regarded as a set of parallel processes performing operations on data objects. Usually, a data object is managed by a single process, but other processes can operate on the object indirectly (e.g. by issuing a remote procedure call requesting the managing process to do the operation). In general, the effects of an operation become visible immediately. Moreover, operations affecting objects on secondary storage become permanent once the operation has been performed. Sometimes this behaviour is undesirable. Consider a program that transfers a sum of money from one bank account (stored on disk) to another, by decreasing the first one and increasing the second one. This simple approach has two dangers. First, if another parallel process adds up all accounts in the database while the first process is in the middle of its transaction, it may observe the new value of the first account and the old value of the second, so it uses inconsistent values. Second, if the process doing the transfer crashes immediately after decreasing the first account, it leaves the database in an inconsistent state. If it is restarted later, it may try to decrease the first account once more.

A solution to these problems is to group operations together in *atomic transactions* (also called *atomic actions* or simply *transactions*). A group of operations (called a transaction) is atomic if it has both the property of *indivisibility* and of *recoverability*. A transaction is indivisible if, viewed from the outside, it has no intermediate states. For the outside world (i.e. all other transactions) it looks as if either all or none of the operations have been executed. A transaction is recoverable if all objects involved can be restored to their initial state if the transaction fails (e.g. because of a processor crash), so the transaction has no effect at all.

Recoverability can be achieved as follows. If a transaction contains an operation that tries to change an object, the changes are not applied to the original object, but to a new copy of the object, called a *version*. If the entire transaction fails (*aborts*), the new versions are simply discarded. If the transaction succeeds, it *commits* to these new versions. All objects changed by the transaction retain the value of their new version. Furthermore, the latest value of each object is also placed on *stable storage* [Lampson, 1981], which has a very high chance of surviving processor crashes and is accessible by all processors.

Indivisibility can be trivially assured by executing all atomic transactions sequentially. In our bank account example, we could deny other processes access to the database while the first process is doing the transfer. Unfortunately, this severely limits parallelism and hence degrades performance. A more efficient approach is to synchronize processes by using finer grained *locks*. The process doing the transfer first locks the two accounts. Other processes trying to access these two accounts are automatically suspended when they attempt to lock them.

Atomic transactions originated in the database world, but they are also used by some programming languages, such as Argus and Aeolus. A programming language can provide convenient abstractions for data objects and invocations of atomic transactions. The language run-time system can take care of many details, like locking and version management. These issues will be discussed in Chapter 4.

3.3.3   Transparent fault tolerance

The mechanisms discussed above provide linguistic support for dealing with partial failures. Some of the problems are solved by the operating system or the language run-time system, but programmers still have to do part of the work. This work has to be done for every new application. Other systems relieve programmers from all worries, by supporting fault tolerance in a fully transparent way.

Borg *et al.* describe a fault-tolerant message-passing system [Borg *et al.*, 1983]. For each process, an inactive *backup* process is created on another processor. All messages sent to the primary process are also sent to its backup. The backup also counts the messages sent by the primary process. If the primary processor crashes, the backup process becomes active and starts repeating the primary process's computations. Whenever it wants to receive a message, the backup process reads the next message saved while the primary process was still alive. If the backup process needs to send a message, it first checks if the primary process had already sent it, to avoid sending messages twice. During normal computations, the primary and backup processes periodically synchronize, to copy the entire state of the primary process (a checkpoint) to the backup. The backup process then can forget all messages previous to the checkpoint.

This approach requires extra processors and will sometimes delay computation while a checkpoint is being made. Strom and Yemini propose a different technique, *optimistic recovery*, to be used in systems consisting of processes that interact only by message passing [Strom and Yemini, 1985b]. (This model is used in their language NIL.) Their technique involves periodic checkpointing and logging of messages on stable storage, rather than a backup process. As a fundamental departure from Borg's approach, these activities proceed *asynchronously* with the normal computations. This has the advantage that, if I/O bandwidth to stable storage is high enough, the normal computation will not slow down. However, the technique requires some bookkeeping overhead to allow a consistent system state to be restored after a crash.

CHAPTER 4

Languages for Programming Distributed Systems

In this chapter we will take a closer look at several languages that have been designed for programming distributed systems. We will first present a detailed survey of the state of the art in this area and then discuss to what extent existing languages meet the goals listed in the introduction to this book.

It is difficult to determine exactly how many languages for distributed programming exist; we know of nearly 100 relevant languages, but there are probably many more. We have selected a subset for closer study. These languages together are representative of research in this area. We have chosen these languages to cover a broad spectrum of ideas. While we have attempted to focus on languages that have been well documented and cited in the literature, we fully admit that any selection of this kind contains a certain amount of subjective choice. We include references to languages not discussed in detail here.

We have organized the languages in a simple classification scheme. First of all, we distinguish between *logically distributed* and *logically nondistributed* languages, as discussed in Section 1.4. In languages based on logical distribution, parallel computations (e.g. processes) communicate by sending messages to each other. The address spaces of different computations do not overlap, so the address space of the whole program is distributed. In a logically nondistributed language, the parallel units have a logically *shared* address space and communicate through data stored in the shared address space. Note that this distinction is based on the *logical model* of the language; the presence of logically shared data does not imply that *physical* shared memory is needed to implement the language. All languages described below that are based on logically shared data have been implemented on distributed computing systems, that is, on computers without shared primary memory.

The languages in the two categories are further partitioned into a number of classes, based on their communication mechanisms. In the first category we include: synchronous message-passing, asynchronous message-passing, rendezvous, remote procedure calls, multiple communication primitives, objects, and atomic transactions. In the second category we distinguish between implicit communication through function results (used in parallel functional languages), shared logical variables (parallel logic languages), and distributed data structures. The classification is illustrated in Figure 4.1.

In each of the following subsections we will discuss one class of languages. Each subsection starts with a table containing several languages of that class together with references to papers on these languages. Each table corresponds to one specific leaf in the tree of Figure 4.1. We have selected at least one language from each table for closer study. We describe the most distinctive features of the example language(s), and discuss how it differs from other members of its class. We emphasize the semantics, rather than the syntax. Our intention is to expose the new key ideas in the language, not to provide a full language description.

For each language, we first provide background information on its design. Next, we describe how parallelism is expressed in the language and how parallel units are mapped onto processors (if the language addresses this issue). Subsequently, the communication and synchronization primitives are discussed. If relevant, we also discuss how the language deals with fault tolerance; several languages ignore this issue, however. Finally, we give information on implementations and user experiences with the language. Issues like support for distributed debugging and commercial availability of language implementations are outside the scope of this survey and are therefore not discussed.

4.1 Languages with logically distributed address spaces

We will now discuss seven classes of languages with logically distributed address spaces: languages supporting synchronous message-passing, asynchronous message-passing, rendezvous, remote procedure calls, multiple communication primitives, operation invocations on objects, and atomic transactions. Languages in the first two classes provide point-to-point messages. Rendezvous-based languages support two-way communication between senders and receivers. A remote procedure call also is a two-way interaction, but its semantics are closer to a normal procedure call. Languages in the fifth class use a variety of one-way and two-way (or even multi-way) communication primitives. Object-based languages also support one or more of the above primitives. Unlike other languages, communication is between objects rather than processes. As objects encapsulate both data and behaviour, these languages may also be thought of as providing some form of data sharing. Finally, we discuss languages based on atomic transactions; these languages are mainly intended for implementing fault-tolerant applications.

4.1.1 Synchronous message-passing

In 1978, Hoare wrote what was later to become a very influential paper, although it described only a fragment of a language [Hoare, 1978]. The language, called Communicating Sequential Processes (CSP), not only generated some criticism [Kieburtz

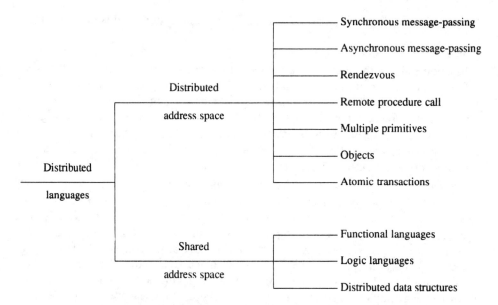

Figure 4.1 *Classification of languages for distributed programming.*

and Silberschatz, 1979; Bernstein, 1980], but also stimulated the design of many other languages and systems (see Table 4.1).

Joyce differs from the other languages of Table 4.1 by supporting *recursive* processes. The model proposed by Hoare consists of a fixed number of sequential processes that communicate only through synchronous message-passing. Below, we describe CSP in some detail and discuss one of its descendants, occam.

CSP

CSP was designed by Hoare as a simple language that allows an efficient implementation on a variety of architectures [Hoare, 1978, 1985]. We describe the original language, outlined in [Hoare, 1978]. The 1985 version has a clearer syntax and uses named channels.

Parallelism. CSP provides a simple parallel command to create a fixed number of parallel processes. A process consists of a name, local variables, and a sequence of statements (body). CSP processes take no parameters and cannot be mapped onto specific processors. An array of similar processes can be created, but their number must be a compile-time constant. As a simple example of a parallel statement

```
[writer:: x: real; ...  ||  reader(i:1..2):: ...]
```

creates three processes, called 'writer,' 'reader(1),' and 'reader(2).' The writer has a local variable *x*. The subscript variable *i* can be used within the body of the reader processes.

Communication and synchronization. CSP processes may not communicate by

Table 4.1 *Languages based on synchronous message-passing*

Language	References
CCSP	[Hull and Donnan, 1986]
CSM	[Zhongxiu and Xining, 1987]
CSP	[Hoare, 1978]
CSP-S	[Patniak and Badrinath, 1984]
CSPS	[Roman *et al.*, 1987]
CSP/80	[Jazayeri *et al.*, 1980]
ECSP	[Baiardi *et al.*, 1984]
GDPL	[Ng and Li, 1984]
Joyce	[Brinch Hansen, 1987]
LIMP	[Hunt, 1979]
occam	[Inmos Ltd., 1984]
Pascal-m	[Abramsky and Bornat, 1983]
Pascal+CSP	[Adamo, 1982]
Planet	[Crookes and Elder, 1984]
RBCSP	[Roper and Barter, 1981]

using global variables. All interprocess communication is done using synchronous **receive** and **send**. The sending process specifies the name of the destination process, and provides a value to be sent. The receiving process specifies the name of the source process, and provides a variable to which the received value is assigned. A process executing either a **send** or a **receive** is blocked until its partner has executed the complementary statement. For example

```
[X:: Y ! 3   || Y:: n: integer; X ? n]
```

In process X's statement, the value 3 is sent to Y. In process Y's statement, input is read from process X and stored in the local variable *n*. When both X and Y have executed their statements, the one-way communication occurs. The net result is assigning 3 to *n*.

Both simple and structured data may be communicated (and assigned), as long as the value sent is of the same type as the variable receiving it. The structured data can be given a name (a *constructor*), such as pair in the following example:

```
[X:: Y ! pair(35,60)  || Y:: n,m: integer;  X ? pair(n,m)]
```

An empty constructor may be used to synchronize two processes without transferring any real data.

The *alternative* construction provides for nondeterminism in CSP. It consists of sets of guards followed by actions to be performed. The guards may contain Boolean expressions and an input statement, as explained in Section 3.2.3. CSP allows a process to receive selectively, based on the availability of input and the name field (constructor) of the incoming communication.

Implementation and experience. CSP is essentially a paper design, but it has influenced the design of several languages (see Table 4.1) that have been implemented and used, most notably the occam language.

Occam

Occam is modelled on Hoare's CSP, and was designed for programming Inmos's Transputer [Inmos Ltd., 1984; May, 1983]. Occam is essentially the assembly language of the Transputer. The language lacks features that have become standard in most modern programming languages, such as data typing, recursive procedures, and modules.

Parallelism. There are three basic actions in occam: *assignment*, *input*, and *output*. Each action is considered to be a little process. Processes can be grouped together in several ways to form more complex processes. Any process can be *named* by prefixing its definition with the keyword PROC, followed by its name and a list of formal parameters. When subsequently referenced, a new instance of the named process is created, with the parameters specified in the reference. Both parallel and sequential execution of a group of processes must be explicitly stated, by heading the group with a PAR or SEQ, respectively.

Arrays of similar processes can be expressed in occam. In the construct

```
PAR i = 0 FOR n
   process...
```

n parallel processes are created, each with a different value for *i*.

Occam provides a facility for assigning processes to processors. Parallel processes may be prioritized by prefixing the group with PRI PAR. The first process in the group is given highest priority, the second, second highest priority, and so on.

Communication and synchronization. Unlike CSP, parallel processes communicate indirectly through *channels*. A channel is a one-way link between two processes. Channel communication is fully synchronous. Only one process may be inputting from, and one outputting to, a channel at a given time. Channels are typed and their names can be passed as parameters to PROC calls.

Occam provides an ALT construct, similar to CSP's alternative statement, to express nondeterminism. The constituents of this construct can be prioritized. If input is available on more than one channel, the one with the highest priority will be accepted.

The current time can be read from an input-only channel declared as a TIMER. A delay until a certain time can be made with the 'WAIT AFTER t' construct. This can be used as a constituent of an ALT construct, for example, to prevent a process from hanging forever if no input is forthcoming.

Implementation and experience. The occam language was intended for use with multiple interconnected Transputers, where a channel would be implemented as a link between two Transputers [May and Shepherd, 1984]. The Transputer implementation is quite efficient (e.g. a context switch takes a few microseconds). This efficiency has been achieved by using a simple communication model (CSP), and by requiring the number of processes and their storage allocation to be determined during compile time. Occam has also been implemented on non-Transputer systems [Fisher, 1986].

Occam is used extensively for applications like signal processing, image processing, process control, simulation, and numerical analysis. A major criticism of the first version of occam is the inability to pass complex objects (e.g. arrays) as part of a single message. Occam-2 has addressed this problem through the introduction of *channel protocols*, which describe the type of objects that may be transferred across a channel [Burns, 1988]. The compiler (sometimes with the help of the run-time system) checks that the input and output operations on a channel are compatible with the channel protocol.

4.1.2   Asynchronous message-passing

The synchronous message-passing model proposed by Hoare and adapted by occam prevents the sending process from continuing immediately after sending the message. The sender must wait until the receiving process is willing to accept the message. This design decision has a major impact on both the programming style and the implementation of a language. Several language designers have chosen to remove this restriction and support asynchronous-message passing, sometimes in addition to synchronous message-passing. Languages in this class are shown in Table 4.2. We discuss NIL in some more detail.

Table 4.2 *Languages based on asynchronous message-passing*

Language	References
AMPL	[Dannenberg, 1981; Milewski, 1984]
CMAY	[Bagrodia and Chandy, 1985]
Concurrent C	[Tsujino *et al.*, 1984]
CONIC	[Kramer and Magee, 1985; Sloman and Kramer, 1987]
DPL-82	[Ericson, 1982]
FRANK	[Graham, 1985]
GYPSY	[Ambler *et al.*, 1977]
LADY	[Nehmer *et al.*, 1987]
MENYMA/S	[Koch and Maibaum, 1982]
NIL	[Strom and Yemini, 1983]
ParMod	[Eichholz, 1987]
PCL	[Lesser *et al.*, 1979]
Platon	[Staunstrup, 1982]
PLITS	[Feldman, 1979]
Port Language	[Kerridge and Simpson, 1986]
Pronet	[LeBlanc and Maccabe, 1982]
ZENO	[Ball *et al.*, 1979]

NIL

NIL (Network Implementation Language) is a high-level language for the construction of large, reliable, distributed software systems [Strom and Yemini, 1983, 1984, 1985a, 1986]. NIL was designed by Robert Strom and Shaula Yemini at the IBM T.J. Watson Research Center.

NIL is a *secure* language. Security implies that one program module cannot affect the correctness of other modules (e.g. by a 'wild store' through a bad pointer). Security in NIL is based on an invention called the *typestate* [Strom and Yemini, 1986]. A typestate is a compile-time property that captures both the type of a variable and its state of initialization. In the following program fragment

```
1.   X,Y: INTEGER;
2.   if condition then X := 4; end if
3.   Y := X + 3;
```

statement 3 is marked as illegal by the compiler, because variable X may not be initialized at this point. X has the right type (integer) but the wrong state. The typestate mechanism imposes some constraints on the structure of the programs (especially on the control flow), but the designers claim that these constraints are not overly restrictive and usually lead to better structured code. NIL avoids features that would make compile-time checking of typestates impossible. It does not provide explicit pointer manipulation (it does provide a higher level construct for building general data structures) and it has an IPC model that disallows sharing of variables.

Parallelism. Parallelism in NIL is based on the so-called *process model* [Strom *et al.*, 1985; Strom, 1986]. A NIL system consists of a network of dynamically created processes that communicate only by message passing over communication channels. In NIL, a process is not only the unit of parallelism, but also the unit of *modularity*. The division of a NIL program into processes should be based on software engineering principles rather than on performance considerations. The mapping of processes onto processors is considered to be an implementation issue, to be dealt with by the compiler and run-time system. This process model makes NIL conceptually simpler than other languages that have separate mechanisms for parallelism and modularity (e.g. tasks and packages in Ada).

Communication and synchronization. Configuration of the communication paths between processes is done dynamically. A *port* in NIL is a queued communication channel. At any given instant, a port has one specific owner. Ownership of a port can be transferred to another process, by passing the port as part of a message or by passing the port as an initialization parameter to a newly created process. A process can connect input ports and output ports owned by it.

Both synchronous and asynchronous communication are supported. A single input port may be connected to several output ports, so there can be multiple pending messages on an input port; these messages are queued. A guarded-command style statement is provided for waiting for messages on any of a set of input ports.

Fault tolerance. Recovery from processor failures is intended to be handled transparently by the NIL run-time system, using the optimistic recovery technique discussed in Section 3.3.3.

Implementation and experience. A NIL compiler generating code for a uniprocessor (IBM 370) has been implemented. Research on distributed implementations has focused on transformation strategies, which optimize NIL programs for specific target configurations [Strom and Yemini, 1985a]. NIL has been used to implement a prototype communication system, consisting of several hundred modules [Strom and Yemini, 1986]. The implementors found the typestate mechanism highly useful in integrating this relatively large number of modules.

4.1.3 Rendezvous

The rendezvous mechanism was first used in Ada and was later employed in some other languages, as shown in Table 4.3. We discuss Ada and Concurrent C below.

Ada
The language Ada was designed on behalf of the US Department of Defense by a team of people led by Jean Ichbiah [US Department of Defense, 1983]. Since its first (preliminary) definition appeared in 1979, Ada has been the subject of an avalanche of publications. A substantial part of the discussion in these publications relates to parallel and distributed programming in Ada [Yemini, 1982; Gehani, 1984a; Mundie and Fisher, 1986; Burns *et al.*, 1987] and to the implementation of Ada's multitasking. Van Katwijk reviews more than 30 papers of the latter category [Van Katwijk, 1987].

Parallelism. Parallelism is based on sequential processes, called *tasks* in Ada. Each task has a certain type, called its *task type*. A task consists of a *specification* part, which describes how other tasks can communicate with it, and a *body*, which contains its executable statements. Tasks can be created explicitly or can be declared, but in neither case is it possible to pass any parameters to the new task. Limited control over the local scheduling of tasks is given, by allowing a static priority to be assigned to task types. There is no notation for mapping tasks onto processors.

Communication and synchronization. Tasks usually communicate through the rendezvous mechanism. Tasks can also communicate through shared variables, but updates of a shared variable by one task are not guaranteed to be immediately visible to other tasks. An implementation that does not use shared memory can keep local copies of shared variables and defer updates until tasks explicitly synchronize through a rendezvous.

The rendezvous mechanism is based on entry declarations, entry calls, and accept statements, as discussed in Section 3.2.1. Entry declarations are only allowed in the specification part of a task. Accept statements for the entries appear in the body of the task. They contain a formal parameter part similar to that of a procedure. It is not possible to accept an entry conditionally depending on the values of the actual parameters, or to control the order in which outstanding requests are accepted. Gehani and Cargill show that an array of entries with the same formal part (a so-called *family*) can

Table 4.3 *Languages based on rendezvous*

Language	References
Ada	[US Department of Defense, 1983]
BNR Pascal	[Gammage *et al.*, 1987]
Concurrent C	[Gehani and Roome, 1989]
MC	[Rizk and Halsall, 1987]

sometimes be used instead of conditional acceptance, although in general this leads to polling [Gehani and Cargill, 1984].

A task can call an entry of another task by using an *entry call statement*, similar to a procedure call statement. An entry call specifies the *name* of the task containing the entry, as well as the entry name itself. Entry names cannot be used in expressions (e.g. they cannot be passed around as parameters). A program can use a pointer to an explicitly created task as a name for that task. Pointers are more flexible than static identifiers, but they cannot point to declared tasks or to entries.

Ada uses a **select** statement similar to CSP's alternative command for expressing nondeterminism. Ada's **select** statement is actually used for three different purposes: to select an entry call nondeterministically from a set of outstanding requests, to call an entry conditionally (i.e. only if the called task is ready to accept it immediately), and to set a timeout on an entry call. So Ada essentially supports input guards and conditional and timed entry calls, but not output guards.

Fault tolerance. Ada has an exception-handling mechanism for dealing with software failures, but the language definition does not address the issue of hardware failures [Burns *et al.*, 1987]. If the processor on which a task T executes crashes, an implementation may (but need not) treat T like an aborted task (i.e. a task that failed because of software errors). If so, other tasks that try to communicate with T will receive a **tasking_error** exception and conclude that T is no longer alive; however, they do not know the reason (hardware or software) why T died, so this support for dealing with processor failures is very rudimentary.

Implementation and experience. Given the fact that the DoD intends to have Ada replace 300 or so other languages currently in use, and that industry has also shown some interest in Ada, the language probably will be used extensively in the future. Many implementations of Ada are now available and several million lines of Ada code have already been written for uniprocessor applications [Myers, 1987].

Burns *et al.* cite 18 papers addressing the issue of how to use Ada in a distributed environment [Burns *et al.*, 1987]. They also review many problems with parallel and distributed programming in Ada. The synchronization mechanism receives a substantial part of the criticism: only input guards (not output guards) are allowed in **select** statements, entry calls are always serviced in FIFO order and cannot be accepted conditionally, and it is not possible to assign priorities to alternatives of a **select** statement. Distribution of programs among multiple processors is not addressed by the definition of Ada, but is left to configuration tools.

Concurrent C

Concurrent C extends the C language [Kernighan and Ritchie, 1978] by adding support for distributed programming. The language is being developed at AT&T Bell Laboratories, by Narain Gehani and colleagues [Gehani and Roome, 1986, 1989]. Concurrent C is based on Ada's rendezvous model, but its designers tried to avoid the problems they observed in this model [Gehani and Roome, 1988].

Parallelism. A process in Concurrent C has a specification part and a body, just like tasks in Ada. The specification part consists of the process's name, a list of formal parameters, and a list of *transactions*. (A transaction is Concurrent C's equivalent to an Ada entry. It should not be confused with atomic transactions.) Processes are created explicitly, using the **create** primitive, which can pass parameters to the created process. The new process can be given a priority (which can later be changed by itself or by other processes) and it can be assigned to a specific processor. The **create** primitive returns an identifier for the new process instantiation. This value can be assigned to a variable of the same process type, and can be passed around as a parameter. For example

```
process buffer pid;
pid = create buffer(100) priority(1) processor(3);
```

starts a process of type buffer on processor 3, giving it priority 1 and passing the number 100 as a parameter to it. A reference to the process is returned in pid, which might be passed to another process to use for subsequent communication with the buffer process.

Communication and synchronization. Processes communicate through the rendezvous mechanism. (Communication through shared variables is not forbidden, but no special language support is provided for it, and it will only work correctly on shared-memory machines.) A transaction in Concurrent C differs from an Ada entry in that a transaction may return a value. In addition, Concurrent C supports *asynchronous* transactions (equivalent to asynchronous message-passing); such transactions may not return a value [Gehani, 1987].

Concurrent C supports a more powerful **accept** statement than Ada. Transactions can be accepted conditionally, based on the values of their parameters. For example

```
accept tname(a,b,c) suchthat (a < b) { ... }
```

Only outstanding transaction calls for which the expression after the **suchthat** evaluates to 'true' will be accepted. The order of acceptance can be controlled using a **by** clause:

```
accept tname(a,b,c) by(c) { ... }
```

Of all outstanding calls to transaction tname, the one with the lowest third parameter will be accepted. The **suchthat** and **by** constructs may also be used in combination with each other.

A transaction call is similar to a function call and can be used as part of an expression (since transaction calls may return values). The transaction call specifies the name of the called process along with the transaction name, and supplies actual parameters. The process name can be any expression that yields a process identifier. The transaction name is a static identifier. A specific transaction of a specific process can be assigned to a *transaction pointer* variable, which can subsequently be used instead of these two names in an indirect transaction call. With this mechanism, the caller need not know the type or name of the called process.

The caller can specify the amount of time it is willing to wait for its request to be carried out, using the following construct:

> **within** N ? pid.tname(params) : expr

If process `pid` does not accept the `tname` transaction call within N seconds, the call is cancelled and the expression `expr` is evaluated instead. This construct is equivalent to Ada's timed entry call, although with an entirely different syntax.

Nondeterminism is expressed through a **select** statement, similar to the one used by Ada. Concurrent C's select statement is somewhat cleaner, because it is used only for dealing with nondeterminism, not for timed or conditional transaction calls.

Fault tolerance. A fault-tolerant version of Concurrent C (called FT Concurrent C) based on replication of processes has been designed [Cmelik *et al.*, 1987].

Implementation and experience. Concurrent C has been implemented on a uniprocessor, a group of executable-code-compatible machines connected by an Ethernet, and a multiprocessor providing shared global memory [Cmelik *et al.*, 1988].

Concurrent C has been used in several nontrivial applications, such as a distributed version of 'make', a robot system, discrete event simulation, and a window manager. The language is being merged with C++ [Stroustrup, 1986] to create a programming language supporting both distributed programming and classes [Gehani and Roome, 1989].

4.1.4   Remote procedure call

Remote procedure call was first introduced by Brinch Hansen in his language Distributed Processes (see below) and has been studied in more detail by Nelson and Birrell [Nelson, 1981; Birrell and Nelson, 1984]. Remote procedures are also used in several other languages, as shown in Table 4.4. (Most languages based on atomic transactions also use remote procedure calls; these are discussed in Section 4.1.7.)

Table 4.4 *Languages based on Remote Procedure Call*

Language	References
Cedar	[Swinehart *et al.*, 1985]
Concurrent CLU	[Hamilton, 1984: Cooper and Hamilton, 1988]
Distributed Processes	[Brinch Hansen, 1978]
LYNX	[Scott, 1985, 1986, 1987; Scott and Cox, 1987]
P+	[Carpenter and Cailliau, 1984]

Distributed Processes

Brinch Hansen's Distributed Processes [Brinch Hansen, 1978] is the successor to Concurrent Pascal [Brinch Hansen, 1975]. Like Concurrent Pascal, DP is oriented towards real-time systems programming. Instead of Concurrent Pascal's monitor-based communication scheme, DP processes communicate using remote procedure calls.

Parallelism. In DP the number of processes is fixed at compile time. The intention is that there be one processor dedicated to executing each process. Each process, however, can contain several threads of control running in pseudo-parallel. A process definition contains an *initial* statement, which may be empty; this is the first thread. It may continue forever, or it may finish executing at some point, but in either case the process itself continues to exist; DP processes never terminate. Additional threads are initiated by calls from other processes. Arrays of processes may be declared. A process can determine its array index using the built-in function **this**.

Communication and synchronization. DP processes communicate by calling one another's *common procedures*. Such a call has the form

    call P.f(exprs, vars)

where P is the name of the called process and f is the name of a procedure declared by P. The expressions are input parameters; the return values of the call are assigned to the (output) variables.

The calling process (and all its threads) is blocked during the call. A new thread of control is created within P. P's *initial* statement and the threads created to handle remote calls execute as pseudo-parallel processes, scheduled nonpre-emptively. They communicate through P's global variables and synchronize through guarded regions.

Like the select statement of CSP and Ada, a guarded region in DP is based on Dijkstra's guarded command. A guarded region allows a thread to wait until one of a number of guards (conditional expressions) is true. When a thread is blocked in a guarded region, other threads in its process can continue their execution. The guards have access to the input parameters of the remote call and to the process's global variables. Since other threads can change the global variables, the guards are repeatedly evaluated, until one or more of them is true. This is a major difference with the select statement and makes the guarded region somewhat more powerful.

Two forms of guarded region are supported by DP. The **when** statement nondeterministically selects one true guard and executes the corresponding statement. The **cycle** statement is an endless repetition of the **when** statement.

Implementation and experience. DP is a paper design and has not been implemented. An outline of a possible implementation is given in [Brinch Hansen, 1978].

4.1.5   Multiple communication primitives

As can be seen from the previous sections, many different communication and synchronization mechanisms exist, each with its own advantages and disadvantages. As there is no general agreement on which primitive is best, some language designers have taken the approach of providing a range of primitives, from which the programmer can choose the one most suited to the application. In addition, programmers can experiment with different primitives while still using the same language. An important issue in the design of such a language is how to integrate all these primitives in a clean and consistent way. Examples of languages in this class are shown in Table 4.5. We discuss SR below.

Synchronizing Resources
Synchronizing Resources (SR) was developed by Gregory Andrews *et al.* at the University of Arizona [Andrews, 1981, 1982; Andrews and Olsson, 1986; Andrews *et al.*, 1988]. SR is a language for programming distributed operating systems and applications. It is based on Modula, Pascal, and DP, and provides several models of interprocess communication.

Parallelism. An SR program consists of one or more *resources*. A resource is a module run on one physical node (either a single processor or a shared-memory multiprocessor). Resources are dynamically created (parameters may be passed), and optionally assigned to run on a specific machine. An identifier for the resource instance is returned by the **create** command.

A resource can contain several processes, and these may share data. Synchronization among these processes is supported by the use of semaphores. Communication with processes in other resources is restricted to *operations*, discussed below. A resource may contain an initialization and a termination process. These are created and run implicitly. A resource terminates when it is killed by the **destroy** command. A program terminates when all its processes terminate or block.

Communication and synchronization. An SR operation definition looks like a procedure definition. Its implementation can either look like a procedure, or an entry point. When implemented as a procedure, the operation is serviced by an implicitly created process. When implemented as an entry point, it is serviced by an already running process in a rendezvous. The two types of implementation are transparent to the invoker of the operation. On the invoker's side, an operation may be called asynchronously using a **send** or synchronously using a **call**. A **send** blocks until the message has been delivered to the remote machine; a **call** blocks until the operation has

Table 4.5 *Languages based on multiple communication primitives*

Language	References
Dislang	[Li and Liu, 1981]
Pascal-FC	[Burns and Davies, 1988]
StarMod	[Cook, 1980; LeBlanc and Cook, 1983]
SR	[Andrews, 1981]

been completed and any return values received. Several **call**s can be grouped in a parallel call-statement, which terminates when all calls have been completed. The operation and its resource instance must be named explicitly in the invocation. This is done using the identifier for the resource returned by the **create** command.

By combining the two modes of servicing operations and the two modes of invoking them, four types of interprocess communication can be expressed as follows:

	call (synchr.)	send (asynchr.)
entry (synchr.)	rendezvous	message passing
proc (asynchr.)	RPC	fork

SR uses a construct similar to the **select** statement to deal with nondeterminism. The SR guarded command, or **alternative** has the following form:

```
entry_point(params) and bool-expr by expr → statements
```

A guard may contain an entry point for an operation, a Boolean expression, and a priority expression. The two expressions can refer to the actual parameters of the operation. An alternative is enabled if there is a pending invocation of the operation and the Boolean expression evaluates to true. The expression in the **by** part is used for prioritization when there are several pending invocations of the same operation. If all Boolean expressions are false, the process suspends.

Fault tolerance. SR supports two rudimentary mechanisms for handling failures. Exception handlers can be used to handle failures detected by the run-time system. For example, a handler attached to an operation invocation is called if the invocation fails. A **when** statement can be used to ask the run-time system to monitor a certain source (e.g. a process or processor) and to invoke a user-supplied operation if the source fails.

Implementation and experience. An implementation of SR on top of UNIX is described in [Andrews *et al.*, 1988]. It runs on collections of SUNs or VAXes® and on the Encore Multimax. SR has been used to implement a parallel Prolog-interpreter and the file system of the Saguaro distributed operating system.

4.1.6 Object-based languages

The object-based approach to programming is becoming increasingly popular, not only in the world of sequential programs, but also for building distributed applications. The need for distributed objects arises when, for example, operating systems and distributed problem solvers are modelled. Exploiting parallelism to speed up programs is usually considered to be a secondary issue, to be dealt with by the language implementation.

In most parallel object-based or object-oriented* languages (see Table 4.6), parallelism is based on assigning a parallel process to each object, so objects become active components. This method is used, for example, in the languages Concurrent-Smalltalk, CLIX, Emerald, Hybrid, Ondine, POOL, Sloop, and in the actor languages Act 1, Cantor, and CSSA. ConcurrentSmalltalk (based on Smalltalk-80) also supports asynchronous message-passing to increase parallelism further. Actor languages [Hewitt, 1977; Agha, 1986] are related to object-oriented languages, but arrange objects in dynamically changing hierarchies, rather than in static classes. Athas and Seitz discuss the usage of the actor language Cantor for programming fine-grain multicomputers [Athas and Seitz, 1988].

ABCL/1 uses asynchronous message-passing and an explicit construct for sending several messages simultaneously to different objects. Orient84/K is a multiparadigm language for programming knowledge-based systems, integrating object-oriented, logic, and parallel programming. OIL is the intermediate language for the FAIM-1 symbolic multiprocessor system. OIL integrates parallel, object-oriented, logic, and procedural programming. Raddle is a language for the design of large distributed systems. EPL is an object-based language based on Concurrent Euclid [Holt, 1982]. EPL is used with the Eden distributed operating system. It influenced the design of Emerald (discussed below) and Distributed Smalltalk, which is based on Smalltalk-80.

Emerald

Emerald is an object-based programming language for the implementation of distributed applications. It was developed at the University of Washington by Andrew Black and colleagues [Black *et al.*, 1986, 1987; Hutchinson, 1987; Jul *et al.*, 1988; Jul, 1988].

Like Smalltalk-80, Emerald considers all entities to be objects. For the programmer, both a file accessible by many processes and a Boolean variable local to a single process are objects. Objects can either be passive (data) or active. Unlike Smalltalk-80, Emerald is a strongly typed language and has no classes or inheritance.

Abstract types are used to define the interface to an object. An abstract type can be implemented by any object supporting at least the operations specified in the interface. The type system was designed to allow multiple implementations of the same type to coexist; new implementations can be added to a running system. The pro-

---

* As discussed in Section 3.1.1, we define a language to be object-oriented if it has inheritance, and object-based if it supports objects but lacks inheritance.

Table 4.6 *Object-oriented, object-based, and actor languages*

Language	References
ABCL/1	[Yonezawa *et al.*, 1986]
Act 1	[Lieberman, 1987]
ALPS	[Vishnubhotia, 1988]
Cantor	[Athas and Seitz, 1988]
CLIX	[Hur and Chon, 1987]
Cluster 86	[Lujun and Zhongxiu, 1987]
ConcurrentSmalltalk	[Yokote and Tokoro, 1986, 1987a, 1987b]
CSSA	[Nehmer *et al.*, 1987]
Distributed Smalltalk	[Bennett, 1987]
Emerald	[Black *et al.*, 1986]
EPL	[Black *et al.*, 1984]
Hybrid	[Nierstrasz, 1987]
Mentat	[Grimshaw and Liu, 1987]
OIL	[Davis and Robison, 1985]
Ondine	[Ogihara *et al.*, 1986]
Orient84/K	[Ishikawa and Tokoro, 1987]
POOL	[America, 1987]
Raddle	[Forman, 1986]
SINA	[Aksit and Tripathi, 1988]
Sloop	[Lucco, 1987b]

grammer can supply different implementations, each tailored to a specific use. Alternatively, the compiler can automatically generate different implementations from the same source code, tailored for local objects or distributed objects.

Parallelism. Parallelism is based on the simultaneous execution of active objects. Since objects in Emerald can be moved from one processor to another (as discussed below), the language essentially supports process migration. This is the most flexible mapping strategy discussed in Section 3.1.2.

Communication and synchronization. An object consists of four parts: a *name*, a *representation*, a set of *operations*, and an optional *process*. The name uniquely identifies the object within the distributed system. The representation contains the data of the object. Objects communicate by invoking each other's operations. There can be multiple active invocations within one object. The optional process runs in parallel with all these invocations. The invocations and the data shared by these invocations can be encapsulated in a monitor construct. The internal process can enter the monitor by calling an operation of its own object. Within a distributed system, many objects can run in parallel. Emerald provides the same semantics for local and remote invocations.

At any given time, an object is on a single processor, called its *location*. In general, programmers do not have to worry about locations, because the semantics of operation invocations are location independent. Some applications, however, are better off when they can control the locations of objects. Two objects that communicate frequently can be put on the same processor. Objects that are replicas of the same data should be located on different processors, to reduce the chance of losing the data after a processor crash. In Emerald, global objects can be moved from one processor to another. Such a move may be initiated either by the compiler (using compile-time analysis) or by the programmer, using a few simple language primitives. One important case is where an object is passed as a parameter in a remote operation. Every access to the parameter object will result in an extra remote invocation. The obvious solution is to pass a *copy* of the object as a parameter, but this changes the parameter mechanism into call-by-value. For object-based languages, call-by-reference is more natural. The solution in Emerald is to optimize such calls by first moving the parameter object to the destination processor, then doing the call, and optionally moving the object back. As this case occurs frequently, Emerald introduces a new parameter passing mode, called *call-by-move*, to accomplish this efficiently (i.e. with low message-passing overhead).

Implementation and experience. An important goal of a good implementation of Emerald is to recognize simple operations on small objects and to treat them efficiently. For example, an addition of two local integer variables is compiled to inline code. Local calls to objects that cannot move essentially take a local procedure call. Global objects (which are allowed to move) are referenced indirectly through an *object descriptor*, which either contains the address of the object if it is local, or indicates where to find the object in the distributed system. When an object moves to another processor, the descriptors on its old and new locations are updated.

A prototype distributed implementation of Emerald has been built, running on DEC MicroVAX II and SUN workstations connected by Ethernet.

Emerald has been used to implement a mail system, a replicated name server, a shared appointment calendar system, and several other applications [Jul *et al.*, 1988].

4.1.7   Atomic transactions

Several languages that were specifically designed for building fault-tolerant applications support atomic transactions in combination with remote procedure calls (see Table 4.7).

Aeolus and Avalon are built on top of existing systems that already support atomic transactions. Aeolus provides language support for the Clouds operating system. Avalon is being implemented on top of the Camelot distributed transaction management system. Camelot applications can also use the Camelot Library, which is a collection of macros and subroutines embedded in the C language. The Camelot Library takes care of many low-level details of transaction and object management, thus facilitating the implementation of Camelot servers and applications. This approach avoids designing a totally new language, while providing higher level primitives than traditional system calls.

Table 4.7 *Languages based on atomic transactions*

Language	References
Aeolus	[Wilkes and LeBlanc, 1986]
Argus	[Liskov and Scheifler, 1983]
Avalon	[Detlefs *et al.*, 1988]
Camelot Library	[Bloch, 1988]

Argus

Argus [Liskov, 1982; Liskov and Scheifler, 1983; Liskov, 1984, 1988; Weihl and Liskov, 1985], being developed at MIT by Barbara Liskov and colleagues, is based on CLU [Liskov *et al.*, 1977] and Extended CLU [Liskov, 1979]. It provides support for fault-tolerant distributed programming, in particular for applications requiring a high degree of reliability and availability, such as banking, airline reservation, and mail systems. Its main features are *guardians* (modules which can survive crashes) and *actions* (groups of atomic executions).

Parallelism. An Argus module, called a *guardian*, contains data objects and procedures for manipulating those objects. A guardian may contain **background** and **recover** sections and may have several **creator** and **handler** procedures. A creator procedure is run when an instance of the guardian is being made. The handler procedures are run on behalf of processes outside of the guardian. The recover section is executed when the guardian is started up again after a crash. The background section is intended for doing periodic tasks and is run continually during the life of the guardian.

A guardian instance is created dynamically by a call to a creator procedure. A creator may take parameters, and the guardian may be explicitly placed on a node:

```
g := GuardianType$create(params) @ machineX
```

More than one process may be running in a guardian instance at a given time. If the guardian contains a background section, a process is created to run it. In addition, each time a call is made to one of the guardian's handlers, a process is created to run the appropriate handler procedure. A guardian can terminate itself by executing the **terminate** statement.

Parallelism results from simultaneous execution of guardians. Pseudo-parallelism results from the implicit creation of a new process for each handler call within a guardian. Pseudo-parallel execution can also be expressed using a **coenter** statement. A **coenter** terminates when all its components have finished, and one component may terminate the rest prematurely by transferring control out of the **coenter** statement.

Communication and synchronization. Processes running in the same guardian instance can communicate using shared variables. Processes belonging to different guardians, however, can only communicate using *handler calls*. A handler call is a form of RPC, with arguments passed by value. Guardian and handler names may be passed as parameters. Argus provides synchronization mechanisms at two levels: one for pseudo-parallel processes, the other for parallel actions.

The **mutex** type provides mutually exclusive access to objects shared by processes within a guardian. The **seize** construct delays a process until it can gain possession of the given mutex object; the process gives up possession again when it finishes executing the seize body. The **pause** call can be made when a process encounters a delay (such as an unavailable resource), and wants to give up the mutex object while it suspends for a while.

In order to allow parallelism of actions, while retaining their atomic semantics, *atomic objects* are used, which are instances of atomic data types. Argus has some built-in atomic types, and users can define their own. The types of atomic object determine the amount of parallelism of actions permitted.

Fault tolerance. Some of the guardian's objects may be declared as **stable**; they are kept on stable storage. If a node crashes, the guardian can be brought up again by retrieving its stable objects from store and executing its recover section.

Argus supports two types of atomic execution: *topactions* and *nested subactions* [Moss, 1981]. Changes only become permanent (and stable objects written back to stable storage) when a topaction commits. A subaction is indivisible, but its effects are not made permanent until its toplevel action commits. If a toplevel action aborts, its subactions have no effect at all. On the other hand, if a subaction aborts, its parent action is not forced to abort. Nested subactions can be used for dealing with communication failures and for increasing parallelism. An action can also start up a new topaction.

Implementation and experience. A UNIX-based implementation of Argus on a collection of MicroVAX II workstations is described in [Liskov *et al.*, 1987].

One Argus application reported in the literature is a distributed collaborative editing system (CES), which allows a group of co-authors to edit a shared document [Greif *et al.*, 1986]. A number of problems with the language design were identified during this experiment. When an action aborts, for example, no user code is activated; the run-time system does all the processing automatically. In some cases, however, the application also needs to do some processing after an abort (e.g. in CES an abort sometimes implies updating a screen). The implementors of CES reported that their task would have been significantly simplified had Argus provided more explicit control over action aborts and commits.

Another application implemented in Argus, a distributed mail repository, is described by Day [Day, 1987].

Aeolus

Aeolus is a systems programming language for implementing fault-tolerant servers for the Clouds distributed operating system. Aeolus provides abstractions for the Clouds notions of *objects*, *actions*, and *processes* and it provides access to the recoverability and synchronization features supported by Clouds. Both Clouds and Aeolus are being developed at the Georgia Institute of Technology by Richard LeBlanc and colleagues [LeBlanc and Wilkes, 1985; Wilkes and LeBlanc, 1986, 1988].

Parallelism. Aeolus is object-based in the sense that it supports data abstractions. Unlike in Emerald, however, objects in Aeolus are passive. Aeolus therefore supports a *process* concept for providing parallel activity.

Communication and synchronization. Communication and synchronization in Aeolus are expressed through operation invocations on objects, as discussed below.

Fault tolerance. We first give a brief description of salient features of Clouds related to fault tolerance and then discuss how Aeolus supports these features. The Clouds distributed operating system supports atomic transactions on *objects*. As in Argus, actions can be nested. A Clouds object is a passive entity that encapsulates data. The data of an object can only be manipulated by invoking operations (remote procedures) defined for the object. Objects are created dynamically. Each instance of an object type has its own *state*, consisting of the global variables used by the implementation of the operations. Objects may be replicated in order to increase availability [Wilkes and LeBlanc, 1988].

Clouds supports so-called *recoverability* and *synchronization* of objects. Recoverability allows objects to survive processor crashes. Synchronization ensures that parallel operation invocations are ordered such that they do not interfere with each other. Both features can be handled automatically by the Clouds kernel, or can be custom programmed for higher efficiency, using semantic knowledge about the problem being implemented. Automatic recovery is based on checkpointing the entire state of the object, while custom recovery need only checkpoint those parts of the object state that have been indicated by the programmer. Automatic synchronization allows multiple read-operations to execute simultaneously, but serializes all operations that modify any part of the object state.

Aeolus gives programming language support for Clouds objects and actions. An object type in Aeolus consists of a *definition part* and an *implementation part*. The former contains the name of the object type and the operations allowed on objects of that type. It also specifies whether recovery should be done by the system, by the programmer, or not at all, and it may specify that synchronization is to be done automatically. Programmed synchronization is based on critical sections (for mutual exclusion) and on explicit locking using various *lock types*. The declaration of a lock type specifies a number of *modes*, a *compatibility* relation between the nodes, and (optionally) a *domain* of values to be locked. For example, a read–write lock type over file names of 14 characters can be declared as

```
type rwlock is lock (read: [read], write: [])
    domain is string(14)
```

This declaration introduces two modes: 'read' and 'write', and specifies that several 'read' locks on file names may be obtained, but that 'write' locks are exclusive, as they are compatible with no other mode. The usage of a domain allows a lock to be separated from the data being locked.

The support provided by Aeolus for programming with actions is rather low level. The language provides direct access to the Clouds primitives. Programmers may write their own *action-event handlers*, procedures that are called when an action event (such as commit or abort) happens.

Aeolus gives the programmer more flexibility than Argus for optimizing recovery and synchronization. On the negative side, the many features thus introduced make Aeolus a fairly complex language.

Implementation and experience. A compiler and run-time system for Aeolus have been implemented. Aeolus has not yet been used for any major distributed applications.

4.2   Languages with logically shared address spaces

We will now turn our attention from languages with logically distributed address spaces to languages providing logically shared address spaces. In particular, we will look at three subclasses: parallel functional languages, parallel logic languages, and languages based on distributed data structures (see Figure 4.1). Languages based on shared variables (e.g. Algol 68, Concurrent Pascal, and Mesa [Geschke *et al.*, 1977]) are not discussed here. They can (at least in principle) be implemented on a distributed system, using techniques like shared virtual memory, but they were designed for shared-memory multiprocessors. (For a detailed discussion of shared-variable languages, we refer the reader to [Andrews and Schneider, 1983].)

4.2.1   Parallel functional languages

Pure functional languages are being studied in several parallel programming projects (see Table 4.8). The implicit parallelism in functional languages is especially suited for architectures supporting fine-grain parallelism, such as dataflow machines; whereas distributed computing systems in general employ more coarse-grained parallelism. Nevertheless, functional languages can be used for programming distributed systems by providing a mapping notation that efficiently distributes computations among processors. This approach is taken by the language ParAlfl (discussed below).

Impure functional languages can also be based on functional parallelism, but they require a mechanism for determining which expressions can be evaluated in parallel. The language FX-87 uses an *effect system* for this purpose. An effect is a static description of the side-effects of an expression. The effect of a function can be specified by the programmer and checked by the compiler. The compiler uses the effect information to do certain optimizations and to determine which expressions to evaluate in parallel.

Multilisp, QLISP, and Concurrent Lisp are intended primarily for shared-memory machines and would be less efficient on distributed systems. Blaze is a Pascal-based language for parallel scientific programming that supports the functional programming model. It uses functional parallelism as well as explicit parallelism through a parallel loop-construct.

Table 4.8 *Parallel functional languages*

Language	References
Blaze	[Mehrotra and Van Rosendale, 1987]
Concurrent Lisp	[Sugimoto *et al.*, 1983]
FX-87	[Jouvelot and Gifford, 1988]
Lisptalk	[Li, 1988a]
Multilisp	[Halstead, Jr., 1985]
ParAlfl	[Hudak, 1986]
PML	[Reppy, 1988]
QLISP	[Gabriel and McCarthy, 1984; Goldman and Gabriel, 1989]
Symmetric Lisp	[Gelernter *et al.*, 1987a, 1987b]

ParAlfl

ParAlfl [Hudak and Smith, 1986; Hudak, 1986, 1988] is a parallel functional language developed by Paul Hudak at Yale University.

Parallelism. ParAlfl employs implicit, functional parallelism. Functional parallelism is usually fine grained, resulting in many small tasks that can be done in parallel. As there may be far more parallel tasks than physical processors, ParAlfl uses a mapping notation to specify which expressions are to be evaluated on which processors. An expression followed by the annotation **\$on proc** will be evaluated on the processor determined by the expression **proc**. This **proc** expression can be relative to the currently executing processor. For example, if the expression

```
(f(x) $on ($self - 1)) + (g(y) $on ($self + 1))
```

is executed by processor P, then processor P-1 executes f(x), processor P+1 executes g(y) (in parallel), and processor P itself performs the addition.

Communication and synchronization. Communication and synchronization between parallel computations is implicit, so there is no need for explicit language constructs. A computation automatically blocks when it needs the result of another computation that is not yet available.

The semantics of ParAlfl are based on *lazy evaluation*, which means that an expression is not evaluated until its result is needed. In general, the programmer need not be concerned with the order in which computations are done. For efficiency reasons, he or she may want to control the evaluation order, however. For this purpose, ParAlfl supports *eager expressions*, which are evaluated before their results are needed, and *synchronizing expressions*, which constrain the evaluation order.

ParAlfl programs are fully deterministic, provided that a few simple restrictions on **proc** expressions are satisfied. This means that the results of such programs do not depend on how the computations are distributed among the processors. In particular, the results of a program will be the same whether executed on a uniprocessor or on a parallel system.

Implementation and experience. ParAlfl has been implemented on the Encore Multimax multiprocessor and on two distributed architectures (hypercubes): the Intel iPSC and the NCube [Goldberg and Hudak, 1986]. The language has been used for implementing several parallel algorithms, such as divide-and-conquer, linear equations, and partial differential equations [Hudak, 1986].

4.2.2   Parallel logic languages

Many of the underlying ideas of parallel* logic programming languages (see Table 4.9) were introduced by Clark and Gregory for their Relational Language.

Most parallel logic languages are based on AND/OR parallelism, shared logical variables, and committed-choice nondeterminism. Examples are Concurrent Prolog and Flat Concurrent Prolog (discussed below), PARLOG (also discussed below), Guarded Horn Clauses (GHC), and Oc. P-Prolog is also based on shared logical variables, but uses a mechanism called *exclusive guarded Horn clauses* for controlling OR parallelism. For a normal guarded Horn clause, if several clauses for a given goal have a guard that evaluates to 'true', then one of them is chosen nondeterministically. For an *exclusive* guarded Horn clause, however, the execution of the goal *suspends*, until exactly one guard evaluates to 'true'. (Note that a guard that initially succeeds can later fail, if one of the variables used by the guard becomes bound.)

BRAVE is a parallel logic language that does not use committed-choice nondeterminism, but supports true OR parallelism. Mandala combines object-oriented and logic programming. Quty combines functional and logic programming.

Delta Prolog is significantly different from the languages mentioned above. It is based on message passing rather than on shared logical variables, it uses only AND parallelism, and it supports Prolog's completeness of search by using distributed backtracking.

Concurrent Prolog

Concurrent Prolog was designed by Ehud Shapiro of the Weizmann Institute of Science in Rehovot, Israel [Shapiro, 1983, 1986, 1987]. Concurrent Prolog uses many of the ideas proposed by Clark and Gregory for their Relational Language. Shapiro and his group, however, have developed several new programming techniques for languages like Concurrent Prolog.

Parallelism. Parallelism in Concurrent Prolog comes from the AND-parallel evaluation of the goals of a conjunction and from the OR parallel evaluation of the guards of a guarded Horn clause. There is no sequential AND-operator, so every goal of a conjunction creates a new parallel process. The textual ordering of the goals has no semantic significance. A mapping notation has been designed for assigning processes to processors, as discussed in Section 3.1.2.

Communication and synchronization. Parallel processes communicate through shared logical variables. Synchronization is based on suspension on *read-only vari-*

---

* The logic programming community has adopted the term *concurrent* logic language rather than *parallel* logic language; for consistency with the rest of this book we use the latter term, however.

Table 4.9 *Parallel logic languages*

Language	References
BRAVE	[Reynolds *et al.*, 1988]
Concurrent Prolog	[Shapiro, 1987]
Delta Prolog	[Pereira *et al.*, 1986]
Guarded Horn Clauses	[Ueda, 1985]
Mandala	[Ohki *et al.*, 1987]
Oc	[Takeuchi and Furukawa, 1986]
PARLOG	[Clark and Gregory, 1986]
P-Prolog	[Yang and Aiso, 1986; Yang, 1987]
Quty	[Sato, 1987]
Relational Language	[Clark and Gregory, 1981]
Vulcan	[Kahn *et al.*, 1986]

ables. A variable is marked as read-only by suffixing it with a '?' Unification of two terms suspends if an attempt is made to instantiate a read-only variable. Thus Concurrent Prolog extends the unification algorithm of Prolog [Robinson, 1965] with a test for read-only variables.

Concurrent Prolog uses guarded Horn clauses to deal with nondeterminism. There is no restriction on the kinds of goal that may appear in a guard, so a guard may create other AND-parallel processes. As these processes may invoke new guards, this may lead to a system of arbitrarily nested guards. This creates a problem, as only the guard of the clause that is committed to may have side-effects. Therefore, a new *environment* is created for every guard of a guarded Horn clause, containing the bindings made by that guard. On commitment, the environment of the chosen guard is unified with the goal being solved. The environments of all other guards are discarded. Maintenance of these separate environments is difficult to implement, even on a single processor machine. The need for environments has been eliminated in a subsequent language, called Flat Concurrent Prolog (FCP) [Mierowsky *et al.*, 1985]. In FCP, guards may only contain a predefined set of predicates, rather than user defined predicates, so nesting of guards is ruled out. This also virtually eliminates OR parallelism, but a method has been designed to compile OR-parallel programs into AND-parallel programs [Codish and Shapiro, 1986].

Implementation and experience. A uniprocessor implementation of Flat Concurrent Prolog exists for several types of UNIX machines [Houri and Shapiro, 1986]. The implementation supports the Logix programming environment and operating system [Silverman *et al.*, 1986]. The novelty in the implementation is its efficient support for the creation, suspension, activation, and termination of lightweight processes. The performance is comparable to conventional uniprocessor Prolog implementations.

A distributed implementation of FCP was developed for the Intel iPSC hypercube [Taylor *et al.*, 1987b]. The key concepts in the implementation are data distribution by demand-driven structure copying and the use of a specialized two-phase locking protocol to implement FCP's atomic unification.

Several applications have been written in Concurrent Prolog. [Shapiro, 1987] contains separate papers on Concurrent Prolog implementations of systolic algorithms, the Maxflow problem (determining the maximum flow through a network), region finding in a self-intersecting polygon, image processing, the Logix system, a distributed window system, a public-key system, an equation solver, a compiler for FCP, and a hardware simulator. Most experiences reported are quite positive; actual performance measurements are absent from nearly all papers.

Several programming techniques have been developed that can be used for systems and application programming in Concurrent Prolog. Streams, bounded buffers, and incomplete messages were mentioned in Section 3.2.2. Streams and merging of streams can be expressed in Concurrent Prolog [Shapiro and Mierowsky, 1984; Shapiro and Safra, 1986]. The 'short-circuit' technique implements distributed termination detection. 'Meta-programming' and 'meta-interpreters' are studied in [Safra and Shapiro, 1986]. Systolic programming is a well-known technique for executing numerical algorithms in parallel on special-purpose hardware [Kung, 1982]. Shapiro [Shapiro, 1984] shows that systolic algorithms can also be expressed in Concurrent Prolog, so they can be run on general-purpose hardware. Concurrent Prolog can also be used for object-oriented programming [Shapiro and Takeuchi, 1983]. Kahn *et al.* have designed a preprocessor language for Concurrent Prolog (called Vulcan), which allows object-oriented programs to be written with less verbosity [Kahn *et al.*, 1986].

PARLOG

PARLOG is a parallel logic programming language being developed at Imperial College, London, by Keith Clark and Steve Gregory [Clark and Gregory, 1985, 1986; Foster *et al.*, 1986; Gregory, 1987; Ringwood, 1988; Clark, 1988]. It is a descendant of IC-PROLOG [Clark *et al.*, 1982] and the Relational Language [Clark and Gregory, 1981]. Like Concurrent Prolog, PARLOG is based on AND/OR parallelism and committed-choice nondeterminism. The main innovation introduced by the language is the use of *mode declarations* to control synchronization.

Parallelism. PARLOG uses AND/OR parallelism that can be controlled by the programmer. There are two different conjunction operators: ',' evaluates both conjuncts in parallel, '&' evaluates them sequentially (left to right). The clauses for a relation can either be separated by a '.' or by a ';' operator. In finding a matching clause for a goal, all clauses separated by a '.' are tried in parallel (OR parallelism). Clauses after a ';' are only tried if all clauses before the separator do not match. In the example below

```
1. A ← (B & C), (D & E);
2. A ← F, G.
3. A ← H & J.
```

clause 1 is tried first, by doing '(B & C)' and '(D & E)' in parallel. If clause 1 fails, clauses 2 and 3 are tried in parallel. F and G are evaluated in parallel, but H and J are done sequentially.

The presence of sequential AND/OR operators requires the implementation to determine when a group of parallel processes has terminated, which is not a trivial task in a distributed environment. For example, in 'B & C', all the processes created by B must have terminated before C is started. This additional complexity is the main reason why Concurrent Prolog supports only the parallel operators.

Communication and synchronization. Processes communicate through shared logical variables and synchronize by suspending on unbound shared variables. PARLOG has a mechanism for specifying which processes may generate a binding for a variable. For every relation, a *mode declaration* must be given that specifies which arguments are input and which are output. For example, the declaration

> **mode** append(list1?, list2?, appended-list^).

defines the first two arguments to the append relation to be input and the third one to be output. An actual argument appearing in an input position will only be used for input matching. If unification of the argument with the corresponding term in the head can only succeed by binding a variable appearing in the input argument, then the unification will *suspend*. The unification will be resumed when some *other* process generates a binding for the variable. After commitment, any actual argument appearing in an output position is unified with the output argument in the head of the clause.

PARLOG uses three specialized unification primitives for input matching, equality testing, and output unification. In contrast, Concurrent Prolog has a general unification algorithm, which also has to take care of read-only variables.

Like Concurrent Prolog, PARLOG uses guarded Horn clauses for nondeterminism. A guard in PARLOG may *test* any input variables and bind local variables of the clause, but it may not bind variables passed in an input argument. This is checked at compile time, using mode declarations. If a guard tries to bind an output variable, the actual binding is established only *after* commitment. Unlike Concurrent Prolog, no environments need be maintained.

Implementation and experience. The compiler can use the information in a mode declaration to increase efficiency. A sequential implementation of PARLOG is described in [Foster *et al.*, 1986]. The compiler first compiles PARLOG programs into a subset called Kernel PARLOG, in which all unifications are performed by explicit unification operators. Kernel PARLOG programs are subsequently compiled to code for an abstract machine, called the Sequential PARLOG Machine (SPM), which is emulated on a real machine.

A distributed implementation of PARLOG on a network of SUNs is described in [Foster, 1988]. The implementation uses some of the ideas of the distributed FCP implementation (see above), but differs in supporting distributed termination and deadlock detection. Also, as PARLOG does not have atomic unification, distributed unification is implemented without using a two-phase locking protocol.

PARLOG has been used for discrete event simulation, the specification and verification of communication protocols, a medical diagnosis expert system, and natural language parsing [Gregory, 1987; Clark, 1988].

4.2.3 Distributed data structures

Distributed data structures are used in Linda (discussed below), SDL, and Tuple Space Smalltalk (see Table 4.10).

Linda

Linda is being developed by David Gelernter and colleagues at Yale University [Gelernter, 1985; Ahuja *et al.*, 1986; Carriero *et al.*, 1986; Carriero and Gelernter, 1989]. Linda is not based on shared variables or message passing, but uses a novel communication mechanism: the tuple space. It supports (but does not enforce) a programming methodology based on distributed data structures and replicated workers. The goal of this methodology is to release the programmer from thinking in terms of parallel computations and simultaneous events, hence making parallel programming conceptually similar to sequential programming.

Parallelism. Linda provides a simple primitive (called **eval**) to create a sequential process.* Linda does not have a notation for mapping processes to processors. With the replicated worker style (discussed below) there is no need for such a notation, as each processor executes a single process.

Communication and synchronization. Linda's underlying communication model, the tuple space, was discussed in Section 3.2.2. Processes communicate by inserting new tuples into tuple space and by reading or removing existing tuples. Processes synchronize by waiting for tuples to be available, using blocking **read** and **in** operations.

Traditional communication primitives (e.g. message passing and remote procedures) can be simulated using operations on tuple space [Gelernter, 1985], so algorithms that split up the work among several communicating processes can be expressed in Linda. Alternatively, Linda programs can use the so-called *replicated worker style* [Ahuja *et al.*, 1986]. Such a program consists of *P* identical (replicated) worker processes, one for each processor. The work to do is stored in a *distributed data structure*, which is implemented in tuple space and is accessible by all worker processes. Each process repeatedly takes some work from the data structure, performs it, puts back the results into the data structure, and possibly generates some more work. All workers essentially perform the same kind of task, until all work is done. The workers are loosely coupled; they only interact indirectly through the data structure. This model is claimed to have several advantages [Carriero *et al.*, 1986]. In principle, any number of processors can be used (including just one). Also, the work is automatically and fairly distributed among the workers. Finally, process management is easy, as there usually is only one process per processor.

Fault tolerance. A fault-tolerant network kernel for Linda, based on replication of the tuple space, has been designed by Xu [Xu, 1988].

Implementation and experience. Implementations exist for running Linda pro-

---

* An earlier version of Linda provided constructs for parallel execution of a group of statements. We describe the current version here, which is based on C.

Table 4.10 *Languages based on distributed data structures*

Language	References
Linda	[Ahuja *et al.*, 1986]
SDL	[Roman *et al.*, 1988]
Tuple Space Smalltalk	[Matsuoka and Kawai, 1988]

grams on Bell Labs' S/Net [Carriero and Gelernter, 1986], an Ethernet based Micro-VAX network, the iPSC hypercube [Gelernter and Carriero, 1986; Bjornson *et al.*, 1989], the Encore Multimax, the Sequent Balance, and other configurations. Different implementation strategies are discussed in [Carriero, 1987].

A hardware coprocessor has been designed by Venkatesh Krishnaswamy that supports Linda communication patterns and tuple matching [Ahuja *et al.*, 1988]. Several (in the order of thousands) nodes, consisting of some CPU and the Linda coprocessor, can be arranged into a grid using this new hardware to form a highly parallel Linda Machine.

One of Linda's main goals is to achieve high speedups for real-life problems. Applications for which Linda programs have been written include DNA-sequence comparison, database search, VLSI simulation, heuristic monitoring, the travelling salesman problem, parameter sensitivity analysis, ray tracing, numerical problems [Gelernter and Carriero, 1988], and a distributed backtracking package [Kaashoek *et al.*, 1989a].

4.3   Evaluation

In this chapter we have described a number of languages designed for distributed programming. We will now elaborate on these languages and see whether they meet the goals listed in the introduction of this book.

We first discuss the issues directly related to distributed programming: parallelism, communication and synchronization, and fault tolerance. Next, we look at the integration of sequential and distributed constructs and at two general programming language design issues: complexity and type security. Finally, we discuss the efficiency of several distributed languages.

4.3.1   Parallelism

One important decision in the design of a language for distributed programming is how to express parallelism, in other words, what to use as the unit of parallelism. In Section 3.1, we surveyed a spectrum of parallel units, including processes, objects, statements, expressions, and clauses. We will now examine this spectrum in more detail. Most languages reviewed above use sequential processes for expressing parallelism, but we will look at the alternative constructs first.

Parallel statements

Parallel statements are used in only a few languages (e.g. occam), as they give little support for the structuring of large parallel programs. Moreover, as Andrews and Schneider [Andrews and Schneider, 1983] point out, they are less powerful than parallel processes and they usually create only a fixed number of parallel units.*

Objects

From a parallel programming point of view, processes and objects are not very different. No doubt, object-oriented programming is a highly important research area and using objects for expressing parallelism does reduce the number of concepts in the language, but it does not by itself solve any problems. Designers of object-oriented parallel languages are faced with exactly the same design choices as designers of other kinds of parallel languages [Carriero and Gelernter, 1989]. The choice between synchronous and asynchronous message-passing, for example, is important to both procedural and object-oriented languages. Asynchronous message-passing has been added to Concurrent C – a procedural language – as well as POOL – an object-oriented language – both of which were originally designed to use synchronous rendezvous only [Gehani, 1987; America, 1988]. The decision whether to use objects as units of parallelism should probably be based on software engineering reasons, rather than on parallel programming considerations.

Expressions

Declarative (functional and logic) languages are frequently claimed to be more suitable for parallel execution than imperative languages. Declarative languages specify *what* has to be computed, whereas imperative languages focus on *how* a result is to be computed through a sequence of simple actions. Imperative languages therefore over-specify the order in which computations are to be performed. A tremendous amount of research has been done on how to use functional and logic languages for parallel programming.

Functional languages have been used for programming dataflow architectures, which give hardware support for managing many short parallel computations [Arvind and Nikhil, 1988]. Distributed systems, on the other hand, are less suitable for executing short computations, because the overhead in creating, scheduling, and synchronizing parallel tasks will far outweigh the gains of parallelism. In other words, the grain of the parallelism is too fine.

Communication overhead can be decreased by using some sort of mapping notation for combining multiple fine-grain units into large-grain units. Such a notation was described in Section 4.2.1 for ParAlfl. Even with such a notation, however, communication overhead still may be too high.

---

* Andrews and Schneider state that '... **cobegin** as defined in any existing language, can be used only to activate a fixed number of processes.' This claim seems to be incorrect, however, as Algol 68 – one of the languages they cite as using **cobegin**s – allows a dynamic number of processes to be created by using recursive procedures.

Hudak has implemented a parallel matrix multiplication program written in ParAlfl on a shared-memory multiprocessor (the Encore Multimax) and a distributed computing system (the Intel iPSC hypercube) [Hudak, 1988]. As matrix multiplication is easy to parallelize, the multiprocessor implementation achieves almost linear speedup. The distributed implementation has a poor speedup, however, because of communication overheads. Currently, functional parallelism seems unsuitable for distributed systems, although the increase of network speeds may make it more attractive in the future.

Clauses

The main representatives of parallel logic languages are Concurrent Prolog and PARLOG. A major disadvantage of these languages (and other parallel logic languages using committed-choice nondeterminism) is the fact that they give up Prolog's completeness of search. Consider, for example, the following set of Concurrent Prolog clauses:

```
a :- g1 | b.
a :- g2 | c.
g1.
g2.
c.
```

The conjunction 'g2 and c' is true, so the goal 'a' logically should succeed (recall that '|' is logically equivalent to 'and'). As the two alternatives for 'a' are tried in parallel and both their guards (g1 and g2) succeed, however, the system may commit to g1 and forget about g2. As the goal 'b' cannot be proven, the first clause will subsequently fail. Hence no solution will be found, although logically a solution does exist. The programmer must ensure that, at the time of commitment, either the right clause is selected, or no clause resulting in a proof exists. To achieve this, the guards can be extended to include 'b' and 'c':

```
a :- g1 , b | .
a :- g2 , c | .
```

This technique should not be used indiscriminately, however, because it restricts the effective parallelism. Any bindings to variables are not made known to the caller of 'a' until commitment, so in the new scheme the caller will have to wait longer for these values to be available. This implies that, in general, guards should be kept as small as possible.

Operationally, there are good reasons for using committed-choice nondeterminism, but the resulting loss of Prolog's completeness of search conceptually is unappealing. Several alternative approaches have been suggested for introducing parallelism into logic languages while preserving completeness. Delta Prolog, for example, uses AND parallelism in combination with message passing. The language supports Prolog's completeness of search by using distributed backtracking on failure of a clause. Unfortunately, this is very hard to implement efficiently, as the communication overhead is high.

Logic languages have a high potential for parallelism and are highly interesting research vehicles. It is not clear yet, however, whether this potential can be realized in an efficient way without compromising one of the main advantages of the sequential logic programming model – completeness of search. The problem is fairly fundamental. Completeness of search is implemented by backtracking, but in a parallel environment, backtracking is highly inefficient.

Processes

As stated before, processes are favoured by most designers of distributed languages, as they are more coarse-grained than the alternative constructs. Below, we look at several important issues related to processes.

One important design issue is how processes are created. Languages like CSP and DP require the number of processes to be a compile-time constant. Although this makes assignment of processes to processors easier, it requires the programmer to know in advance how many processes to use. In Amoeba, for example, all users share a large *pool* of processors, so the number of processors that can be allocated to a certain application depends on the current load of the system. This number is not known until the application is executed. It would be highly inefficient to recompile a program each time before it is executed. It is therefore more flexible to create processes dynamically through some sort of **create** language construct.

Preferably, the **create** construct should allow parameters to be passed to the newly created process. This is supported, for example, by Concurrent C. Ada allows processes to be created dynamically, but it is not possible to pass any parameters to them. Instead, parameters should be sent using explicit communication. This has been criticized by Yemini [Yemini, 1982], who shows that the absence of parameters may cause serial bottlenecks if thousands of processes have to be created at once. Although there are solutions to this problem [Burns *et al.*, 1987] it seems more practical to use the Concurrent C approach and allow processes to have parameters. Moreover, allowing parameters to be passed to procedures and entries but not to processes is not very orthogonal.

Another important issue is how to assign processes to physical processors. This issue is referred to as *mapping*. Some of the languages discussed above (e.g. NIL and Ada) ignore the mapping issue or leave it to the implementation. This means that the programmer can only specify which computations may logically be executed in parallel. For high-performance applications, however, programmers want to benefit from physical parallelism, so they also need to specify on which processors the parallel computations are to be executed. A better approach therefore is to allow the programmer to control this mapping. In languages like Concurrent C, SR, and Argus, processes can be assigned to specific processors when they are forked off. Each processor is identified by a unique number. In Concurrent C, for example, the following statement

create slave(12,50) **processor**(3);

creates a new process slave on processor 3. In this way, the programmer can specify which processes should be run on which processor.

In some cases, the programmer may even want to worry about the physical inter-connection structure of the communications network. On a first-generation hyper-cube, for example, sending a message to a neighbouring node is much cheaper than sending the same message to a processor that is several hops away. If two processes communicate frequently, one may assign them to two neighbouring nodes, so they can run physically in parallel while communication overhead is kept low.

If processors are numbered systematically, such assignments can be expressed in a language by allowing the **processor** part of the **create** statement to contain arbitrary expressions. ParAlfl is one example of a language supporting such a notation. As communications networks become more homogeneous, however, the need for com-plex mapping notations that take the network structure into account becomes less urgent. Current hypercubes use special I/O processors for forwarding messages through the network, so the latency time of a message hardly depends on the number of hops it has to go [Athas and Seitz, 1988].

Linda avoids mapping notations altogether, by using the replicated worker style. With this model, one basically executes a single worker process on each available pro-cessor. The language only requires the underlying run-time system or operating sys-tem to schedule different processes on different processors.

4.3.2 Communication and synchronization

The second issue related to distributed programming is the design of the interprocess communication (IPC) mechanism. The two oldest paradigms for IPC in parallel languages are shared variables and message passing. Shared variables were already used decades ago for the construction of operating systems for uniprocessors. Such systems were frequently designed as collections of pseudo-parallel processes that communicated through shared variables. Message passing was already used in the RC4000 operating system [Brinch Hansen, 1973], and was later introduced by Hoare as a language construct [Hoare, 1978].

Simple shared variables are hardly ever used as IPC mechanisms for distributed programming. Several recent IPC mechanisms, however, provide some form of shared data that can be implemented efficiently without using physical shared memory. Such primitives are based on *logically shared data*. Below, we will first look at communication based on message passing. Subsequently we will consider alternative models that are based on logically shared data.

Communication through message passing

Probably the most controversial issue related to message passing is whether communication should be synchronous or asynchronous. Synchronous mechanisms, such as synchronous point-to-point messages, rendezvous, and remote procedure call, are claimed to be easier to program [Tanenbaum and Van Renesse, 1985]. On the other hand, they force the sender to wait until the receiver has accepted the message. For applications that aim at achieving high speedups this may be a severe limitation. In principle, this problem can be solved by somehow simulating asynchronous message-passing, for example by introducing 'agent' processes between the sender and receiver [Burns *et al.*, 1987] or by making the sender multithreaded (see Section 2.3.2 and Section 2.4.2). This causes some overhead, however, as the extra threads have to be created and scheduled. Moreover, it makes the structure of the program more complicated. It is significant that several languages exist that were originally designed to use synchronous message-passing exclusively, but that were at a later stage (on requests from users) extended with asynchronous primitives (e.g. Concurrent C [Gehani, 1987] and POOL [America, 1988]). So in practice synchronous message-passing seems to be too restrictive.

Another important issue is the *expressive power* of the IPC mechanism. As discussed in Section 3.2, sometimes a process wants to control which messages to accept from which processes. One way of doing this is to use a nondeterministic language construct, for example the **select** statement. This construct allows a process to wait for an incoming message that satisfies some conditions (guards).

According to Bloom [Bloom, 1979], the following information may be useful in guard expressions:

1. The type of the message,
2. The order in which messages arrive,
3. The parameters of the message,
4. The state of the receiver.

Ada, for example, has several major shortcomings in this area, as shown by Gehani and Roome [Gehani and Roome, 1988] and Burns *et al.* [Burns *et al.*, 1987]. In Ada, it is very hard to write servers that need any of the following features:

- Give preference to a certain type of request (e.g. give priority to read operations over write operations in a database).
- Serve requests of the same type in any but FIFO order.
- Serve requests of different types in order of their arrival.
- Accept a request conditionally, based on information in the request.

These problems are due to the restrictions of the Ada synchronization mechanism mentioned in Section 4.1.3: entry calls are always serviced in FIFO order; the guards in a **select** statement may not reference the actual parameters of the entry call; no priorities can be associated with different alternatives of a **select** statement.

Nondeterministic constructs increase the expressive power of the synchronization mechanism, but they also have their disadvantages. First, they make the implementation of the language more complicated. More significantly, nondeterministic programs are notoriously hard to test and debug, because the output of such programs is not fully determined by their inputs [Tai and Carver, 1988]. Different runs of the same program with the same input may result in different outputs. Usually, such behaviour is caused by a synchronization error in the program. As such errors cannot be easily reproduced, they are very hard to repair: this is one of the reasons why distributed programming in such languages is harder than sequential programming.

Communication through logically shared data

The main problem with the message-passing model is the fact that applications cannot easily use global state information. In Chapter 2 we discussed two applications requiring global data – branch-and-bound and alpha-beta search – and showed how these could be implemented using RPC – a form of message passing – by simulating shared data. If global data could have been used, however, implementing these algorithms would have been much simpler.

In Chapter 3 we discussed two communication primitives based on logically shared data: the tuple space, used in Linda, and the shared logical variable, used in languages like Concurrent Prolog and PARLOG. Below, we will take a closer look at these primitives.

The first example of logically shared data is Linda's tuple space. The tuple space model has simple and clean semantics. In particular, mutual exclusion synchronization for access to tuples is done automatically.

Some problems with the tuple space model are discussed in [Kaashoek *et al.*, 1989a]. One problem is the variety of ways for representing a given data structure in tuple space. A 10K bit-vector, for example, can be stored in any of the following ways:

- As 10K single-bit tuples,
- As a single 10K-bit tuple,
- Any combination in between these two extremes (e.g. 32 tuples of 320 bits each).

Each representation calls for a different locking scheme and allows different amounts of parallelism.

The first case allows the most parallelism, as all bits of the bit vector can be read or written simultaneously. On the other hand, synchronizing access to the shared data structure must be done carefully. To invert several bits of a bit vector in one indivisible action, the programmer must write code for locking the bit vector (or the individual bits); the tuple space model itself only synchronizes operations on single tuples. Also, the overhead of having many small tuples will be high.

In the second case – one 10K tuple – synchronization is easy but parallelism is limited. Moreover, changing a single bit of the bit vector will be expensive, as there is no assignment operator for changing tuples in tuple space. Instead, the 10K tuple first has to be copied into a local data structure (using the **in** operation); next, the local data structure must be changed and stored back in a new tuple (using **out**). (A clever optimizing compiler might be able to recognize such patterns and avoid copying tuples in some cases, but this has not been implemented yet.)

Sometimes, the third case – an intermediate form – may be most suitable, although it is a rather ad hoc solution. It reduces the overhead to acceptable proportions while still allowing a high degree of parallelism. As a disadvantage, the programmer still has to take care of locking, as in the first case.

Another important issue is the overhead in execution- and communication-time of the tuple space operations. As all tuples can be accessed by all processors, communication overhead potentially is high. But even if the tuple being accessed is stored locally, there is still the execution-time overhead of *searching* the tuple in local memory, because tuples are referenced associatively rather than by address.

The designers of Linda have paid considerable attention to this issue, however, and have come up with implementations of tuple space that have quite acceptable performances. The communication overhead is reduced by carefully distributing (i.e. replicating and partitioning) tuple space among the local memories of the processors. The costs of associative addressing are decreased through compile-time optimization techniques [Carriero, 1987].

Still, operations on tuple space are significantly more expensive than operations on local variables. If shared data are accessed very frequently, it may be necessary to maintain copies of the data in local variables (outside tuple space). In the travelling salesman problem, for example, processes need to read the value of the shared variable `minimum` very frequently (see Section 2.3). To implement TSP efficiently in Linda, one has to store a local copy of this variable on every processor [Bjornson *et al.*, 1988]. The burden of updating the copies lies in the hands of the programmer.

We will now turn our attention to another primitive based on logically shared data: the shared logical variable. In Section 3.2.2 we described how several communication patterns can be expressed using shared logical variables despite the single-assignment property of such variables. On the other hand, the shared logical variable also has its problems. Although it is possible to implement shared data structures like streams and queues using shared logical variables, only a single process can add elements to such data structures [Gelernter, 1984]. In the producer/consumer example of Section 3.2.2, only one producer can append elements to the shared stream. If there are multiple producers, each one should have its own output stream. All these output streams should then be *merged* and fed into the consumer. Although merging of streams can be expressed in parallel logic languages [Shapiro and Safra, 1986], the easy solutions merge only a statically fixed number of streams; for many parallel programming problems, however, this is unacceptable.

4.3.3 Fault tolerance

The third issue related to distributed programming is fault tolerance. In principle, distributed applications can survive hardware failures because of the partial failure property of distributed architectures. Achieving this goal, however, is far from easy. As discussed in Section 3.3, there are three different ways for obtaining fault tolerance: letting the programmer solve all the problems; providing language constructs (atomic transactions) for dealing with partial failures; or letting the language implementation make failures transparent.

Before discussing these three approaches in turn, we note that, in this book, we are mainly interested in running high-performance, parallel applications on distributed systems. Unlike, say, a distributed banking system, such applications do not have fault tolerance as a main objective. Rather, fault tolerance is considered to be a convenient property that makes such applications easier to use. The main reason for distributing high-performance applications is to achieve speedup through parallelism, so fault tolerance should not be achieved at the cost of a significant decrease in speed. Therefore, the costs of the fault-tolerance mechanisms will be central to our discussion.

Programming fault tolerance
As far as the language designer is concerned, the easiest way for achieving fault tolerance is to let the programmer do it. In general, the language need only supply a mechanism for detecting processor failures. One way of doing this is to return an error status to every process that tries to communicate with a crashed processor. Another way is to let the programmer define an error-handling routine that is called automatically when some process or processor crashes (e.g. the exception-handling facility of SR and Ada).

The applications described in Chapter 2 can easily be made fault tolerant without using any further support from a language. These applications were modelled as a master process that repeatedly hands out work to side-effect-free slave processes. If a slave fails, the master simply retransmits the work to another slave.

Not every application can be structured in such a way, however. Consider, for example, the parallel sorting algorithm of Horiguchi and Shigei [Horiguchi and Shigei, 1986]. With their algorithm, each of the P processors first takes N/P data elements and sorts them. Next, the processors repeatedly exchange some of their elements with their left and right neighbours and merge the new elements with the elements they had sorted already. This iterative process continues until the leftmost processor contains the N/P lowest numbers, the second processor contains the next N/P numbers, and so on. If one of the processors crashes during the merge phase, chaos will result, because the numbers currently stored on that processor are lost. Recovering from failures in such applications will require a lot of work from the programmer.

Although the exception-handling approach to fault tolerance is easy to understand and involves little overhead, it is too low level to be of general use. Programmers frequently will not be prepared to write significant amounts of extra code for making applications fault tolerant.

Atomic transactions

Another approach to fault tolerance is to provide powerful language constructs that make it easier to deal with failures. The atomic transaction is by far the most important language construct that has been proposed for this purpose.

An atomic transaction consists of multiple actions; either all of the actions of a transaction are executed, or none of them are. In the distributed sorting example described above, one might consider grouping together all exchange operations of the same iteration into one atomic transaction. If the data elements are also stored on stable storage, it will probably be relatively easy to make this application fault tolerant. On the other hand, the costs of doing this may be prohibitively high.

The actual costs of atomic transactions depend on the underlying language implementation. For one language based on atomic transactions, Argus, performance figures of an implementation are reported in the literature [Liskov *et al.*, 1987]. The costs of committing a transaction are several hundreds of milliseconds, depending on the number of processes involved in the transaction. Roughly, a transaction is one or two orders of magnitude more expensive than a remote procedure call. Also, the overhead of locking is substantial. If a write lock on an object is required, the object first has to be copied (i.e. a new version of it is created). For large objects (e.g. an array of 1000 elements), this may take well over a millisecond. All these overhead costs may be quite acceptable for applications like distributed banking, but for parallel sorting they would be far too high.

Transparent fault tolerance

The third approach to fault tolerance, hiding processor failures from the programmer, has been used by only a few languages. As the language implementation does not have any knowledge about the application, it cannot distinguish between those processes (or data) that are vital to the application and those that are less important. Consequently, the implementation will have to take gross measures and treat every process or piece of data as being important. The overhead of such a scheme may be very high.

For NIL, a technique called *optimistic recovery* has been developed [Strom and Yemini, 1985b]. This technique, which is based on checkpointing of processes and replaying of logged messages, makes processor failures fully transparent. Unfortunately, no measurements of its performance are reported in the literature.

A somewhat more conservative approach is taken by Concurrent C [Cmelik *et al.*, 1987]. In a recent extension of this language (called Fault Tolerant Concurrent C), the programmer may request certain processes to be replicated, as in

create master(parameters) **copies**(3);

The programmer must also assure that all replicas of the same process behave in the same way. Usually, it is sufficient to let each replica execute the same code. Apart from this, the programmer need not be aware of the presence of replicated processes. Whenever a request is sent to a replicated process, the run-time system automatically sends it to all replicas of the process. If a replicated process calls an entry of another process, each replica will issue the entry call. Only the first of these entry calls is actually executed by the called process; the run-time system discards all other calls. If a replicated process contains a **select** statement, the run-time system makes sure all replicas select the same alternative.

The price paid for adding fault tolerance in this way is determined by two factors. First, a process that is replicated N times will need N physical processors, rather than 1. As processors are a scarce resource, fewer processors will be available for doing real work. If a parallel program shows linear speedup, for example, replicating each process on two processors will cost a factor two in speed. Second, the communication overhead of the replicated processes is nontrivial. An entry call to a replicated process must be sent to each replica. Moreover, a distributed consensus protocol among the copies of the same process is needed for dealing with the problems of outgoing entry calls and **select** statements. All in all, the price of fault tolerance will be high.

4.3.4   Integration of sequential and distributed programming

Above, we discussed issues related directly to distributed programming. We will now turn our attention to more general programming language design issues. First of all we will look at the integration of language constructs for distributed programming with other, sequential, constructs. As we will show, several of the languages discussed above have shortcomings in this area.

Many languages for parallel or distributed programming are designed as extensions to existing sequential languages or models. In this way, programmers only have to learn a few new primitives and can continue using their favourite language. Except for Cobol, virtually every sequential language X of some importance has a parallel extension, usually called 'Concurrent X'. The disadvantage of this approach is also clear: language constructs designed for sequential programs are not necessarily suitable for distributed programming.

Some language designers have worked the other way around, starting with a distributed model and extending it with sequential language constructs. Again, there is room for conflict between sequential and parallel constructs, as we will see. Below, we will give specific examples of this friction between sequential and distributed programming.

If a sequential language is extended with support for parallel or distributed programming, one would like the extensions to fit well with the existing constructs. The parameter mechanism in a **send** or **fork** primitive, for example, should be similar – if not the same – to the parameter mechanism already used for procedures. Many sequential languages have a parameter mechanism that is totally unsuitable for this purpose, however. In the C language, for example, data structures like arrays are passed by reference (i.e. by passing a pointer to the array as actual parameter). Similarly, if a procedure has to change one of its parameters, a pointer to a variable is supplied. In a distributed implementation, this causes severe problems, because pointers are only meaningful within a single machine.

Several distributed languages that are based on C suffer from this problem. In Concurrent C, one cannot pass arrays as part of an entry call (**transaction**) or **fork**; also, entries cannot have output parameters as in Ada. In C/Linda (Linda embedded in C) the array problem is addressed through a so-called LINDA_BLOCK data type, which represents a linear sequence of machine words. With this feature, the programmer can put any data structure in a tuple, after first writing explicit code for converting between the data structure format and the linear representation. Undoubtedly, the LINDA_BLOCK feature is useful, but it is far from elegant. Moreover, it will take a nontrivial amount of programming to put a complex data structure (e.g. a graph) in a tuple.

Even if the parameter mechanism is designed with distributed programming in mind, there still may be other sources of problems. Ada, for example, uses approximately copy-in/copy-out semantics, which can be used for procedures as well as entries. (Recall that processes in Ada do not take parameters.) The Ada reference manual states that 'The parameter modes defined for parameters of the formal part of an entry declaration are the same as for a subprogram declaration and have the same meaning' (Section 9.5 of [US Department of Defense, 1983]). It is convenient to define the semantics in such a concise way, but unfortunately this rule totally ignores the problem of passing a pointer variable as an argument to an entry. In a sequential language like Pascal it is no problem to pass pointers as arguments to procedures. Passing a pointer to a local data structure as an argument of a remote entry call, however, is very hard to implement without shared memory. Stammers calls this problem the 'central heap assumption' of Ada [Stammers, 1985]. The problem is clearly inherited from the underlying Pascal storage model.

The central heap problem in Ada could be solved by disallowing entry call parameters to contain pointers. This would mean that, for example, arrays could be passed as parameters – because they are built-in data types – while linked lists built out of pointers could not. Other solutions, such as performing pointer dereferences at the caller's machine or copying the part of the heap reachable from the pointer argument, are equally unattractive, however.

A final example of a problem inherited from a sequential language is the global variable. Most procedural languages support variables that can be accessed directly in all (or many) procedures of a program. If such a language is extended to distributed programming, these procedures may be executed by different processors, so the global variables would automatically become shared variables. If the underlying hardware lacks shared memory, however, shared variables are hard to implement; at the very least, they need special run-time support.

One example of this phenomenon is Concurrent C. In the distributed implementation of this language, each physical processor has its own instance of each global variable. The instance is shared among the processes on that machine [Cmelik *et al.*, 1988]. If a process on one processor changes a global variable X, the instance of X on other processors is not affected. In a shared-memory implementation of Concurrent C, on the other hand, X would be put in the global memory and be shared among all processes in the system. So the semantics of a Concurrent C program depend on whether the program is executed on a distributed system or a multiprocessor, a highly undesirable result.

Occam is an example of a language based on a distributed model rather than being an extension to a sequential language. The underlying model of occam is Hoare's Communicating Sequential Processes. Occam was designed as a highly efficient language based on CSP. Efficiency has been achieved in occam by sacrificing some flexibility. Most notably, the process structure of the model is fully static. Although this has some disadvantages (see Section 4.3.1), one might be willing to live with it, as it makes the implementation more efficient. Occam, however, also puts severe restrictions on the usage of procedures, in order to keep the number of processes determinable at compile time. In particular, procedures are not allowed to be recursive. So occam lacks a feature that most people (except BASIC hackers) would say is very important to sequential programming.

It seems that the proper way of designing a language for distributed programming is to deal with the distributed and sequential mechanisms simultaneously. This has been done with reasonable success, for example, in the design of SR.

4.3.5 Complexity of the language design

Any designer of a programming language, whether sequential or distributed, should aim at both minimizing the complexity of the language and keeping the semantics clean and simple. These issues are of great concern to both the implementors and the users of the language. Still, there are many examples of languages that fail to achieve these goals [Hoare, 1981].

Of the distributed languages discussed above, Ada has the questionable honour of receiving the most criticism for being too big. According to Wichmann, Ada could not be cut down in size significantly, because each feature is needed by at least some of the applications Ada was intended for [Wichmann, 1984]. Strom *et al.* have argued, however, that significant simplifications are possible by combining multiple features into a single language construct [Strom *et al.*, 1985]. In particular, they suggest using a single model, the *process model*, for dealing with modularity, parallelism, and naming.

With respect to complexity, the Ada tasking model certainly is not inferior to the rest of the language. Burns *et al.* need three pages of complicated state transition diagrams just to give a rough overview of how the tasking model may be implemented [Burns *et al.*, 1987]. They describe 17 different states for Ada tasks and use 34 possible transitions between these states. This complexity is due to the large number of features the tasking model has to support, such as exception handling, process abortion, conditional entry calls, timed entry calls, and collaborative termination.

Some of the other languages described in this chapter also strike as being more complex than necessary. Aeolus, for example, supports a large variety of low-level features for optimizing recovery and synchronization. Occam started out as a very simple language, omitting features that are not absolutely necessary. Its successor, occam 2, is already much more complex [Burns, 1988]. For example, occam 2 contains a whole sublanguage for describing channel protocols, which just optimize the transmission of data structures over a Transputer link. SR is another fairly big language, but this is due to its design objective of supporting multiple communication primitives. Its designers managed to keep the number of language features within acceptable limits, by using a highly orthogonal approach. In contrast to the above languages, Linda sets an example in simplicity; its tuple space model essentially uses only four primitives, which are very easy to understand.

4.3.6   Type security

The concept of type security is defined in Section 1.5.1. Security implies that all violations of the language rules should be detected, either by the compiler or by the run-time system. Many frequently used languages (e.g. C) or their implementations violate this principle and allow errors to cause an arbitrary amount of havoc, before generating a core dump. This applies especially to array bound errors and to flaws in dynamic storage management. According to Hoare, 'In any respectable branch of engineering, failure to observe such elementary precautions would have long been against the law' [Hoare, 1981].

For distributed programming, security is even more important than for sequential programming. First, distributed programs are hard to debug even if a clear error message is produced, because such programs usually are nondeterministic. Second, an undetected error in one process may affect the correctness of other processes that run in the same address space. In Concurrent C, for instance, all processes executing on the same machine share one address space [Cmelik *et al.*, 1988]. As C is not a type-secure language, a process can accidentally change the local variables of any other process on the same machine. Such errors are very hard to trace.

Several of the languages described above use insecure constructs. Concurrent C and C/Linda are based on C and are therefore insecure. Ada addresses the issue of security up to a certain point (e.g. array bound checking), but it also has insecure constructs (e.g. unchecked type conversion or storage deallocation). In fact, the language reference manual reserves the term 'erroneous execution' for denoting conditions that violate the language rules but that need not be detected by the implementation. The reference manual states that 'The effect of erroneous execution is unpredictable.' NIL is an example of a secure language; security in NIL is realized through the typestate concept.

4.3.7 Efficiency considerations

As we intend to use distributed hardware for speeding up programs, the efficiency of the language being used is an important issue. Unfortunately, it is very hard to make a fair comparison of the relative efficiencies of the languages, as many different hardware configurations have been used for implementing them. Moreover, several languages have not actually been implemented on distributed hardware yet. For those that have been implemented, actual performance data are frequently omitted in research papers on the language.

The costs of the language primitives critically depend on the hardware being used. Most languages are implemented on top of an existing operating system, so their costs also depend on the efficiency of the operating system. The most important factor is the time needed for sending a message reliably from one processor to another. For comparison, Amoeba currently claims to be the fastest distributed operating system around; it uses 1.4 ms for doing an RPC (with one integer argument) between two SUN-3/50s [Van Renesse *et al.*, 1988].

Performance figures for a distributed implementation of Concurrent C on a collection of VAX 11/780s connected by an Ethernet are given in [Cmelik *et al.*, 1988]. The implementation uses the socket streams provided by BSD 4.2 UNIX for interprocess communication. The cost of a Concurrent C remote operation with one argument and one return value is reported to be 31 ms, which is quite slow compared to Amoeba's 1.4 ms. A local Concurrent C transaction in a uniprocessor implementation takes 270 μs. The performance could probably be improved by implementing transactions directly on the hardware, rather than on UNIX.

The most efficient distributed version of Linda is the S/Net implementation [Carriero and Gelernter, 1986; Carriero, 1987]. The S/Net is a multicomputer consisting of MC68000 processors connected by an 80 Mbit/second bus that supports reliable broadcast. On this system, an **in** or **out** takes roughly 1 ms for small tuples; a **read** takes about 0.5 ms. This performance has been obtained by replicating the entire tuple space and updating the replicas with reliable broadcast messages. The shared-memory implementations of Linda (on the Encore Multimax and Sequent Balance) are about 10 times faster. A Linda machine is under construction that is expected to decrease communication costs even further [Ahuja *et al.*, 1988].

The performance of Emerald on MicroVAX II workstations connected by an Ethernet is discussed in [Jul *et al.*, 1988]. An operation invocation on a local object takes less than 20 μs, whereas a remote operation invocation costs about 30 ms. An important goal of the Emerald implementation is to reduce network traffic by migrating objects to wherever they are used most frequently. For one application, a distributed electronic mail system, object mobility more than halved the number of messages sent.

Argus has been implemented on the same hardware – MicroVAX IIs with Ethernet. A handler call (i.e. an RPC) without any arguments takes 17.5 ms [Liskov *et al.*, 1987]. Locking of objects costs several hundreds of microseconds. Committing a toplevel transaction takes hundreds of milliseconds, as discussed in Section 4.3.3.

For most declarative languages, relevant performance figures are hard to find in the literature. Some indication of the efficiency of ParAlfl is given in [Hudak, 1988]. Coincidentally, one of the example applications used for ParAlfl, multiplication of two 50 x 50 matrices, is also implemented in C/Linda [Carriero, 1987], using the same hardware – the Encore multiprocessor. (It is not clear, however, whether the ParAlfl version uses floating-point arithmetic – as the Linda version does – or integer arithmetic.) The Linda version is more than three times as fast; both implementations achieve nearly linear speedup. The same problem implemented in ParAlfl on a hypercube is significantly slower.

Most of the implementations discussed above use a LAN for communication between processors. The performances of the LAN-based implementations are quite disappointing, given the speed of systems like Amoeba. One reason why communication overheads are in the order of milliseconds rather than microseconds is the unreliability of message passing on LANs. A substantial part of the overhead goes into software protocols for making message passing reliable.

One way to avoid this overhead is to use a communications network supporting reliable message-passing, such as a hypercube. In the first generation hypercubes, sending a message between two nodes also takes several milliseconds and increases with the distance (number of hops) between the nodes. Athas and Seitz expect communication times for hypercubes to decrease dramatically in the future [Athas and Seitz, 1988]. For the next two generations of hypercubes, they project communication times to drop to 5 µs (1988–1992) and 0.5 µs (1993–1997). Language implementations will probably become much faster using such hardware.

4.4   Conclusions

In the preceding sections, we have looked at several languages for distributed programming. It turns out that there exists a large number of such languages, probably well over a hundred. We partitioned these languages into ten different classes, using a simple classification scheme (see Figure 4.1). For each class, we have described one or two representative languages. Finally, we have evaluated several language designs to see whether they are suitable for implementing parallel algorithms on distributed systems and meet our design goals of simplicity, expressiveness, type security, and efficiency.

We feel that none of the languages described in this chapter adequately fulfils all of the above requirements. To be fair, several languages were designed with somewhat different design objectives in mind. Ada, for example, was designed primarily for embedded systems, rather than parallel programming. Argus and Aeolus are languages for implementing fault-tolerant applications. Many languages were designed for systems programming or for implementing distributed services, rather than for general applications programming. Owing to these differences in design objectives, these languages frequently support features that are unnecessary or even undesirable for applications programming and lack features that would be useful.

Most languages for distributed programming fall in one of the message-passing categories of Figure 4.1. These languages do not allow programs to contain any global state information. Also, several message passing languages (e.g. Ada) suffer from many other subtle problems (see Section 4.3.2). Finally, the synchronous versions of message passing limit parallelism, or at least need additional mechanisms for obtaining a high degree of parallelism.

Languages based on atomic transactions are mainly useful for implementing fault-tolerant applications. For parallel applications, however, fault tolerance is of minor importance and should not be obtained at the cost of a significant decrease in performance. Unfortunately, atomic transactions turn out to be very expensive and therefore are not well suited for our purpose.

Functional languages are highly interesting research vehicles for parallel programming, as functional programs have a high potential for parallelism. For dataflow machines they are used extensively. For distributed systems, however, they have not yet been shown to be useful. The main problem is the high communication overhead, which is due to the low granularity of parallelism in functional programs. In the long run these problems may be solved, either through software or hardware solutions, but that remains to be seen. The decreasing communication overhead of distributed systems (e.g. the new generation of hypercubes), however, may make functional languages more attractive. Also, one can envision the programmer or compiler increasing the level of granularity by combining several fine-grain parallel computations into larger chunks. This idea has been pursued by Hudak, but it is not yet proven to be practical [Hudak, 1988].

Logic languages also have a high potential for parallelism. As with functional languages, this parallelism is rather fine-grained. The main problem with most parallel logic languages, however, is the tendency of moving away from the ideal of a fully declarative language. Languages like Concurrent Prolog and PARLOG still let programmers think in terms of processes communicating through message passing. Although these languages certainly are interesting and also have many useful properties, they are less declarative than sequential Prolog, since they lack completeness of search. As message-passing languages, they also have several disadvantages, as shown by Gelernter [Gelernter, 1984].

The last class of Figure 4.1 contains languages based on distributed data structures. The major language in this category is Linda, the first language to advocate this paradigm. The distributed data structure paradigm has several advantages, especially if it is used in combination with the replicated worker style. The model allows processes to share data and it makes distribution of work among the processors easy. Linda supports the distributed data structure paradigm through the tuple space model. Although this model is easy to understand and has clean semantics, we feel it also has some problems, as explained in Section 4.3.2. In particular, its support for complex data structures like sets and graphs is rather low level.

Besides the problems summarized above, existing languages for distributed programming also have other shortcomings, like poor integration of sequential and distributed constructs, high complexity, and lack of type-security. Although these issues are not directly related to distributed programming, they are important and need more attention.

Taking all the factors discussed in the previous four chapters together, we come to the unfortunate conclusion that no existing technique or language provides a fully satisfactory base for distributed programming. Each of the models has something to offer, but each has substantial disadvantages as well. A convenient-to-program yet efficient-to-implement language is not available. In the remaining chapters of this book we will propose a new language that we regard as a first step in the right direction. We will also discuss its use and give numerous examples and provide actual measurements of its implementation to support our conclusions.

## CHAPTER 5

The Shared Data-object Model

In the previous two chapters we have surveyed models for distributed programming and we have briefly described one or two representative languages for each model. We have also noticed several problems with these models and languages. Owing to these problems, existing languages fail to meet the goals set out in the introduction. In this chapter we will propose a new model for distributed programming and a new language based on this model.

First, we will look at the most important design alternatives for such a model. In particular, we will discuss whether parallelism, communication, and partial failures are to be dealt with by the programmer or the implementation (i.e. the compiler and run-time system). As we will see, our model differs from most other models for distributed programming by hiding physical communication from the users. Instead, it allows different parts of a program to communicate through logically shared data. We review some existing work in this area – the simulation of shared data in distributed systems – and then introduce a new model, the *shared data-object model*. Finally, in Section 5.4 we discuss the design of a new language, *Orca*, based on the shared data-object model.

5.1 Design alternatives

As discussed extensively in Chapters 3 and 4, the issues that are most important to the design of a model for distributed programming are parallelism, communication, and handling of partial failures. For all three issues, there is a choice between making the issue explicit in the model or hiding it in the implementation (i.e. having the compiler or run-time system handle it automatically). The model may either let the programmer specify which computations are to be executed simultaneously (explicit parallelism) or it may require the implementation to discover opportunities for parallel execution (implicit parallelism).

Models that hide parallelism typically also hide communication and partial failures.

With explicit parallelism, on the other hand, communication and handling of failures can be either explicit or implicit. Sending messages between processes is a form of explicit communication, while exchange of information through shared variables is more implicit, since it hides the physical communication. Finally, the model may require the programmer to deal with processor failures or it may let the implementation try to make crashes transparent.

The decisions as to whether parallelism, communication, and partial failures are to be explicit or implicit are fundamental to the design of a model. Below, we will compare the alternatives and see which ones are most appropriate for our purpose.

5.1.1   Implicit versus explicit parallelism

The most important design issue concerning parallelism is the choice between *explicit* and *implicit* parallelism. In the first case, parallelism is directly visible to the programmer; in the second case, parallelism is hidden from the programmer and is managed by the implementation.

As an advantage of implicit parallelism, programmers do not have to worry about which computations to run in parallel and how to synchronize them. The catch, of course, is how to implement a compiler that takes full advantage of the available parallel processing power. Whether or not implicit parallelism is suitable depends on whether such a parallelizing compiler can be implemented. This in turn depends on the parallel architecture being used. Below, we will take a brief look at parallelizing compilers for some architectures.

For dataflow and vector machines implicit parallelism has been applied successfully in the implementations of some languages. Id, for example, is a functional language for the MIT Tagged-Token Dataflow Architecture that uses implicit parallelism [Nikhil, 1988]. For vector computers, several language implementations exist that automatically detect parallelism [Padua and Wolfe, 1986; Almasi and Gottlieb, 1989].

Implicit parallelism in asynchronous MIMD machines has been studied, for example, in the ParaScope project [Callahan *et al.*, 1988]. The PFC system developed in this project translates ordinary FORTRAN programs into a dialect that can execute different iterations of loops in parallel. Although PFC performs a very sophisticated dependency analysis, it frequently fails to do automatic parallelization because it is unable to disprove one or more dependencies. After years of experience, its designers have come to the conclusion that 'automatic techniques will not be sufficient to achieve high performance on asynchronous parallel systems' and that 'our research has convinced us that the programmer will need to be involved in the specification of parallelism at some level.'

The ParaScope project is concerned with numerical applications, hence its focus on parallelizing loop statements. For symbolic applications, automatic parallelization may even be harder to accomplish. Consider, for example, parallel game-tree search. There are several different ways of employing parallelism for game-tree search [Bal and Van Renesse, 1986], of which tree-splitting – searching different parts of the tree in parallel – is most effective for MIMD machines. Even if a compiler is clever enough to detect this kind of parallelism, it still has not solved the real problem, which is how to find an efficient parallel search strategy that minimizes the number of nodes to be searched [Marsland and Campbell, 1982]. In general, the best strategy depends on many different factors, like how the search tree is constructed and the rules of the game being played. As even human beings find it very difficult to figure out the best strategy, there is little hope for a compiler to make optimal usage of parallelism by just looking at the source code.

A compiler that efficiently explores parallelism in applications like game-tree search would probably have to use knowledge about the application, much like expert systems do. Such compilers are far beyond the current state of the art. Our conclusion is that current compilers are unable to take optimal advantage of implicit parallelism on MIMD machines, of which distributed systems are a subclass.

With explicit parallelism, the programmer's task potentially becomes more complicated. Some people claim that programming is already difficult as is, and adding explicit parallelism will make it far more difficult. The speedup obtained through parallelism, however, may also have positive effects on programming productivity. It is not uncommon for programmers to spend weeks optimizing their programs, sometimes even rewriting parts in assembly code. The performance gained by switching from sequential to distributed programming may take away the need for such low-level optimizations. Moreover, one may sacrifice part of the performance gains by using a less efficient yet much higher level language. Very high level languages (e.g. SETL [Schwartz *et al.*, 1986]) make programming significantly easier, but unfortunately they also are very inefficient. On distributed hardware, the performance may be more acceptable. Also, one may employ part of the extra processing power to make programs more type secure, for example by enabling array bound checking and range checking.

In conclusion, we feel that, given the current state of the art in compiler technology, explicit parallelism is more effective than implicit parallelism for distributed systems. With explicit parallelism, the programmer gets the extra job of managing the parallelism. On the other hand, the performance gains can be used to ease the programmer's task by using a higher level, type-secure language. Consequently, our model will be based on explicit parallelism.

5.1.2   Implicit versus explicit communication

Most models for distributed programming are based on message passing. These models can be mapped efficiently onto the distributed hardware, which also supports message passing. A drawback, however, is the lack of support for global data. Applications that need global state information are hard to program using message passing.

The literature contains numerous examples of distributed applications and algorithms that would greatly benefit from support for shared data, even if no physical shared memory is available. Bisiani and Forin, for example, describe a distributed speech recognition system that is implemented on a conceptual shared memory [Bisiani and Forin, 1987]. Li mentions linear equation solving, three-dimensional partial differential equations, the travelling salesman problem, and split-merge sort as applications for his shared virtual memory system [Li, 1988b]. Cheriton discusses how logically shared memory could ease the implementation of distributed system services (e.g. name service, time service), global scheduling, and replicated files [Cheriton, 1985]. Chess programs frequently maintain a database (the *transposition table*) of positions they have already looked at, to avoid evaluating the same position twice. In a distributed chess program, the transposition table should be shared among all processors, to prevent two processors from accidentally having to evaluate the same position [Felten and Otto, 1988].

In Chapter 2 we looked at two specific applications requiring global data and discussed how they could be implemented with message passing. To achieve an acceptable performance, the programmer has to replicate global data and write code for updating all copies of the same data. As discussed in Section 2.3.3, keeping all copies up to date is far from easy. It is therefore desirable to put the task of replicating global data in the hands of a language implementation, rather than letting programmers worry about it.

Message-passing models may either be synchronous (synchronous message-passing, rendezvous, remote procedure call) or asynchronous. Both categories have their own additional problems, in addition to the lack of support for global data.

Synchronous message-passing limits parallelism, because the sender has to wait for the receiver to be ready. Other mechanisms can be used for obtaining parallelism, such as lightweight processes, but this frequently leads to complicated program structures. Synchronous message-passing therefore is not a very convenient model for implementing parallel, high-performance applications.

Conversely, asynchronous models are more flexible, but they also are hard to program. If an asynchronous message is sent from process A to process B, it may take an arbitrary amount of time before the message is accepted by B. In the mean time, lots of other events may happen. Because of this delay, distributed programs based on asynchronous messages are frequently hard to understand and debug [Tanenbaum and Van Renesse, 1985].

In conclusion, a message-passing model is relatively easy to implement, but it also has many disadvantages. The possibility of implicit communication through logically shared data frequently makes programming easier, although such a communication model is more complicated to implement efficiently on distributed systems. As our main concerns lie with the (application) programmer, we will base our model on logically shared data and accept the increased complexity of the language implementation.

5.1.3 Implicit versus explicit handling of partial failures

Like parallelism and communication, partial failures can be made explicit (visible to the programmer) or implicit (hidden from the programmer). In Chapters 3 and 4 we have described several explicit and implicit mechanisms. We will now see which of these are suitable for our model.

One way of making partial failures visible to the programmer is through exception handling. With this method, the run-time system merely detects processor crashes, but the problem of getting the system back into a consistent state has to be solved by the programmer. As shown in Section 4.3.3, this is, in general, a difficult task. For critical applications like monitoring an aircraft or factory, this effort is certainly worthwhile. Our model, however, is mainly intended for noncritical tasks, like parallel, high-performance applications. It is doubtful whether implementors of such applications are willing to write significant amounts of code for making programs more fault-tolerant, especially as processor crashes are rare.

Another explicit mechanism for dealing with partial failures is the atomic transaction. An atomic transaction executes multiple operations on several data items in an all-or-nothing fashion. If any of the operations fail (e.g. because of a processor crash), the whole transaction is aborted and all data items are left unchanged. Atomic transactions are mainly useful for atomic updating of important data that must always be consistent, such as bank accounts or flight reservations. Parallel, high-performance applications, on the other hand, usually do not manage such vital data. Nonetheless, atomic transactions could sometimes be useful for such applications as well, as illustrated by the sorting algorithm of Section 4.3.3. Unfortunately, the costs of this mechanism are very high, as all data affected by the transaction have to be copied before being changed. Moreover, an expensive protocol is needed for committing the transaction. Again, it is doubtful whether such an expensive mechanism would be used frequently by parallel-application programmers.

In conclusion, none of the explicit mechanisms are suitable for our purpose. We will therefore not include explicit mechanisms for handling partial failures in our model. Instead, partial failures should be handled implicitly by the implementation. The run-time cost for doing this, however, must be weighed against the risks of using a program that aborts if a processor fails. Frequently, the risks of program failures will be quite acceptable, especially if the program is not subject to hard timing constraints. In some cases, it may be necessary to spend part of the processing power to protect programs against processor failures. (As stated in Section 1.5.1, however, we will not discuss fault-tolerant implementations of our language in this book.)

5.1.4 Summary

In the preceding sections we discussed the three most important design alternatives for a distributed programming model, namely implicit or explicit parallelism, communication, and handling of partial failures. We conclude that, for our purpose, it is desirable to have explicit, programmer-controlled parallelism and implicit communication through logically shared data; partial failures should be dealt with by the implementation, provided that the cost for doing so is justifiable.

As the model is to be implemented on systems that do not have shared memory, the requirement for supporting shared data is not easy to fulfil. Therefore, we will first look at proposals for sharing data in distributed systems. Next, we will develop a new model based on logically shared data.

5.2   Sharing data in distributed systems

In theory, a shared variable can simply be simulated on a distributed system by storing it on one processor and letting other processors read and write it through remote procedure calls. In most distributed systems, however, a remote procedure call is two to four orders of magnitude slower than reading local data. This difference makes a straightforward simulation of shared variables unattractive.

Instead, the systems described below offer primitives that have some properties of shared variables and some of message passing. The semantics are somewhere in between shared variables and message passing. Often, the data are only accessible by some of the processes and only through some specific operations. These restrictions make the primitives more secure than regular shared variables and make an efficient distributed implementation possible.

5.2.1   Ada's shared variables

One example of logically shared data is Ada's shared variables. Shared variables in Ada are normal variables that happen to be visible to several tasks, as defined by the Ada scope rules. In an attempt to make the language implementable on memory-disjoint architectures, special rules for shared variables were introduced (Section 9.11 of the language reference manual [US Department of Defense, 1983]). Between synchronization points (e.g. normal rendezvous communication), two tasks sharing a variable cannot make any assumptions about the order in which the other task performs operations on the variable.

In essence, this rule permits a distributed implementation to use copies (replicas) of shared variables and to update these copies only on rendezvous. The semantics of Ada's shared variables are quite different from normal shared variables, as updates do not have immediate effect. Moreover, there are many deficiencies of shared variables in Ada, as discussed in detail by Shulman [Shulman, 1987]. All in all, introducing shared data this way does not seem like a major breakthrough in elegant language design.

5.2.2   Problem-oriented shared memory

Cheriton [Cheriton, 1985] has proposed a kind of shared memory that can be tailored to a specific application, the so-called *problem-oriented shared memory*. The shared memory can be regarded as a distributed system service, implemented on multiple processors. Data are stored (replicated) on one or more of these processors, and may also be cached on client workstations.

The semantics of the problem-oriented shared memory are tuned to the needs of the application using it. In general, the semantics are more relaxed than those of shared variables. In particular, inconsistent copies of the same data are allowed to coexist temporarily, so a 'read' operation does not necessarily return the value stored by the most recent 'write'. There are several different approaches to deal with these *stale* data, for example to let the applications programmer worry about it, or to let the shared memory guarantee a certain degree of accuracy (e.g. a shared variable containing the 'time of the day' can be kept accurate within, say, five seconds).

The implementation significantly benefits from the relaxed semantics. Most important, it does not have to use complicated schemes to update atomically all copies of the same data. For some applications, the weak semantics provided by this model may not be a problem. Still, the proposal is too ad hoc to serve as a sound basis for a general language for programming distributed applications.

5.2.3   The Agora shared memory

The Agora shared memory allows processes written in different languages and executing on different types of machines to communicate [Bisiani and Forin, 1987]. It has been implemented on closely coupled as well as loosely coupled architectures.

The memory contains shared data structures, accessible through a (extensible) set of standard functions. These functions are available (e.g. as library routines) in all languages supported by the system. A shared data structure is organized as a set of immutable data elements, accessed indirectly through (mutable) *maps*, each of which maps an index (integer or string) onto the address of a data element. To change an element of the set, a new element must be added and the map updated accordingly. Elements that are no longer accessible are automatically garbage collected.

Exclusive access to a data structure is provided by a standard function that applies a user function to a data structure. The implementation is based on replication of data structures on reference. As in Cheriton's model, read operations may return stale data.

5.2.4   Linda's tuple space

Linda's tuple space was discussed in Section 3.2.2. Although the semantics of tuple space are significantly different from shared variables (e.g. it lacks assignment), the tuple space clearly gives the illusion of a shared memory. The tuple space has been implemented on several memory-disjoint machines (iPSC hypercube, S/Net, Ethernet-based network of MicroVAXes). The S/Net implementation, for example, replicates the entire tuple space on all processors and updates all these copies using multicast [Carriero and Gelernter, 1986].

5.2.5   Shared virtual memory

Kai Li has extended the concept of *virtual memory* to distributed systems, resulting in a *shared virtual memory* [Li, 1986]. This memory is accessible by all processes and is addressed like traditional virtual memory. Li's system guarantees memory *coherence*: the value returned by a 'read' always is the value stored by the last 'write'.

The address space is partitioned into a number of fixed-size *pages*. At any time, several processors may have a *read-only* copy of the same page; alternatively, a single processor may have a *read-and-write* copy.

If a process tries to write on a certain page while its processor does not have a read-and-write copy of it, a 'write page-fault' occurs. The fault-handling routine tells other processors to *invalidate* their copies, fetches a copy of the page (if it did not have one yet), sets the protection mode to read-and-write, and resumes the faulting instruction.

If a process wants to read a page, but does not have a copy of it, a 'read page-fault' occurs. If any processor has a read-and-write copy of the page, this processor is instructed to change the protection to read-only. A copy of the page is fetched and the faulting instruction is resumed.

The shared virtual memory can be used to simulate true shared variables, with exactly the right semantics. The implementation uses the hardware memory management unit and can benefit from the availability of multicast (e.g. to invalidate all copies of a page). Several strategies exist to deal with the problem of multiple simultaneous writes and to administrate which processors contain copies of a page [Li, 1986]. The entire scheme will perform very poorly if processes on many different processors repeatedly write on the same page. This situation arises if multiple processors write the same variable, or if they write different variables placed on the same page. Nevertheless, unlike most of the other proposals, this one has well-defined semantics. Its problem is the difficulty of implementing it efficiently.

5.2.6   Shared logical variables

Shared logical variables were discussed in Section 3.2.2. Shared logical variables have the *single-assignment* property: once they are bound to a value (or to another variable) they cannot be changed. (In 'sequential' logic languages, variables may receive another value after backtracking; most concurrent logic languages eliminate backtracking, however.)

The single-assignment property allows the model to be implemented with reasonable efficiency on a distributed system. An implementation of Flat Concurrent Prolog on a hypercube is described in [Taylor *et al.*, 1987b]. If a process tries to read a logical variable stored on a remote processor, the remote processor adds the process to a list associated with the variable. As soon as the variable becomes bound (if it was not already), its value is sent to all processes on the list. These processes will keep the value for future reference. In this way, variables are automatically replicated on reference. Although this method also works and has clean semantics, it is not very general and only applies to programs written in parallel logic languages.

5.2.7   Discussion

Although the systems discussed above differ widely in their semantics, there is a striking similarity in their implementations: they all *replicate* data. Replication of data has already been used for a long time in distributed databases to increase the availability of data in the presence of processor failures. Replication introduces a severe problem: the possibility of having inconsistent copies of the same logical data. For databases, several solutions exist [Bernstein and Goodman, 1981]. Typically, multiple copies of the same data are accessed when reading or writing data.

The techniques discussed in this section use replication to decrease the *access time* to shared data, rather than to increase availability. Therefore, it is unattractive to consult several processors on every access to the data. Instead, just the local copy should suffice for as many accesses as possible. With this restriction, different solutions must be found to deal with the consistency problem.

The systems discussed above use three different ways of dealing with inconsistency. Ada, the problem-oriented shared memory, and the Agora shared memory relax the semantics of the shared memory. The latter two systems allow 'read' operations to return stale data. Higher level protocols must be used by the programmer to solve inconsistency problems. Ada requires copies to be updated only on rendezvous.

The second approach (used for tuple space and shared logical variables) is to replicate only *immutable* data (data that cannot be changed). This significantly reduces the complexity of the problem, but it may also introduce new problems. The approach is most effective in languages using single-assignment. Such languages, however, will need a complicated distributed garbage algorithm to remove unaccessible data. In Linda, tuples are immutable objects. A tuple can conceptually be changed by first taking it out of tuple space, and storing it in normal (local) variables. After changing these local data, they can be put back in a new tuple. As tuples are accessed by contents, it makes little difference that the old tuple has been replaced by a new one, instead of being modified while in tuple space. As a major advantage of doing the modification outside tuple space, updates by different processes are automatically synchronized. On the other hand, unless clever compiler optimizations are applied, a small modification to a large tuple will be expensive, since the tuple has to be copied twice.

The third approach to the consistency problem is exemplified by the shared virtual memory: use protocols that guarantee memory coherence. Before changing a page, all copies of the page are invalidated, so subsequent reads will never return stale data. Great care must be taken in the implementation, however, to avoid thrashing. For badly behaving programs, the system may easily spend most of its time moving and invalidating pages.

In summary, none of the above models provides the semantics and efficiency we would like to have. In the next section, we will look at an alternative model, the shared data-object model.

5.3   A new model based on logically shared data

In this section we will present a new model for interprocess communication based on logically shared data, the *shared data-object* model. This model is designed to support shared data structures that can be manipulated by arbitrary operations in a clean way, with well-defined semantics, while still allowing an efficient implementation on distributed systems.

For the description of our model, we assume that parallelism is expressed through explicit creation of processes. Also, we do not address fault tolerance in our discussion, but assume this issue is dealt with by the implementation of the model.

As discussed above, replication is the key to efficient sharing of data in a distributed system. Each of the systems described above somehow replicates shared data. Unfortunately, having multiple copies of the same data introduces inconsistency problems, which, if not dealt with properly, result in a model with unclear semantics.

The idea behind the shared data-object model is to make replication of shared data transparent to the programmer. The model is designed to let the implementation (compiler and run-time system) manage the physical distribution of shared data among the available processors. In particular, the implementation takes care of consistent updating of replicated data.

Another important objective of the model is to synchronize automatically access to shared data. If two processes simultaneously try to write (or read and write) the same data structure, then the result should be well defined. In contrast, shared variables as used in, say, Algol 68, need separate synchronization mechanisms (e.g. semaphores) for this purpose.

5.3.1   Data

The most important issue addressed by our model is how data structures can be shared among distributed processes in an efficient way. In most multiprocessor languages, shared data structures are stored in the shared memory and accessed in basically the same way as local variables, namely through simple load and store instructions. If one process is going to change part of a shared data structure and it does not want other processes to interfere, it locks that part. The underlying assumption is that all these operations (loads, stores, locks) on shared data structures involve very little overhead, because access to shared memory is hardly more expensive than access to local memory. However, on large systems with many processors and many memory modules connected by omega switching networks, even this may not be true.

In a distributed system, the access time of data depends on their location. Accessing data on remote processors may be orders of magnitude more expensive than accessing local data. It is therefore infeasible to apply the multiprocessor model of programming to distributed systems. The operations used in this programming model are far too low-level and will have tremendous overhead on distributed systems.

The starting-point in our model is to access shared data structures through higher level operations. Instead of using low-level instructions for reading, writing, and locking shared data, we propose to let programmers define composite operations for manipulating shared data structures.

Shared data structures in our model are encapsulated in so-called data objects that are manipulated through a set of user-defined operations. Data objects are best thought of as instances (variables) of *abstract data types*. The programmer specifies an abstract data type by defining operations that can be applied to instances (data objects) of that type. The actual data contained in the data object and the executable code for the operations are hidden in the implementation of the abstract data type.

(We will sometimes use the term 'object' as a shorthand notation for data object. Note, however, that this term is also used in object-oriented and object-based languages and systems, with various different meanings. Most important, objects in our model are purely passive. We will come back to this issue in Section 5.3.4.)

Although data objects logically are shared among processes, their implementation does not need physical shared memory. In the worst case, an operation on an object located on a remote processor can be implemented with a remote procedure call. The general idea, however, is for the implementation to take care of the physical distribution of data objects among processors and to decrease access costs as much as possible. As we will see in Chapter 6, one mechanism for achieving this goal is to replicate shared data-objects.

In the following sections, we will elaborate the basic idea by looking at the issue of synchronization. Two types of synchronization can be distinguished: *mutual exclusion synchronization* prevents multiple simultaneous writes (or reads and writes) to the same data from interfering with each other; *condition synchronization* allows processes to wait for a certain condition to become true [Andrews and Schneider, 1983]. We discuss both types of synchronization in turn.

5.3.2   Mutual exclusion synchronization

If two or more processes simultaneously try to access the same shared data structure, race conditions can arise. In particular, if two processes try to modify the same part of a shared data structure, they must be prohibited from interfering with each other. This type of synchronization is called mutual exclusion.

Shared-variable languages usually provide some kind of *locking* construct for mutual exclusion synchronization. In a distributed environment, however, such locking primitives are too low-level and have a high overhead. In our model, mutual exclusion is done implicitly, by executing all operations on objects *indivisibly*. Conceptually, each operation locks the entire object it is applied to and releases the lock only when it is finished. To be more precise, the model guarantees *serializability* [Eswaran *et al.*, 1976] of operation invocations: if two operations are applied simultaneously to the same data object, then the result is as if one of them is executed before the other; the order of invocation, however, is nondeterministic.

An implementation of the model need not actually execute all operations one by one. To increase the degree of parallelism, it may execute multiple operations on the same object simultaneously, as long as the effect is the same as for serialized execution. For example, operations that only read (but do not change) the data stored in an object can easily be executed in parallel.

As operations are indivisible, mutual exclusion synchronization to shared data-objects is taken care of automatically. Consider, for example, an object encapsulating an integer variable, with the following operations:*

```
operation Value(): integer;  # return current value
operation Assign(val: integer);  # assign new value
operation Add(val: integer);  # add val to current value
```

If two processes sharing such an object simultaneously try to apply the `Assign` operation to the object, the resulting value will either be that of the first or second operation, but the value will never be some strange mixture of the bits. Similarly, if two processes simultaneously increment the value of an object by invoking the operation `Add(1)`, the value will always be incremented twice, because the operations are serialized.

On the other hand, *sequences* of operations are not executed indivisibly. For example, the sequence

- get value of object (through `Value`)
- increment this value
- store result back (through `Assign`)

---

* We use the Orca syntax for comments here: a comment starts with a '#' and is terminated by an end-of-line.

is not an indivisible action. If multiple processes apply this sequence to the same object, the value may be incremented once or twice. This rule for defining which actions are indivisible and which are not is both easy to understand and flexible: single operations are indivisible; sequences of operations are not.

Our model does not support indivisible operations on multiple objects, as languages like Argus and Aeolus do. Such operations would require some sort of distributed locking protocol, which is complicated to implement efficiently. Instead, we prefer to keep our basic model as simple as possible and implement more complicated actions on top of it. Operations in our model therefore apply to single objects and are always executed indivisibly. However, the model is sufficiently powerful to allow users to construct locks for multi-operation sequences on different objects, so arbitrary actions can be performed indivisibly.

5.3.3   Condition synchronization

Condition synchronization allows processes to wait (*block*) until a certain condition becomes true. The simplest form of condition synchronization in a shared-variable language is repeated testing (*busy waiting*) of a shared variable, until it has a certain value. As busy waiting wastes computing cycles, however, most languages use a separate condition synchronization mechanism, like a semaphore, event count, or condition variable.

The shared data-object model described so far can be extended in one of two ways to support condition synchronization. One approach is to add a separate synchronization primitive, independent of the mechanism for shared objects. Another approach is to integrate condition synchronization with the shared-object model by allowing operations to block. In the latter case, processes synchronize implicitly through operations on shared objects. To illustrate the difference between these two alternatives, we will first look at a specific example.

Consider a Queue object with operations to append elements to the tail and retrieve elements from the head:

```
operation Append(x: item);  # append to tail
operation Get(): item;  # get from head
```

Queue data structures can be used, for example, for storing work generated by a master process and picked up by slave processes. A slave process trying to fetch an element from an empty queue should not be allowed to continue. In other words, the number of Get operations applied to a queue should not exceed the number of Append operations. This is an example of a *synchronization constraint* on the order in which operations are executed. There are at least two conceivable ways for expressing such constraints in our model:

1. Processes trying to execute `Get` should first check the status of the queue and block while the queue is empty. Doing a `Get` on an empty queue results in an error.
2. The `Get` operation itself blocks while the queue is empty. Processes executing a `Get` on an empty queue therefore block automatically.

In both cases, a new primitive is needed for blocking processes. In the first case this primitive would be used directly by user processes; in the second case only operations on objects would use it. Also, the first approach calls for an extra operation on queues that checks if a given queue is empty. (For both approaches, unblocking the process and removing the head element from the queue should be done in one indivisible action, to avoid race conditions.)

The first approach has one major drawback: the *users* of an object are responsible for satisfying synchronization constraints. This is in contrast to the general idea of object-based programming to hide implementation details of objects from users. The second approach is much cleaner, as the *implementor* of the object takes care of synchronization and users just use the operations. We therefore use the second approach and do condition synchronization inside the operations. The model allows operations to block; processes can only block by executing operations that block.

An important issue in the design of the synchronization mechanism is how to provide blocking operations while still guaranteeing the indivisibility of operation invocations. If an operation may block at any point during its execution, operations can no longer be serialized. Our solution is to allow operations only to block *initially*, before modifying the object. An operation may wait until a certain condition becomes true, but once it has started executing, it cannot block again.

The implementation of an operation has the following form:

```
operation name(parameters)
    condition → statements
```

The condition (guard) is a side-effect-free Boolean expression that depends only on the internal data of the object and the parameters of the operation. The statements may read or modify the object's data.

If the operation is applied to a certain object, the operation blocks until the guard is true. If the guard initially fails, it can succeed at a later stage after another process has modified the internal data of the object. As soon as the guard succeeds, its statements are executed.

The testing of the guard and the execution of the statements together are an indivisible action. As long as the guard fails, the operation has no effect at all, as the object's data can only be modified by the statements. This means that serializability is still easy to achieve, so all operation invocations are executed as indivisible actions.

5.3.4   Comparison with other models

In this section, we will compare the shared data-object model with several related communication models. In particular, we will look at objects (as used in parallel object-oriented languages), monitors, and Linda's tuple space.

Objects

Objects are used in many other languages for parallel or distributed programming, as discussed in Section 4.1.6. Objects in such languages typically have two parts:

1. Encapsulated data.
2. A *manager process* that controls access to the data.

The data are accessed by sending a message to the manager process, asking it to perform a certain operation on the data. As such objects contain a process as well as data, they are said to be *active*.

Although, in some sense, parallel object-oriented languages allow processes (objects) to share data (also objects), their semantics are closer to message passing than to shared variables. Access to the shared data is under full control of the manager process. In ALPS [Vishnubhotia, 1988], for example, all operations on an object go through its manager process, which determines the order in which the operations are to be executed. Therefore, the only way to implement the model is to store an object on one specific processor, together with its manager process, and to translate all operations on the object into remote procedure calls to the manager process.

The shared data-object model does not have such centralized control. Objects in this model are purely passive: they contain data, but no manager process. Access control to shared data-objects is much more distributed; it is basically determined by only two rules:

1. Operations must be executed indivisibly.
2. Operations are blocked while their guards are false.

Therefore, the model can be implemented by replicating data objects on multiple processors. We will not go into the details of the implementation here – these are discussed in Chapter 6 – but one can envision, for example, an implementation where each processor contains its own local copy of each object. An operation that only *reads* the data stored in the object can easily be applied to the local copy, without any message passing being involved. Moreover, processes located on different processors can apply the read operations simultaneously, without losing any parallelism. If an operation *writes* an object (i.e. it changes the data stored in the object), some cooperation will be needed among the processors to update all the local copies in a consistent way.

Monitors

The idea of encapsulating shared data in abstract data types also has been used in several languages based on *monitors* [Brinch Hansen, 1973; Hoare, 1974], such as Concurrent Pascal, Mesa, and Pascal-Plus [Welsh and Bustard, 1979]. A monitor is a program module encapsulating shared data and operations on the data. Processes can only access the data through these operations. The semantics of the monitor construct guarantee that only one process at a time will be executing an operation. The restriction is usually enforced by the compiler, which recognizes monitor operations and automatically inserts lower level primitives such as semaphores. Most monitor languages use condition variables for condition synchronization. A WAIT(v) on a condition variable blocks the currently executing process and a SIGNAL(v) reactivates one process blocked in a WAIT(v).

In most languages, monitors are compile-time constructs, although Mesa and Concurrent Pascal allow monitors to be created dynamically. The monitor operations are not executed indivisibly, as they may block at any point during their executing (by invoking WAIT). The monitor construct merely provides mutual exclusion; two operations of the same monitor cannot execute simultaneously, but operations need not be completed before others are allowed to enter the monitor.

The main problem with monitors, however, is again the centralized control to the shared data. Monitors were designed for uniprocessors and shared-memory multiprocessors rather than for distributed systems. They could be implemented on distributed systems in much the same way as parallel object-oriented languages are. This would be vastly inefficient, however, as each monitor operation would essentially require a remote procedure call.

Linda's tuple space

Linda is one of the first languages to recognize the disadvantages of central manager processes for guarding shared data. Linda supports so-called *distributed data structures*, which can be accessed simultaneously by multiple processes. In contrast, object-based and monitor-based languages typically serialize access to shared data structures. As we discussed in Chapter 3, Linda uses the tuple space model for implementing distributed data structures.

In general, distributed data structures in Linda are built out of multiple tuples. Different tuples can be accessed independently of each other, so processes can manipulate different tuples of the same data structure simultaneously. In principle, multiple **read** operations of the same tuple can also be executed simultaneously. Tuples are (conceptually) modified by taking them out of tuple space first, so modifications of a given tuple are executed strictly sequentially.

Although the idea of distributed data structures is very appealing, we feel the support given by the tuple space for implementing such data structures is too low-level. In Section 4.3.2, we discussed some problems related to the tuple space model. For distributed data structures built out of single tuples, mutual exclusion synchronization is done automatically; operations on complex data structures (built out of multiple tuples), however, have to be synchronized explicitly by the programmer. In essence, tuple space supports a fixed number of built-in operations that are executed indivisibly, but its support for building more complex indivisible operations is too low-level.

In the shared data-object model, on the other hand, programmers can define operations of arbitrary complexity on shared data structures; all these operations are executed indivisibly, so mutual exclusion synchronization is always done automatically by the run-time system. This means it is the job of the implementation (the compiler and run-time system) to see which operations can be executed in parallel and which have to be executed sequentially. As discussed above, one way of doing this is by distinguishing between read and write operations and executing reads in parallel on local copies; more advanced implementations are also feasible.

There are also other differences between the tuple space and shared data-object models. Tuple space is addressed associatively, which is potentially expensive. Although several optimizations are possible to decrease the costs significantly [Carriero, 1987], it is not clear whether access time of tuples can be reduced to that of local variables. Conversely, shared data-objects are addressed directly. The inherent overhead of accessing a local copy of an object approximately is that of a local procedure call; these costs can be decreased further through inline substitution, which is a standard optimization technique [Bal and Tanenbaum, 1986].

Another difference between the two models is the way shared data are modified. Shared data-objects are modified directly, much like normal (local) variables. Tuples, however, cannot be modified directly, but first have to be taken out of tuple space and later have to be put back. For large data structures, there may be a significant overhead involved in copying data from and to tuple space. This overhead may be optimized away in some cases, but existing implementations of tuple space have not yet addressed this issue.

5.4   A language based on the shared data-object model

The shared data-object model is used to design a new language for distributed programming, called *Orca*, which will be described in this section. We will first give a general overview of the language, focusing on the design principles behind it. Next, we will discuss the most important issues in more detail, starting with distributed programming issues. Then we illustrate our discussions with short fragments of Orca code. Example Orca applications will be presented in Chapter 7, to illustrate the language and its use. The appendices contain the complete Orca source code for some of these applications.

5.4.1   Design overview

Orca is a new language for distributed applications programming. Unlike the majority of other languages described in Chapter 4, it is not an extension to an existing sequential language. Instead, its sequential and distributed constructs have been designed together, in such a way that they integrate well.

As Orca is intended for applications programming, it lacks low-level features that would only be useful for systems programming. Another approach to reducing complexity is to avoid language features aimed solely at increasing efficiency, especially if the same effect can be achieved through an optimizing compiler. Finally, the principle of orthogonality [Ghezzi and Jazayeri, 1982] is used with care, but it is not a design goal by itself.

As debugging of distributed programs is a hard job, one needs all the help one can get. Although the development of debugging tools is outside the scope of this book, we have paid considerable attention to easing debugging. Most important, Orca is a type-secure language. The language design allows the implementation to detect many errors during compile time. In addition, the language run-time system does extensive error-checking.

Orca is a procedural, strongly typed language. Its statements and expressions are fairly conventional and comparable to those of Modula-2. The data structuring facilities of Orca, however, are substantially different from those used in Modula-2. Orca supports records, unions, dynamic arrays, sets, bags, and general graphs. Pointers have intentionally been omitted to provide security.

5.4.2   Processes and procedures

Parallelism in Orca is based on explicit creation of sequential processes through **fork** statements. Processes are conceptually similar to procedures, except that procedure invocations are serial and process invocations are parallel.

One important design issue concerning processes is how the sharing of data objects among processes is expressed. We will look at this issue first. Sharing of data can be expressed in several ways, as shown by the systems of Section 5.2. The shared virtual memory and Linda's tuple space provide a global memory that can be accessed by all processes, so all shared data in the system are global. In contrast, languages using shared logical variables (Concurrent Prolog, PARLOG) require shared variables to be passed as arguments to goals. In Ada, a shared variable can be accessed by all processes that are in the scope of the declaration of the variable, so the lexical level of the variable declaration determines which processes can access the variable.

It is worth noting that a similar classification exists for sequential languages, only here the classification concerns global variables and procedures, rather than shared variables and processes. In languages with flat name spaces, like C and FORTRAN, all procedures can (potentially) access all global variables. In block structured languages (e.g. Algol 60, Algol 68, Pascal), variables declared within a certain block can be used by procedures within that block, but not by procedures at a higher lexical level. Finally, pure functional and logic languages do not have global variables at all.

For consistency, a language should use similar access rules for shared variables as for global variables. This is illustrated by the languages mentioned above. Linda supports global variables – at least the C/Linda version does – and provides a global shared memory. Concurrent Prolog and PARLOG do not have global variables. Ada is block structured and uses nested scopes for defining the access rules of shared as well as normal variables.*

For our language we have chosen the functional approach to sharing data. The language lacks any form of global data: neither processes nor procedures are allowed to share global variables. Instead, sharing of data must be achieved by passing *parameters* to processes or procedures. Although this restriction requires programmers to do some extra work, we feel it has several major advantages. First of all, programs lacking global variables are, in general, easier to read and understand than programs with global variables [Wulf and Shaw, 1973; Ghezzi and Jazayeri, 1982]. Also, the distributed implementation of logically shared data will be simplified, as only part of the processes can access the shared data. Hence shared data will not have to be replicated on all processors.

Procedures

A procedure in Orca has the following form:

```
function name(formal-parameters): ResultType;
    local declarations
begin
    statements
end;
```

The result type is optional. Procedures may only access their own local variables and parameters. There are no global variables (or static local variables). There are three kinds of formal parameter for procedures:

1. Input (value)
2. Output
3. Shared

By default, parameters are input.

A formal input parameter stands for a local variable that is initialized with the value of the actual parameter, which may be any expression of the same type as the formal. A formal output parameter is a local variable whose value is copied into the actual parameter on return of the procedure. A formal shared parameter denotes the actual parameter, which must be a variable; this is similar to call-by-reference in Pascal. Actual parameters may not be aliases [Ghezzi and Jazayeri, 1982] of each other; this is enforced by either compile-time or run-time tests.

A procedure can read and write shared parameters and it can return several results, either through a result value or through output parameters. Apart from this, a procedure does not have any side-effects on its environment. To emphasize this fact, we

---

* In fact, nontrivial algorithms are needed for distinguishing between shared and nonshared variables in Ada [Hummel, 1988]. Ada supports a pragma 'SHARED,' but this pragma cannot be used for structured types.

use the keyword **function** rather than **procedure**. Note, however, that Orca is not a functional language, as procedures may have call-by-reference parameters.

Processes

A process definition in Orca consists of a name, parameter specification, and body (local declarations and statements):

```
process name(formal-parameters);
    local declarations
begin
    statements
end;
```

A process definition does not create any processes; it merely defines how actual processes should be invoked and it describes the behaviour of such processes.

Initially, an Orca program consists of a single process, but new processes can be created explicitly through the **fork** statement:

```
fork name(actual-parameters);
```

This statement creates a single new process. We will refer to the process executing the **fork** statement as the *parent*; the newly created process is said to be a *child* process. (The relation between a parent and its children is purely dynamic, as there is no static nesting of processes.) Note that the child process is anonymous, as the **fork** statement does not return a value. In our model, there is no need to refer to individual processes.

A process can take parameters, as specified in its definition. Two kinds are allowed: input and shared.

A process may take any kind of data structure as value (input) parameter. In this case, the process receives a copy of the actual parameter, which is passed by its parent (creator) in the **fork** statement. The data structures in the parent and child are thereafter independent of each other – changing one copy does not affect the other – so they cannot be used for communication between parent and child.

The parent can also pass any of its data objects as shared parameter to the child. In this case, the data object will be shared between the parent and the child. The parent and child can communicate through this shared object, by executing the operations defined by the object's type. This mechanism can be used for sharing objects among any number of processes. The parent can spawn several child processes and pass objects to each of them. The children can pass the objects to *their* children, and so on. In this way, the objects are distributed among some of the descendants of the process that created them. If any of these processes performs an operation on the object, they all observe the same effect, as if the object were in shared memory, protected by a lock variable.

Unlike procedures, processes do not return a value or have output parameters. This difference is due to the asynchronous nature of process creation. In principle, it would be possible to add a construct to Orca that blocks the parent until the child has finished and then transfers result values from the child to the parent. (Mesa, for example, has such a **join** construct [Lampson and Redell, 1980].) Such a construct is not strictly necessary, however, as synchronization and transmission of results can also be achieved using shared data-objects.

Mapping of processes to processors

An important issue related to process creation is the *mapping* of processes to processors. In Chapter 3 we identified three types of mapping notation, depending on whether the processor is fixed at compile time, fixed at run time, or not fixed at all. The first type is mainly useful if sharing of data is to be restricted to processes executing on the same physical processor. In our model, any two processes can share data, so it is not necessary to require the mapping to be static.

The third type of mapping essentially allows processes to migrate during their lifetime. The applications for which Orca is intended, however, seldom need this complexity. In Emerald, for example, a process that frequently accesses remote data is sometimes migrated to the processor containing the data. As we will see in Chapter 6, Orca implementations may transparently migrate (or replicate) the shared data in such cases, so there is no need for migrating the process.

The notation of Orca for mapping processes to processors falls in the second class – fixed at run-time. All processors participating in a program are numbered sequentially. These numbers are used for differentiating physical processors, but otherwise have no significance. We do not specify how processors are allocated to programs. We assume that the user somehow negotiates with the operating system and is allotted a certain number of processors for executing a parallel program. The total number of processors available to a program can be obtained through the standard function NCPUS. When a process is created, it can optionally be assigned to a specific processor by specifying the processor's identifying number, as in

```
fork name(actual-parameters) on(processor-number);
```

The processor-number can be any expression yielding an integer result. (If the **on** part is omitted, the new process will be run on the same processor as its parent.) As an example, the following code creates one worker process on each available processor:

```
for p in 1 .. NCPUS() do
    fork worker(actual-parameters) on(p);
od;
```

This notation is quite sufficient for most distributed architectures. In some cases, however, programmers may want to benefit from the physical interconnection structure of the processors (e.g. a Transputer grid). In a processor grid, for example, the latency time for a message depends on the distance (number of hops) between the sending and receiving processor, so communication between two processes can be sped up by assigning them to adjacent nodes.

An implementation of Orca could make the interconnection topology visible to the programmer by systematic numbering of the processors. For example, if the processors of a grid are numbered row by row and left to right within a row, it is easy to identify the four neighbours of a processor. Programs using such a notation, however, may execute inefficiently on other network topologies.

5.4.3   Abstract data types

Processes in Orca communicate through shared data-objects. The type of such an object is essentially an *abstract data type*, as it defines a number of operations on data, but hides the actual implementation of the data structure and the operations. Orca therefore provides an abstract data type facility for defining shared data-objects. Of course, abstract data types are just as useful for encapsulating nonshared, local data. They have also been proposed, for example, to aid the construction of reliable sequential programs [Guttag, 1977]. During our discussion, we will take this issue into account.

Design alternatives for the abstract data type mechanism

An important design issue is whether the same abstract data typing facility should be used for encapsulating shared and nonshared data. If two different mechanisms are used, the implementor of an abstract data type has to decide whether the type is to be used for shared data (i.e. shared data-objects used for interprocess communication) or local (nonshared) data. The advantage of having one mechanism is the possibility of implementing abstract types that can be used for both shared and nonshared data. On the other hand, programmers may need different primitives for implementing shared and nonshared types. This flexibility can only be obtained by distinguishing between shared and nonshared types. Before deciding on this issue, we will look at the most important differences between the two uses of abstract data types.

One difference is caused by the condition synchronization mechanism of our model. As explained in Section 5.3.3, operations on shared data-objects may block until the data satisfy a certain condition. If the object is not shared, however, it makes no sense to let operations block, because no other process can possibly change the object's data. On the other hand, allowing the invoking process to continue even when the guard of the operation fails, frequently will also be undesirable. The synchronization mechanism is only useful for shared objects, not for local objects.

A second difference is the limitation of the shared data-object model to apply operations to single objects only. This rule is the key to a simple and efficient implementation of the model, as it takes away the need for complicated distributed locking protocols on multiple objects. For nonshared objects, however, this limitation is not strictly necessary, as such objects need not be locked.

Despite these two differences, we feel it is much cleaner to use a single, general facility that covers both cases. Many abstract data types will be useful to both sequential and distributed programming, so splitting up abstract types into two disjoint categories is not very attractive. We therefore use a single abstract data type mechanism. Each abstract type can be used for creating shared as well as nonshared objects.

As a consequence of this decision, it is syntactically correct to apply a blocking operation to a nonshared object. The run-time system can easily detect such a situation, however, and generate an error message. Another consequence is the inability to implement operations that change multiple objects, even if the objects are not shared. An operation can take any number of objects as input parameter, however, so it can read (but not modify) multiple objects.

Abstract data type definitions

Abstract data types are used in several modern languages, such as CLU, Ada, and Modula-2. In Ada, for example, the specification part of a module (package) may declare a type to be *private*, which means that users of the module cannot access the internals of the data type. The representation of the abstract data type (the internal data) is not textually hidden from its users, but is included in a separate (private) part of the module specification. Information in the private part is used by a compiler for determining the storage requirements of variables of the private type.

Modula-2 does not have such a private part, but it demands the representation type be a pointer type, so compilers always allocate the same amount of storage for variables of abstract data types. The implementation of the abstract data type can use any amount of storage, however, by allocating it dynamically and binding the pointer to this dynamically allocated area (usually a record). Still, it seems far more convenient not to bother programmers with such implementation details. In Orca, therefore, we hide the representation type from the users and do not impose any restrictions on it.

An abstract data type definition (or *object definition*) in Orca is a separate program unit, much like a module in Modula-2. Like modules, object definitions consist of two parts that can be compiled separately: a *specification* part (Figure 5.1) and an *implementation* part (Figure 5.2). Unlike modules in Modula-2, an object type definition in Orca does not allocate any data by itself; rather, it is a template from which multiple instances (objects) can be created dynamically, each containing the data specified in the definition. (In this sense, an object definition is similar to a class definition in Simula 67.)

```
object specification name;
    operation op1(formal-parameters): ResultType;
    operation op2(formal-parameters): ResultType;
    ...
end;
```

Figure 5.1 *Specification part of an Orca abstract data type definition.*

The specification part only specifies the operations that can be applied to objects of this type. It does not specify the data stored in such objects. An operation has zero or more parameters and may (but need not) return a result. The parameters are either input or output parameters. Input parameters are passed by value. Output parameters are similar to result values: on return of the operation, the current value of the formal parameter is copied into the actual parameter, which must be a variable of the same type. Unlike procedures and processes, operations do not take shared parameters. An operation should be thought of as affecting a single object and returning zero or more results.

The implementation part of an object type definition (see Figure 5.2) consists of the following:

1. A specification of the internal data contained by objects of this type.
2. The code implementing the operations declared in the specification part.
3. The code that initializes objects of this type.

Each instance (object) of the abstract data type contains the data declared in the object implementation. These data may be variables of any type, including dynamically sized data structures (e.g. arrays or graphs). The variables are only visible inside the operations and initialization code.

An operation implementation is similar to a procedure. The operation can access only three kinds of variable:

1. The local (internal) data of the object it is applied to.
2. The parameters of the operation.
3. The local variables of the operation.

As described in Section 5.3.3, operations in our model may *block* until a certain condition becomes true. In fact, Orca allows the body of an operation to specify a number of conditions. The general form of such an operation is as follows:

```
operation op(formal-parameters): ResultType;
    local declarations
begin
      guard condition₁ do statements₁ od;
      guard condition₂ do statements₂ od;
      ...
      guard conditionₙ do statementsₙ od;
end;
```

The operation invocation blocks until one or more of the conditions (guards) are true. Next, one true condition is selected nondeterministically and its corresponding statements are executed.

Objects are created by declaring variables of an object type. The declaration does

```
object implementation name;
    declarations for internal data

    operation op1(formal-parameters): ResultType;
        local declarations of op1
    begin
        code for op1
    end;

    operation op2(formal-parameters): ResultType;
        local declarations of op2
    begin
        code for op2
    end;
    ...
begin
    code that initializes internal data
    (executed whenever a new object is created)
end;
```

Figure 5.2 *Implementation part of an Orca abstract data type definition.*

not need to specify whether the object will be shared. When an object is created, the run-time system allocates memory for the local variables (internal data) of the object and executes the initialization code.

Objects declared local to a process may be shared with other (child) processes by passing them as shared parameters when the children are created. (This was discussed above.) Each process sharing an object can invoke the operations listed in the specification part of the object's type. An operation on an object X is invoked as

```
X$op(actual-parameters)
```

The operation with the given name is applied to object X. The actual parameters should match the formal parameters of the operation specification.

An example object type definition

As a simple example, we will show how an object type IntObject, encapsulating a single integer, can be defined. The definition of an object type consists of a specification part and an implementation part.

The specification part (Figure 5.3) specifies a number of indivisible operations on objects of this type. The implementation part (Figure 5.4) specifies the internal data of the objects (an integer), and it contains the implementation code of the operations as well as code that initializes objects.

Objects of this type are created through variable declarations. Operations are invoked as shown below.

object specification IntObject;
   operation Value(): integer;   # return value
   operation Assign(v: integer); # assign new value
   operation Inc(by: integer); # indivisibly increment value
   operation Dec(by: integer); # indivisibly decrement value
   operation AwaitValue(v: integer); # wait for certain value
end;

Figure 5.3 *Specification part of an object type IntObject.*

object implementation IntObject;
   x: integer; #internal data

   operation Value(): integer;
   begin
      return x;
   end;

   operation Assign(v: integer);
   begin
      x := v;
   end;

   operation Inc(by: integer);
   begin
      x := x + by;
   end;

   operation Dec(by: integer);
   begin
      x := x - by;
   end;

   operation AwaitValue(v: integer);
   begin
      guard x = v **do od**;
   end;
begin
   x := 0; # initialize objects to zero
end;

Figure 5.4 *Implementation part of an object type IntObject.*

```
Obj: IntObject;
tmp: integer;
   ...
Obj$Assign(1989);
Obj$Inc(4);
tmp := Obj$Value();
Obj$AwaitValue(2000);
```

Nested objects

Abstract data types are useful for extending a language with new types. Instead of having a large set of built-in types, a language provides a limited number of standard types and allows users to define new ones. Preferably, this method for building new types should be hierarchical: existing abstract data types should be usable for building new ones. An abstract data type `LinearList`, for example, may be useful for implementing a new type `SymbolTable`.

It is therefore desirable to allow objects to be nested. In other words, the internal data of an object may themselves be objects. Suppose we have an existing object type `OldType`, specified as follows:

```
object specification OldType;
    operation OldOperation1(): boolean;
    operation OldOperation2();
end;
```

We may want to use this object type in the implementation of another type (we omit the specification of this type):

```
object implementation NewType;
    NestedObject: OldType;   # a nested object
    operation NewOperation();
    begin
        guard NestedObject$OldOperation1() do
            ...
            NestedObject$OldOperation2();
        od;
    end
end;
```

Objects of the new type contain an object, `NestedObject`, of type `OldType`. The latter object is called a *nested* object, because it is part of another object. Note that instances of `NewType` are still *single* objects whose operations are executed indivisibly. The nested object is invisible outside its enclosing object, just like any other internal data.

The implementor of NewType can be seen as a *user* of OldType. So, the implementor of NewType does not know how OldType is implemented. This lack of information about the *implementation* of the operations on OldType causes two problems.

The first problem is illustrated by the usage of OldOperation1 in the guard of NewOperation. The guard expressions may not have any side-effects, as they may have to be evaluated several times. Unfortunately, we do not know whether the invocation of OldOperation1 has any side-effects. If the operation modifies NestedObject, it does have side-effects. We can only tell so, however, by looking at the implementation of this operation, which is against the idea of abstract data types.

The second problem is more subtle. Suppose a process declares an object NewObject of type NewType and shares it with some of its child processes. If one of the processes invokes NewOperation on NewObject, the implementation of this object will invoke OldOperation2 on the nested object. The problem is that the latter operation may very well block. If so, we violate the rule that operations are only allowed to block *initially*. In this situation, there are two equally unattractive options:

1. Suspend the process invoking NewOperation, but allow other processes to access the object. This means, however, that the operation will no longer be indivisible.
2. Block the calling process, but do not allow any other processes to access the object. This implies that the process will be suspended forever, because no other process will be able to modify NestedObject.

One could solve this problem by disallowing blocking operations on nested objects, but again this requires looking at the implementation of an operation to see how it may be used.

Cooper and Hamilton have observed similar conflicts between parallel programming and data abstraction in the context of monitors [Cooper and Hamilton, 1988]. They propose to extend operation specifications with information about their implementation, such as whether or not the operation suspends or has any side-effects. We feel it is not very elegant to make such concessions, however.

Our solution to these two problems is as follows. An operation repeatedly tries to evaluate its guards and then tries to execute the statements of a successful guard. Before evaluating a guard, however, the operation creates a copy of the entire object, including any nested (or deeply nested) objects. This copy is used during the evaluation of the guard and execution of the statements. The operation *commits* to a certain alternative, as soon as both of the following occur:

1. The guard succeeds (evaluates to true), and
2. The corresponding statements can be executed without invoking any blocking operations on nested objects.

As soon as a guard fails or its statements invoke a blocking operation, the copy of the entire object is thrown away and another alternative is tried. So, an operation does not commit until it has finished executing a successful guard and its corresponding statements, without invoking any blocking operations on nested objects. If all alternatives of an operation fail, the operation (and the process invoking it) blocks until the object is modified by another process. If an operation commits to a certain alternative, the object is assigned the current value of the copy (i.e. the value after evaluating the selected guard and statements).

This scheme solves both of the above problems. An operation on a nested object used inside a guard (e.g. OldOperation1 in the code above) may have side-effects; these side-effects will not be made permanent until the guard is actually committed to. An operation on a nested object may also block. As long as all guards of that operation fail, however, the alternative containing the invocation will never be committed to. The operation has no effects until it commits to a certain alternative. Before commitment, it may try some alternatives, but their effects are thrown away. If the operation commits to an alternative, both the guards and statements of the alternative are executed without blocking. Therefore, operation invocations are still executed indivisibly.

As an example, suppose we have an object X of type NewType (defined above) and we want to apply the operation NewOperation to X:

```
X: NewType;  # creates an object of type NewType
X$NewOperation();  # apply NewOperation to X
```

This will result in the execution of the following code:

```
do  # forever
    TMP := copy(X);  # create a copy of object X
    # evaluate guard of NewOperation, using TMP:
    if TMP.NestedObject$OldOperation1() then
        # try to execute body of NewOperation, using TMP:
        if TMP.NestedObject$OldOperation2() succeeds
                    without blocking then
            X := TMP;  # commit: assign copy to X
            exit;  # done; exit do-loop
        else
            throw away TMP  # get rid of copy of X
        fi;
    fi;
    block until X has been changed;
od;
```

TMP is a temporary variable of type NewType. The notation TMP.NestedObject denotes the nested object of this temporary variable. Before trying a guard, a copy of object X is created and this copy is used for executing the guard and body of the operation. If the guard succeeds and the body does not invoke a blocking operation on a nested object, the operation commits and the current value of the copy is assigned to the object.

The price paid for this solution is efficiency. It may be quite expensive to copy objects before trying each alternative. In most cases, however, the compiler will be able to optimize away the need for copying objects. Many object types will not have any nested objects, so they do not suffer from the problems described above. Also, an optimizing compiler will sometimes be able to verify that the operations used in a guard are side-effect free and that all operations applied to nested objects are non-blocking. To do so, it needs to access the implementation code of nested objects. This is not any different from other global optimizations (e.g. inline substitution), which basically need to access the entire source program. Also, the same mechanism can be used to test for circularities in nested object definitions.

Our solution therefore preserves abstraction from the programmer's point of view, but sometimes requires global optimizations to be efficient. This is a specific example of our design principle to keep the language simple and rely on optimization techniques for achieving efficiency.

5.4.4 Data structures

We will now turn our attention to the data structuring facilities of Orca. Data structures are important to the design of any language, whether sequential or distributed. Languages having flexible support for complicated data structures are frequently easier to program than languages lacking such support. The very high level language SETL, for example, owes much of its expressiveness to its sophisticated data structuring capabilities.

In Orca, new data structures will frequently be designed as abstract data types. The language needs some basic primitives, however, on top of which more general (abstract) types can be built. These basic primitives were designed with two basic principles in mind: distribution and security.

First, we want data structures to be treated similarly to scalar variables. In particular, any data structure can be passed as a parameter to processes and operations. This is especially important if data structures are encapsulated within abstract data types, because we want to be able to pass an input or shared parameter to a remote process, no matter what its internal data look like. In contrast, most other distributed languages only allow scalar data or arrays to be sent to a remote process (see Section 4.3.4).

Second, we want the data structuring mechanism to be type secure. Erroneous usage of data structures should be detected either during compile time or run time, but should never wreak havoc and generate a core dump. This issue is highly important, as it makes debugging of distributed programs easier.

The basic idea behind the data structuring mechanism of Orca is to have a few built-in primitives that are secure and suitable for distribution. More complicated data structures can be defined using the standard types of the language (integer, real, boolean, char) and the built-in data structuring capabilities. Frequently, new data structures will be designed as abstract data types. To increase the usefulness of such types, Orca supports *generic* abstract data types, which will be described in Section 5.4.5.

There is a trade-off between having a certain type built in or user defined (as an abstract data type). In general, it is desirable not to have too many built-in types, as that complicates the language. Built-in types, however, have several advantages over user-defined types:

- The syntax of operations on built-in types usually is somewhat clearer than that for user-defined types.
- A language may provide a notation for denoting values (constants) of built-in types (e.g. an array aggregate in Ada), while no such notations exist for values of user-defined abstract types.
- Built-in types can often be optimized more easily.
- Some built-in types are related to other language constructs. A **for** statement, for example, may iterate over a set, which is a built-in type.

In Orca, the following type constructors are built-in: arrays, records, unions, sets, bags, and graphs. These are discussed below.

Arrays

An array contains a number of components of the same type. The components are indexed by an index type, which must be a discrete scalar type (e.g. the standard type integer). The range of permissible index values is determined dynamically and is not considered to be part of the type. Moreover, array variables of the same type but with different index ranges can be assigned to each other.

As an example, consider the following array type definition and variable declarations:

```
type table = array[integer] of boolean;
A: table[1..10];
B: table[30..100];
```

Components of an array are accessed through an indexing notation, as in

```
A[i] := B[j+1];
```

Trying to access a component outside the current index range results in a run-time error.

The array bounds appearing in the variable declarations provide the initial values for the actual bounds. These bounds need not be compile-time constants, so arrays of dynamic size can be allocated. If the bounds are omitted in the variable declaration, the index range of the variable is initially empty. The array bounds can be changed by assigning a new value to the array variable, as in:

```
A := table:[true, false, true];
    # assign 3-element array aggregate of type table to A
B := A;
    # both A and B now have bounds 1 and 3
```

Assignment for array variables is similar to assignment for scalar variables: the old value of the variable is lost and the right-hand-side value is copied to the variable. This may cause the bounds of the array variable to be changed. (Note that a similar convention holds for flexible arrays in Algol 68.) In the example above, A is assigned an array aggregate (a composite value) of type table containing three Booleans; subsequently, the value of A is assigned to B. As a result, both A and B get lower bound 1 and upper bound 3. The current bounds of an array variable can be retrieved through the standard functions LB and UB.

Records and unions

A record contains one or more fields, possibly of different types. For example, the following code:

```
type rr =
    record
        i: integer;
        x: real;
        b: boolean;
    end;

r: rr;
```

defines a record type with three fields and declares a variable of this type. The fields of a record variable can be accessed as follows:

```
r.i := 12;
r.x := r.x + 3.14;
r.b := true;
```

Records are basically the same as in Modula-2, except that they do not contain variants. Orca provides union types instead of variants. A union consists of a tag field and one or more other fields, only one of which may be accessed, as determined by the current value of the tag. Consider, for example, the type declaration

```
type uu =
    union (t: integer)
        1 => i: integer;
        3 => b: boolean;
        9 => r: real;
    end;
```

and the following variable declarations:

```
u: uu(3);
v: uu(9);
```

The type definition defines a union type with an `integer` tag field and three other fields. Two variables are declared, with initial tag values 3 and 9. The fields of these variables can be accessed as follows:

```
u.b := true;
v.r := 2.89;
```

Accessing a field that does not correspond to the current value of the tag results in a run-time error, as in:

```
u.i := 20;
v.b := true;
```

Assigning to the tag field directly is not allowed and results in a compile-time error. Assigning to a union variable as a whole is permitted, however, and may change the current value of the tag:

```
u := v;
u.r := 4.9;
```

Both records and unions can contain as fields any structures, such as records, unions, and graphs.

Sets and bags

Sets and bags contain zero or more elements of a given *base* type. In contrast to Modula-2, the base type is not restricted to a subrange of integers, but can also be a structured type. Unlike arrays, sets and bags are unordered and there is no notation for denoting individual elements of them. A set does not contain any duplicates, so adding an element that is already a member of the set has no effect. In contrast, bags may have duplicate elements. Removing a nonexisting element from a set also has no effect.

Several standard operators and statements are defined for manipulating sets and bags. This is illustrated by the following piece of code:

```
type IntSet = set of integer;
S: IntSet;   # sets are initially empty
e: integer;

S := IntSet:{2, 8, 16};  # assign set-aggregate to S
insert (30, S);   # add 30 to S
delete (8, S);   # delete 8 from S
S +:= IntSet:{5, 7, 16};  # union of S and {5,7,16}
assert (2 in S);   # test for membership
for e in S do Write(e); od;
     # iterate over S; prints random permutation
     # of 2, 5, 7, 16, 30
```

Graphs

The main problem in designing a type-secure data structuring mechanism that is suitable for distributed systems is the support for *general* data structures. In most procedural languages (e.g. Pascal), data structures like graphs, trees, and lists are built out of dynamically allocated and deallocated blocks of memory, linked together through *pointers*. As we will discuss below, this approach is often insecure and unsuitable for distributed programming. During our discussion, we will focus on graphs, as these are the most general data structures. We will use Pascal as representative of the large class of languages that use pointers for building general data structures.

First of all, giving the programmer explicit control over allocation and deallocation of memory usually violates security. As an example, consider the following piece of Pascal code:

```
var p, q: ^integer;   {p and q are pointers to integers}
...
new(p);         {allocate memory for one integer}
q := p;         {copy the pointer p}
dispose(p);     {deallocate the memory}
...
p^ := 10;       {modify the deallocated memory}
q^ := 20;       {modify the same deallocated location}
```

After the dispose statement, the pointer variables p and q point to an unallocated location in memory; they are called *dangling references*. The indirect assignments through p and q therefore modify the same random word in memory. This word may be part of any data structure that has been allocated after the dispose statement. Such errors may easily lead to obscure program behaviour and are very hard to trace. Note that the problem cannot be solved by simply marking disposed pointers illegal, since their value may have been copied, as is illustrated by the usage of q.

This problem can be attacked in two different ways. First, deallocation of memory can be left to the system rather than the programmer. With this approach, called *automatic garbage collection* [Cohen, 1981], the run-time system tracks down pieces of memory that can no longer be accessed and deallocates them. The second way of fixing the security problem is by making pointers safe. Lomet [Lomet, 1985], for example, proposes mechanisms for dealing with dangling references during run time, at the cost of losing some efficiency.

The second disadvantage of using pointers for building graphs is the difficulty in transmitting such data structures to remote machines. Pointers, if implemented as addresses, are only meaningful within a single machine, so they need special treatment before being transmitted. Even more important, most languages do not consider such graphs to be first-class objects, so it is hard to determine *what* has to be transmitted. In Pascal, a graph is identified by a pointer to one of its nodes. Given such a pointer, however, it is not clear which blocks of dynamically allocated memory are part of the graph. In other words, there is no denotation in Pascal for the collection of nodes that together constitute a graph. Consequently, graphs in Pascal cannot be passed as value parameter to a procedure; neither can one graph variable be copied into another through an assignment statement. In contrast, such limitations do not hold for records and arrays, which are first-class objects in Pascal.

In Orca, these problems are solved through the introduction of a graph data type, analogous to the array, set, and record types described above. A graph in Orca consists of zero or more *nodes*, each having a number of *fields*, similar to the fields of a record. Also, the graph itself may contain *global fields*, which are used to store information about the entire graph (e.g. the root of a tree or the head and tail of a list). Individual nodes within a graph are identified by values of a *nodename* type.

As an example, a binary-tree type may be defined as follows:

```
type node = nodename of BinTree;
type BinTree =
    graph  # global field:
        root: node; # name of the root of the tree
    nodes  # fields of each node:
        data: integer;
        LeftSon,
        RightSon: node;  # names of left and right sons
    end;
```

This program fragment declares a graph type `BinTree`. Each node of such a graph contains a data field and fields identifying the left and right sons of the node. Furthermore, the graph has one global field, identifying the root node of the tree.

A tree data structure is created by declaring a variable of this type, for example

```
t: BinTree;
```

Initially, the tree is empty (it contains zero nodes), but nodes can be added and deleted dynamically as follows:

```
n: node; # local temporary variable of type node

n := addnode(t); # add a node to t, store its name in n
deletenode(t, n);   # delete the node with given name from t
```

If a new node is added to a graph, the run-time system automatically allocates memory for the node. In this sense, **addnode** is similar to the standard procedure new in Pascal. As a crucial difference between the two primitives, however, the **addnode** construct specifies the data structure for which the new block of memory is intended. Unlike in Pascal, the run-time system of Orca can keep track of the nodes that belong to a certain graph. This information is used whenever a copy of the graph has to be created, for example when it is passed as a value parameter to a procedure or remote process. Also, the information is used to delete the entire graph at the end of the procedure in which it is declared.

The global fields of a graph and the fields of its nodes are accessed through designators that are similar to those for records and arrays:

```
t.root := n;  # access the global field of t
t[n].data := 12;   # access data field of node n
t[n].LeftSon := addnode(t);   # create left son of n
```

Note that the designator for the field of a node specifies the name of the node as well as the graph itself. This is in contrast to Pascal, where nodes are identified by pointers only. The notation of Orca may be somewhat more cumbersome, but it has the advantage that it is always clear which data structure is accessed. This property is a basis for making the data structuring mechanism type-secure, as explained below.

If a certain node is deleted from a graph and subsequently one of its fields is accessed, a run-time error occurs, as illustrated by the following piece of code:

```
n := addnode(t);
deletenode(t, n);
t[n].data := 12;  # causes a run-time error
```

The run-time system checks whether the graph t contains a node with the given name. Furthermore, each invocation of **addnode**(t) returns a different name, so the same nodename will not be reused for denoting a different node. Whenever a node has been deleted from a graph, any future reference to the node will cause a run-time error. (The implementation of this mechanism will be discussed in Chapter 6.)

The data structuring mechanism of Orca has some properties of arrays and some of Pascal-like data structures. The mechanism supports dynamic allocation of memory through the **addnode** primitive. Like arrays, graphs in Orca are first-class entities, which has several advantages: they can easily be passed to remote processes; assignment is defined for graph variables; functions may return a value of a graph type; and graphs are automatically deallocated at the end of their enclosing procedure. The latter feature makes automatic garbage collection of nodes less necessary. Nodenames in Orca have the safety advantages of both pointers and array indices. Like pointers, they cannot be manipulated through arithmetic operations; like array indices, any illegal usage of a nodename will be detected at run time.

The graph type of Orca also has some disadvantages, if compared to pointers. With pointers, for example, any two data structures can be hooked together through a single assignment statement. With graphs, this is not so easy. If the programmer anticipates the join, the data structures can be built using a single graph. If separate graphs are used, one will have to be copied into the other.

5.4.5 Generic abstract data types

The data structuring capabilities of Orca can be used for building other data structures, like lists, queues, and trees. Usually, such new data structures will be defined as abstract data types. There is one potential problem, however, in defining such types on top of the language rather than having them built in. The data structuring mechanisms built into the language can be applied to any type. For example, one can define arrays of integers, arrays of reals, and so on. So, an array is not an actual type, but a *constructor* (or *schema*) from which actual types can be derived. For user-defined types one would like to have the same flexibility. Programmers should be able to define, say, a list type constructor and use it for building lists with any type of elements.

The abstract data typing facility described so far does not have this flexibility. It only allows specific types (e.g. a list of integers) to be defined, but not type constructors. In general, there are several ways for achieving this flexibility [Cardelli and Wegner, 1985]. For Orca, we have chosen for *generic* types, as this mechanism is easy to understand and implement.

Below, we will describe how generic abstract data types can be defined and used. Orca also supports generic modules; these are similar to generic abstract data types and will not be discussed here.

Generic type specifications and instantiations

A generic abstract data type is an abstract type that is parametrized with other types. It is not an actual type itself, but it can be used to create several real types through a process called *instantiation*. Like normal abstract type definitions, generic abstract types consist of a specification part and an implementation part. Consider, for example, the following generic type specification:

```
generic (type T)
object specification GenericQueue;
    operation Append(x: T);
    operation Get(): T;
end generic;
```

This code specifies a generic abstract data type `GenericQueue`, parametrized with a formal type `T`, which is the type of the elements of the queue. The generic type is a *template* from which nongeneric abstract data types can be instantiated. Such an instantiation supplies an actual type parameter for the formal parameter `T`, as in:

```
object IntQueue = new GenericQueue(integer);
```

The type `IntQueue` introduced by this instantiation can be used as if it were specified directly as

```
object specification IntQueue;
    operation Append(x: integer);
    operation Get(): integer;
end;
```

Note that the formal parameter `T` has been replaced by the actual parameter `integer`. Generic types can therefore be regarded as a controlled macro-substitution mechanism.

Generic type implementations

The implementation part of a generic object type definition is similar to the implementation part of nongeneric type, except that it contains the keyword **generic**. Inside the implementation part, the formal types can be used just like normal types. A critical issue, however, is which operators may be applied to variables of such types. Like any procedural language, Orca supports several standard arithmetic and relational operators. Unfortunately, each operator applies only to a certain class of values. The '+' operator, for example, can be used for adding integers or reals, but not Booleans or records. Inside the implementation of a generic type, however, it is not known to which class a formal type belongs.

There are many different solutions to this problem. In principle, a compiler could check whether the operators used in the implementation are defined for the actual type supplied during the instantiation. For example, if the implementation of `Generic-Queue` would apply the '+' operator to values of type `T`, then the instantiation

```
object BoolQueue = new GenericQueue(boolean);
```

would cause a compile-time error message, as '+' is not defined for Booleans. Whether or not the generic type may be instantiated with a given type parameter would depend on the implementation of the generic type. This is an undesirable property.

The solution we have taken is similar to that of Ada. A generic definition may impose a restriction on the actual types supplied during instantiation. We distinguish three cases:

1. If no restriction is imposed on the actual type, no operators may be applied to values of the formal type. Such values can only be manipulated through assignments or parameter passing.
2. If the actual type is required to be a *scalar* type (integer, real, char, boolean, and the enumeration types), the relational operators may be used.
3. If the actual type is required to be a *numeric* type (integer or real), one may use the relational and arithmetic operators.

This categorization leads to three significantly different classes of type. Any additional operations (or constants) needed in the implementation part can be supplied as formal parameters of the generic definition, just as in Ada.

Example of a generic abstract data type

As an example of a generic abstract data type definition, we will show the specification and implementation of a generic type GenericAnnualReport, which encapsulates a table with 12 values, one for each month. The specification part (see Figure 5.5) contains two formal parameters.

The first parameter, the formal type T, is restricted to be a numeric type, as shown in the first line of the specification part. The second parameter is a function print, which presumably prints values of type T. The specification lists operations for initializing and increasing table entries and for printing the entire table.

The implementation part looks very much like a normal object implementation, except for the keywords **generic** at the beginning and end (see Figure 5.6). The internal data of objects of this type consist of a table of 12 entries of type T. The first operation, AssignToMonth, assigns a value to the entry specified as parameter; recall that assignment is always allowed within the body of a generic unit. The second operation, AddToMonth, increments a table entry by using the '+' operator (or rather the *add-and-becomes* operator '+:='); as T is declared to be numeric, this operator may be used throughout the implementation part. Finally, the third operation, PrintReport, calls the formal parameter print to print the entries of the table.

The generic abstract data type is instantiated by specifying an actual type and a print function, for example:

```
object AnnualIncome =
    new GenericAnnualReport(real, WriteReal);
```

or

```
generic  (numeric type T; function print(x: T) )
object specification GenericAnnualReport;
    operation AssignToMonth(month: integer; amount: T);
    operation AddToMonth(month: integer; amount: T);
    operation PrintReport();
end generic;
```

Figure 5.5 *Specification part of a generic object type definition.*

```
generic
object implementation GenericAnnualReport;
    table: array[integer 1 .. 12] of T;

    operation AssignToMonth(month: integer; amount: T);
    begin
        table[month] := amount;
    end;

    operation AddToMonth(month: integer; amount: T);
    begin
        table[month] +:= amount;   # here '+' is allowed
    end;

    operation PrintReport();
        i: integer;
    begin
        for i in 1..12 do
            print(table[i]);   # print is a formal parameter
        od;
    end;
end generic;
```

Figure 5.6 *Implementation part of a generic object type definition.*

```
object AnnualProduction =
    new GenericAnnualReport(integer, WriteInt);
```

The type AnnualIncome can subsequently be used for creating objects that record incomes on a monthly basis. The second type, AnnualProduction, is useful for discrete entities, like the number of items produced during each month.

5.4.6 Program structure

An Orca program consists of definitions of object types and modules. Modules are static entities, similar to packages in Ada. Both object type and module definitions consist of a specification and an implementation part. The specification part provides information on how to use the object type or module; the implementation part contains the actual code. A specification and its implementation may be compiled as separate units.

An object definition introduces a new abstract data type. Each object type may have multiple instances (variables). In contrast, a module is fully static and does not have any instances. Modules do not contain data, but are used for grouping together definitions of constants, types, procedures, and processes.

All entities declared in the specification part of a module are made available to users of the module. The specification does not contain any executable code. If a module specification declares any procedures or processes, their implementations should appear in the module implementation. Both the specification part and the implementation part may contain instantiations of generic units.

The mechanism for importing identifiers from other modules is similar to that of Modula-2. Each compilation unit may contain **import** clauses, specifying the names of other modules or objects used by this unit. Identifiers defined in the specification part of these modules or objects are made available to the unit being compiled. If an imported identifier is used, it has to be qualified with the name of the unit from which it was imported. As in Modula-2, Orca also supports unqualified imports of the form

> **from** unit-name **import** ident1, ident2, ... ;

In this case, the imported identifiers can be used directly. Also, if a unit imports an object definition, all operations declared in the object's specification are directly visible. Operations defined by different object types can have the same name; the type of the object to which an operation is applied is used to avoid ambiguity.

The module structure of Orca is simple. Unlike in Modula-2 and Ada, there is no nesting of modules or procedures. Procedures can only access their own local variables and arguments, so nesting of procedures would not be very useful. Moreover, as Clarke *et al.* argue, nesting of procedures is somewhat superfluous in a language that supports modules [Clarke *et al.*, 1980].

## CHAPTER 6

Implementation

Although Orca is a language for programming distributed systems, its communication model is based on shared data. The language implementation therefore should hide the physical distribution of the hardware and simulate shared data in an efficient way. Also, the implementation should allow any kind of data structure to be exchanged between processes, which may not have access to a common memory. These and other aspects of the implementation are the subject of this chapter.

Unlike, say, occam and Aeolus, our language is not designed for one specific hardware or software configuration. Our discussion therefore will be more general than just describing a specific implementation. We will outline the problems involved in the language implementation, classify the possible solutions, and later illustrate these solutions by means of actual implementations on real systems.

The structure of this chapter is as follows. First, we delimit the range of target systems we have in mind for running Orca programs. Next, we distinguish between the two basic components of any implementation: the compiler and the run-time system (RTS). While the Orca compiler uses mainly conventional compiler technology, the RTS raises many new research issues. We will discuss these issues first. They concern the management of shared data-objects, processes, and complex data structures. Subsequently, we will describe the implementation of the compiler, focusing on its novel aspects and on the optimizations it carries out. Finally, we will illustrate our ideas by briefly describing prototype implementations of three different run-time systems, two of which run on distributed hardware, and third of which, for comparison purposes, runs on a shared-memory multiprocessor.

6.1 Assumptions about the execution environment

Orca is designed as a portable language that can be implemented on a range of distributed systems. In this section, we will take a closer look at the systems on which Orca may be implemented. The environment (target system) in which Orca programs execute is determined not only by hardware factors (CPU types and network topology) but also by software factors (e.g. the operating system running on the target system). Both factors are important when it comes to portability.

The diversity of CPU types found in today's – distributed and uniprocessor – architectures complicates the portability of language implementations. Modern compilers overcome this problem, however, by using retargetable code generators [Ganapathi *et al.*, 1982] and machine-independent optimizers [Leverett *et al.*, 1980; Tanenbaum *et al.*, 1982; Bal and Tanenbaum, 1986].

For distributed systems, an additional problem may be the presence of different types of CPU within a single system. Systems with this property are said to be *heterogeneous*. In heterogeneous distributed systems, communication between processors becomes complicated if the processors have different word sizes and byte orderings. Although a heterogeneous implementation of Orca is conceivable, we will not address the issue in this book, and assume all CPUs are the same.

The second hardware factor is the communications network. Many different networks exist, such as grids, hypercubes, rings, stars, LANs, and WANs. They differ in their topology (interconnection structure), message latency time, number of messages that can be handled simultaneously, support for multicast messages, and so on.

For our discussion, we will use a simplified model for the network topology and assume that each processor can communicate directly with every other processor. For networks like hypercubes and grids, which are not fully interconnected, this model can be implemented by software protocols that forward messages through the network. We note, however, that future (and even some current) generation hypercubes contain special I/O processors that forward messages automatically. Physically, such a network is not fully connected, but this fact is hidden almost completely from the programmer.

The execution environment for Orca programs is determined further by the existing systems software running on the distributed hardware. In the extreme case, there is no software at all (except for a bootstrap loader in ROM), so programs run on the bare hardware. The implementation thus takes care of every detail involved in physical communication. Alternatively, there may be an existing layer of software dealing with physical communication, such as a communications kernel or a distributed operating system.

Unless stated otherwise, we assume there is some layer of communications software running on each processor. This layer provides at least local process creation and reliable, order preserving point-to-point message passing (i.e. messages between two processors are delivered reliably, in the same order they were sent). Optionally, this layer may also support reliable or unreliable multicast or broadcast. We will not discuss how reliable message-passing primitives are to be implemented on top of the bare hardware.

6.2   Compiler and run-time system

The implementation of Orca consists of two parts: the *compiler* and the *run-time system*. The compiler is conceptually similar to a compiler for a sequential language. The RTS, however, is distributed. Each processor contains its own incarnation of the RTS; these incarnations cooperate in executing programs.

The compiler translates Orca source programs into machine code for the target CPUs. The code produced by the compiler invokes primitives implemented by the RTS. The tasks of the compiler can be classified into three categories:

1. Syntactic and semantic analysis of Orca programs.
2. Various optimizations that improve efficiency.
3. Code generation for the target system.

The first task is machine independent; the latter two tasks need information about the target CPUs.

The most important jobs of the RTS are the management of shared data-objects and the management of processes. Orca gives the illusion that objects are shared among processes, even if the processes and objects are on different machines. In reality, remote objects can only be accessed through explicit message-passing; these messages have to be generated by the RTS. The RTS should try to minimize the number of messages needed by carefully distributing objects among processors.

The RTS also implements complex data structures (e.g. graphs). This part of the RTS is independent of the topology of the target system. Conversely, the part that implements shared objects depends on the target system. The RTS may, for example, use different implementation strategies for networks that provide multicast and networks that only support point-to-point messages.

For simplicity, we assume the RTS is constructed as a collection of subroutines linked together with the machine code produced by the compiler (see Figure 6.1). The resulting executable file is subsequently loaded into one or more processors and then executed.

The above scheme may be optimized in many ways. In principle, the compiler can generate separate executable files for each processor, stripping code that will not be executed by that processor. Also, part of the RTS can be integrated with the operating system, as will be discussed in Section 6.7.2.

6.3   Management of shared data-objects

The first (and probably most important) issue in the design of a distributed RTS for Orca is the management of shared data-objects. A naive implementation of the shared data-object model would incur a huge communication overhead. We attack this problem by replicating objects. We will first look at the advantages of replication and at how to decide on which processors to replicate data. Next, we will deal with the

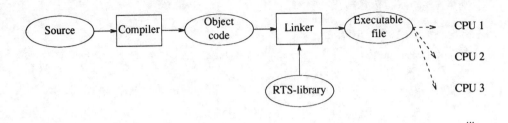

Figure 6.1 *Overview of the compilation and loading procedure. The boxes are programs; the ellipses are files. The executable file is loaded into one or more CPUs.*

problem of consistent updating of replicated data. Finally, we will explain the problem in detail and then give a spectrum of solutions.

6.3.1   Replication of shared data-objects

The technique of data replication in distributed systems has been studied by several researchers [Gifford, 1979; Joseph and Birman, 1986; Van Renesse and Tanenbaum, 1988]. This research typically aims at increasing the availability and reliability of the data in the presence of processor failures. For example, if multiple copies of the same logical data are stored on different processors, the data can still be accessed if part of the processors are down.

In contrast, we use replication primarily for speeding up access to shared data and for decreasing the communication overhead involved in sharing data. The general idea is to replicate an object on those processors that frequently access it. A copy may be accessed by all processes running on the same processor, as shown in Figure 6.2.

It is useful to distinguish between *read* operations and *write* operations on replicated data: a read operation does not modify the data, while a write operation (potentially) does [Joseph and Birman, 1986]. For Orca, we define a read operation as an operation that does not change the internal data of the object it is applied to. Objects of type IntObject (see Figure 5.4), for example, have two read operations: Value and AwaitValue. The remaining operations modify the object's data and are therefore said to be write operations.

The primary goal of replicating shared data-objects is to apply read operations to a local copy of the object, without doing any interprocess communication. On a write operation, all copies of the object must somehow be updated, so a write operation involves communication. This is a departure from most of the replication techniques cited above, which in general need interprocess communication for every read and write operation.

The second goal of replication is to increase parallelism. If an object is stored on only one processor, every operation has to be executed by that processor. This proces-

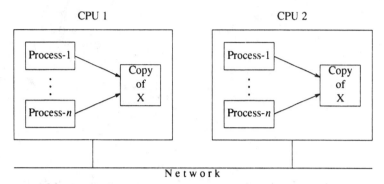

Figure 6.2 *Replication of data objects in a distributed system. Each processor contains multiple processes running in pseudo-parallel. These processes belong to a single job and run in a single address space, so they can share copies of objects.*

sor may easily become a sequential bottleneck. With replicated objects, on the other hand, all processors can simultaneously read their own copies.

The effectiveness of replication depends on the ratio of read to write operations and on the costs of these operations. If a given object is modified frequently and read infrequently, it probably is undesirable to replicate it, especially if updating copies is expensive. In general, we can distinguish between several *strategies* for replication:

No replication: Each object is stored on one specific processor.
Full replication: Each object is replicated on all processors.
Partial replication: Each object is replicated on part of the processors, based on
                (a)   compile-time information, or
                (b)   run-time information, or
                (c)   a combination of both.

The first approach is used by most object-oriented languages. In this case, all operations on a given object are executed by the same processor. As discussed in Section 5.3.4, this may easily lead to sequential bottlenecks and high communication overhead.

The second approach indiscriminately replicates all shared objects on all processors. It will be most effective for architectures supporting fast, reliable, multicast messages, since these will allow efficient updating of all copies.

The third strategy selectively replicates objects, based on information gathered by either the compiler, or the RTS, or both. With this approach, several scenarios are possible. For example, the compiler may disable replication of objects that do not have any read operations at all. (Instantiations of the object type `GenericQueue` fall in this class.) Also, if a processor does not contain any processes that share a given object, it is unnecessary to store a copy of the object on that processor.

The most advanced scheme based on partial replication is to let the RTS decide dynamically where to replicate each object. For example, the RTS may keep track of read and write operations on an object issued by each processor, to determine which processors frequently read the object. If the read/write ratio exceeds a certain threshold, a replica of the object is created dynamically on that processor. This strategy is most suitable if communication is slow, so the overhead of maintaining statistics is worthwhile. Lucco, for example, has implemented a Linda run-time system on a hypercube, using a similar approach; he observed significant savings in communication costs [Lucco, 1987a].

If a write operation is applied to a replicated object, its copies have to be updated. This can be done in two ways:

1. Send the new value of the object to each processor, or
2. Send the operation and its actual parameters to each processor and let each processor apply the operation to its local copy of the object.

The first approach is most effective for small objects which do not contain large amounts of data. If an object contains a large data structure of which the operation modifies only a small part, applying the operation to all copies will be more efficient. With this approach, operations must be executed in a deterministic way, to make sure all copies receive the same value. In particular, the implementation must be careful with operations containing multiple guards.

6.3.2   The inconsistency problem

The presence of multiple copies of the same logical data introduces the *inconsistency problem*. If the data are modified, all copies must be modified. If this updating is not done as one indivisible action, different processors may temporarily have different values for the same logical data. In Chapter 5, we described two systems, the problem-oriented shared memory and the Agora shared-memory, that suffer from this problem. The inconsistency problem pops up in many other areas using replication, for example replicated file systems and CPU caches [Cheriton *et al.*, 1986].

The inconsistency problem potentially affects the semantics of operations on shared data. The semantics of operation invocations in the shared data-object model were defined in Section 5.3. Essentially, each operation is to be executed as an indivisible action. If multiple processes simultaneously perform operations on the same object, the effect should be as if the operations were executed in some (undefined) sequential order. Below, we will discuss how these semantics can even be fulfilled if objects are replicated. We will first look at multiple operations on single, replicated objects. Next, we consider multiple operations on different objects.

Semantics of multiple operations on a single object

We will first consider multiple processes that simultaneously access a *single* object (which may, of course, be replicated). We distinguish three cases, depending on whether the processes are writing, reading, or both writing and reading the object.

If multiple processes try to write the object, these operations are serialized (i.e. executed one by one), to prevent the data from becoming garbled. This statement holds for replicated as well as nonreplicated objects.

If multiple processes try to read the object, these operations can safely be executed simultaneously on different copies of the object. As read operations do not modify the object's data, the effect will be as if the operations had been executed sequentially.

The most important case is where one process writes the object and one or more other processes read it. It is important to note that, although the operations conceptually are serialized, the actual order in which they are to be executed is not defined. In other words, there is no strict *temporal* ordering among the operations. This is typical for MIMD-like systems, in which processors are executing asynchronously. Processors in such systems are not synchronized by physical clocks.

Each sequential process in an asynchronous system performs a sequence of computation steps: C_0, C_1, ... , C_i , ... Within a single process, these steps are *totally* ordered; C_n happens after C_m if and only if $n > m$. There is no total ordering, however, between computation steps of different processes [Lamport, 1978]. There is only a *partial* ordering, induced by explicit interactions (like sending a message or setting and testing shared variables).

As the ordering is not defined, it is perfectly valid to do the following:

1. Execute zero or more of the read operations in parallel; each of these will use the old value of the object;
2. Next, execute the write operation;
3. Next, execute the remaining read operations in parallel; each of these will use the new value of the object.

In conclusion, read operations executed at the same time need not use the same value of the object; the time at which they are executed is not used to impose a total ordering on the invocations.

Semantics of multiple operations on different objects

Above, we only considered operations on single objects. We will now look at multiple operations on different objects. As we will show, the inconsistency problem is of much greater concern here. We will illustrate this by looking at a simple but incorrect update protocol that does not take the inconsistency problem into account.

Suppose we implement our model as follows. To update an object X, a message containing the new value of X is sent to all processors containing a copy of X. Such a processor updates its copy and then sends back an acknowledgement. When all messages have been acknowledged, the write operation is finished and the process invoking it may continue. (For the moment, we ignore the possibility of multiple simultaneous writes to the same object.)

As an example of what is wrong with this protocol, consider the code of Figure 6.3. This program fragment uses two shared objects, both of type `IntObject`. Process P_1 repeatedly increments object X; P_2 tries to keep Y up to date with X; P_3 verifies that X is greater than or equal to Y. Clearly, the latter condition should always be true.

Now suppose X and Y are replicated as shown in Figure 6.4. Object X is replicated on all three processors; object Y is replicated on P_2 and P_3.

The following sequence of events may happen:

1. X is incremented and becomes 1; P_1 sends an update message to P_2 and P_3.
2. P_2 receives the update message, assigns 1 to the variable Y and sends an update message for Y to P_3.
3. P_3 receives the update message from P_2, puts the value 1 in its copy of Y, and is surprised to see that Y now is greater than X (which still contains 0).
4. P_3 receives the update message from P_1, and stores the value 1 in its copy of X.

P_3 observes the changes to X and Y in the wrong order. The problem is caused by the arbitrary amount of time that messages may take to travel from the source to the destination and by the inability to transfer information simultaneously from one source to many destinations. Such an implementation basically provides message-passing semantics disguised in shared variable syntax.

The best way to solve the consistency problem depends on the architecture of the underlying distributed system. In general, there are two different approaches:

1. Instead of updating all copies, *invalidate* all but one copy of the object.
2. Use a protocol that guarantees *consistent* updating of all copies (as opposed to an inconsistent protocol like the one outlined above).

Kai Li's shared virtual memory, for example, uses invalidation: before a page is changed, all its copies are removed. In our model, invalidation is indeed feasible, but it has some disadvantages. First, if an object is big it is wasteful to invalidate its copies, especially if an operation changes only a small part. In this case, it is far more efficient to apply the operation to all copies, hence updating all copies. Second, if an object is small, sending the new value is probably just as expensive as sending an invalidation message. Although update algorithms are more complicated than invalidation algorithms, we think it is useful to study them.

6.3.3   Consistent update protocols for shared data-objects

In this subsection, we look at various protocols for updating shared data-objects in a consistent way. With a consistent update protocol, all processes observe changes to

```
X,Y: IntObject;   # initially 0
xval, yval: integer;

Process P₁:
      do
          X$Inc(1);   # increment X by 1
      od;

Process P₂:
      do
          yval := Y$Value(); xval := X$Value();
          if xval > yval then Y$Assign(xval); fi;
      od;

Process P₃:
      do
          yval := Y$Value(); xval := X$Value();
          assert xval ≥ yval;
      od;
```

Figure 6.3 *Fragment of an Orca program illustrating the inconsistency problem.*

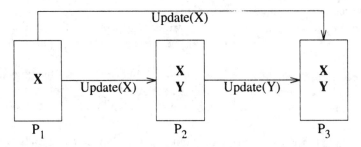

Figure 6.4 *Distribution of the shared objects* x *and* y *used in the program of Figure 6.3. The arrows indicate messages.*

shared objects *in the same order*. The naive protocol described above fails to meet this requirement, because it ignores the arbitrary delays involved in message passing. Below, we give a spectrum of consistent protocols. It depends on the communications network of the target system which of these protocols is most efficient.

In principle, each protocol can be used in combination with each – full or partial – replication strategy; during our discussion, however, we assume all objects are replicated on all processors. For sake of clarity, we will use a simplified view of our shared data-object model. Without lack of generality, we assume an object contains a single integer and supports only two operations:

```
operation read(): integer;       # return current value
operation write(val: integer);   # store new value
```

Our protocols update the copies of an object by transmitting its new value.

The primary distinguishing factor among the protocols is the way they synchronize simultaneous write operations on the same object. As discussed above, such operations should be serialized. Serialization can be achieved in two ways. One way is to appoint one copy of an object as *primary copy* and direct all write operations to this primary copy; the effects of a write operation are subsequently propagated to all other copies, called *secondary copies*. An alternative way for achieving serialization is to treat all copies as equals and use a *distributed update protocol* that takes care of mutual exclusion.

The first approach conceptually is the simplest. Moreover, it allows one important optimization: the primary copy can be migrated to the processor that most frequently changes the object, making updates more efficient. In particular, if only a single processor changes the object, the overhead of mutual exclusion can be eliminated by storing the primary copy on that processor. (This optimization requires the RTS to detect which processor most frequently changes a given object; it is therefore most appropriate for the partial replication strategy based on run-time information.)

With the second approach – a distributed update protocol – there is no distinction between primary and secondary copies. Instead, each processor can initiate a write operation on an object. Some cooperation among the processors is needed to prevent simultaneous write operations on the same object from interfering with each other.

Below, we first look at primary-copy update protocols. We will discuss three different protocols, based on point-to-point messages, reliable multicast, and unreliable multicast. Finally, we discuss a distributed update protocol.

Primary-copy update protocol with point-to-point messages
As described above, we assume the target system supports at least reliable point-to-point message passing. In such a system, objects can be updated in a consistent way through a *two-phase update* protocol. During the first phase, the primary copy is updated and locked, and an update message is sent to all processors containing a secondary copy. Unlike in the incorrect protocol outlined above, all secondary copies are locked and remain locked before being updated. A user process that tries to read a locked copy blocks until the lock is released during the second phase. When all update messages have been acknowledged (i.e. all copies are updated and locked), the second phase begins. The primary copy is unlocked and a message is sent to all processors containing a secondary copy, instructing them to unlock their copies.

To implement the protocol, we use one *object manager* for every processor. An object manager is a collection of one or more processes that takes care of updating the local copies of all objects stored on its processor. (We will sometimes use the shorthand 'manager' instead of 'object manager'. Note, however, that unlike the manager processes used for object-oriented languages, an object manager in our model does *not* serialize access to objects; its only task is to update local copies of objects.)

We assume the object manager and user processes on the same processor can share part of their address space. Objects (and replicas) are stored in this shared address space. Write operations on shared objects are directed to the object manager of the processor containing the primary copy; user processes can directly *read* local copies, although they may temporarily block, as described above. Each manager may contain multiple processes (threads of control). One thread communicates with remote managers; the remaining threads are created dynamically to handle write operations. Multiple write operations on different objects may be in progress simultaneously; write operations to the same object are serialized, as discussed below.

If an object manager receives a request from a (possibly remote) user process W to perform an operation 'X$write(Val)', the manager creates a new thread of control for handling the request. Its code looks like:

```
receive write-req (X, Val) from W →
    fork handle_write(X, Val, W);
```

The process 'handle_write' is defined by the following algorithm:

```
process handle_write(X, Val, W);
begin
    set write-lock on X;
    store Val in X;
    let S = set of processors having a copy of X;
    # first phase
    forall P ∈ S do
        send lock-and-update(X, Val) to manager of P;
    for i := 1 to |S| do
        receive ack;
    # second phase
    forall P ∈ S do
        send unlock(X) to manager of P
    unlock X;
    send ack to W;
end;
```

The process issuing the write request waits until it receives an acknowledgement. A manager responds as follows to messages from remote managers:

```
receive lock-and-update (X, Val) from P →
    set write-lock on local copy of X;
    store Val in local copy of X;
    send ack to P;
```

```
receive unlock (X)   →
    unlock local copy of X;
```

The two-phase update protocol guarantees that no process uses the new value of an object while other processes are still using the old value. The new value is not used until the second phase. When the second phase begins, all copies contain the new value. Simultaneous write-operations on the same object are serialized by locking the primary copy. The next write-operation may start before all secondary copies are unlocked. New requests to *lock-and-update* a secondary copy are not serviced until the *unlock* message generated by the previous write has been handled (recall that point-to-point messages are received in the order they were sent).

Deadlock is prevented by using multithreaded managers. Setting a write lock on a primary copy may block one thread of a manager, but not an entire manager. Locking a secondary copy always succeeds within a finite amount of time, provided that all read operations terminate properly.

If an object has N secondary copies it takes $3 * N$ messages to update all these copies (N *lock-and-update* messages, N acknowledgements, and N *unlock* messages). Reading a remote object takes two messages (one request, one reply). So, objects should only be replicated on processors that read the object at least twice before it is changed again. This can be determined (or estimated) dynamically, as discussed earlier. The protocol can easily be optimized into a one-phase update protocol if an object has only one secondary copy.

For a small object that is frequently changed, it may be more efficient to invalidate copies when the object is changed and to replicate it on reference. The first read operation after a write fetches the object from a remote processor and creates a local copy. Subsequent reads use this local copy, until it is invalidated by a modification to the object.

Primary-copy update protocol with reliable multicast messages

The two-phase update protocol adequately solves the consistency problem, although at the cost of some communication overhead. The semantics provided by the implementation closely resemble those of shared variables. If a write-operation completes at time T_w, read operations issued at time $T_r > T_w$ return the new value.

As discussed above, the lack of total ordering allows an implementation of shared data-objects to relax slightly the semantics without affecting the underlying programming model. Suppose process P_1 executes 'X$write(Val)' and process P_2 executes 'X$read()'. If there is no precedence relation between these two actions (i.e. neither one of them comes before the other in the partial ordering of events), the value read by P_2 may be either the old value of X or the new value. Even if, physically, the write is executed before the read, the read still can return the old value. The major difference with systems that allow read operations to return arbitrary old (stale) data is that our model supports a consistent logical ordering of events, as defined implicitly in the program. Programs like those of Figure 6.3 still execute as expected.

In a distributed system supporting only point-to-point messages, a consistent logical ordering is difficult to obtain, because messages sent to different destinations may arrive with arbitrary delays. Some distributed systems (e.g. broadcast-bus systems) give hardware support to send a single message to several destinations simultaneously. More precisely, we are interested in systems supporting *indivisible reliable multicasts*, which have the following properties:

- A message is sent reliably from one source to a set of destinations.
- If two processors simultaneously multicast two messages (say m_1 and m_2), then either all destinations first receive m_1, or they all receive m_2 first, but not a mixture with some receiving m_1 first and others receiving m_2 first.

With this multicast facility we can implement a simple update protocol. A 'X\$write(Val)' request is handled as follows by the object manager of the processor containing the primary copy of X:

> **receive** *write-req* (X, Val) **from** W →
>   set write-lock on X;
>   store Val in X;
>   **let** S = set of processors having a copy of X;
>   **multicast** *update*(X, Val) **to** manager of every P ∈ S;
>   unlock X;
>   **send** *write-ack* (W) **to** manager of W;

After the *write-req* message has been handled, the acknowledgement is sent to the manager of W (the process that issued the request). The manager forwards it to W. This guarantees that the local copy of X on W's processor has been updated when W resumes execution. The manager can be a single-threaded process in this implementation. A manager handles all incoming *write-req*, *update*, and *write-ack* messages in the order they were sent. A manager containing a secondary copy responds as follows to messages from remote managers:

> **receive** *update* (X, Val) →
>   set write-lock on local copy of X;
>   store Val in local copy of X;
>   unlock local copy of X
> **receive** *write-ack* (W) →
>   **send** *ack* **to** W;

If a processor P reads a new value of an object X, an *update* message for X containing this value has also been sent to all other processors. Other processors may not have handled this message yet, but they certainly will do so before they handle any other messages. Any changes to shared objects initiated by P will be observed by other processors after accepting the new value of X. Problems like those in Figure 6.4 do not occur.

Primary-copy update protocol with unreliable multicast messages

A cost-effective way to build a distributed system is to connect a collection of workstations through a local area network. Such workstation LANs are easy to build and easy to extend. Many distributed operating systems have been designed with this model in mind [Tanenbaum and Van Renesse, 1985].

Many LANs have hardware support for doing multicasts or broadcasts. An Ethernet, for example, physically sends a packet to every computer on the net, although usually only one of them reads the packet. There is no difference in transmission time between a multicast and a point-to-point message.

Unfortunately, multicasts in a LAN are not totally reliable. Occasionally, a network packet is lost. Worse yet, one or more receivers may be out of buffer space when the packet arrives, so some destinations may not receive it. In practice, multicast is highly reliable, although not quite 100 per cent. Unreliable multicast can be made reliable by adding an extra software protocol, at the cost of some communication overhead. Below, we take a different approach and describe an update protocol that directly uses unreliable multicasts.

The basic algorithm is the same as that for reliable multicast. When a shared variable X is updated, some (or all) processors containing a secondary copy of X may fail to receive the *update*(X,Val) message. They will continue to use the old value of X. This is not disastrous, as long as the partial (logical) ordering of events is obeyed, as described above. To guarantee a consistent ordering, processors that failed to receive the *update*(X,Val) message must detect this failure before handling other update messages that logically should arrive after X's message.

Failure detection is realized as follows. Update messages are multicast to *all* processors participating in the program, not just to those processors containing a secondary copy. Every processor counts the number of update messages it sends. This number is called its *mc-count*. Every processor records the *mc-counts* of all processors. These numbers are stored in a vector, called the *mc-vector* (initialized to all zeros). For processor P, *mc-vector*[P] always contains the correct value of P's *mc-count*; entries for other processors may be slightly out of date.

Whenever a processor multicasts a message, it sends its own *mc-vector* as part of the message. When a processor Q receives a multicast message from P, it increments the entry for P in its own *mc-vector* and then compares this vector with the *mc-vector* contained in the message. If an entry R in its own vector is less than the corresponding entry in the message, Q has missed a multicast message from processor R. Q updates the entry for R in its own vector. As Q does not know which variable should have been updated by R's message, Q temporarily invalidates the local copies of all variables that have their primary copy on processor R. It sends reliable (i.e. acknowledged) point-to-point messages to the object manager of R, asking for the current values of these variables. The reply messages from R also contain *mc-vectors*, and undergo the same procedure as for multicast messages. Until the copies are up to date again, local read operations of these copies block.

It is possible that lost update messages will remain undetected for a while. Suppose processor Q misses an update message for a variable Y from processor R and then receives an update message for X from processor P. If P also missed R's message, the entry for R in the *mc-vector* of P and Q will agree (although they are both wrong) and the copy of X will be updated. However, as P contained the old value of Y when it updated X, the new value of X does not depend on the new value of Y, so it is consistent to update X.

If a process misses an update message for X, this failure will eventually be detected while handling subsequent messages. The assumption is that there will be subsequent messages. This assumption need not be true. For example, a process may set a shared flag-variable and wait for other processes to respond. If these other processes missed the flag's update message, the system may very well come to a grinding halt. To prevent this, each object manager periodically generates dummy update messages, which do not update any copy, but just cause the *mc-vectors* to be checked.

The update protocol outlined above has one considerable advantage: it takes a single message to update any number of copies, provided that the message is delivered at all destinations. There is a penalty, however, on losing messages. As modern LANs are highly reliable, we expect this to happen infrequently. As another disadvantage, update messages must be sent to every processor. Each message contains extra information (the *mc-vector*), which must be checked by all receiving processors. The execution-time overhead of checking the vector is proportional to the number of processors. For a limited number of processors, say 32, we think this overhead is acceptable. The protocol can be integrated with the two-phase update protocol described above. For example, objects that are replicated on only a few processors can be handled with the two-phase update protocol while objects replicated on many processors are handled by the multicast protocol.

A distributed update protocol

With the primary-copy update protocols, simultaneous write operations on the same object are synchronized by the object manager of the processor containing the primary copy of the object. Each write operation must first be forwarded to the object manager, which takes an extra message. In this subsection, we will discuss how objects can be updated in a consistent way without using primary copies.

One approach to synchronizing write operations without using primary copies is to lock all copies of an object prior to changing the object. A write operation is then implemented in three steps:

1. Lock all copies of the object.
2. Send new value of the object to other processors containing a copy.
3. Unlock all copies of the object.

(As an optimization, step 2 can be combined with step 1 or 3.) Unfortunately, the locking phase is quite complicated, because multiple processors simultaneously may try to lock the same object. Distributed locking protocols that take such situations into account do exist (see [Maekawa *et al.*, 1987]), but they are expensive. Note that the primary-copy update methods do not need a distributed locking protocol, because only the processor containing the primary copy locks the object.

Below, we will discuss an alternative protocol for updating an object without locking all copies of the object. This protocol uses reliable, indivisible multicast messages, as defined above. Each update message is multicast to all processors participating in the program. As multicast is indivisible, all processors receive all messages in the same order.

With this protocol, each processor maintains a queue of messages that have arrived on the processor but that have not yet been handled. As all processors receive all messages in the same order, the queues on all processors are basically the same, except that some processors may be ahead of others in handling the messages at the head of the queue.

If a process wants to execute a write operation 'X$write(Val)' on a shared object X, it multicasts a message *update*(X, Val) to all object managers (including the one on its own processor) and subsequently blocks:

```
X$write(Val) =
    multicast update(X, Val) to all managers;
    block current process;
```

The update message will be appended to the tail of each local queue.

The object manager of each processor handles the messages in its queue in strict FIFO order. A message may be handled as soon as it appears at the head of the queue. To handle a message *update*(X, Val), the message is removed from the queue, the local copy of X is locked, the value Val is stored in the local copy, and finally the local copy is unlocked. If the message was sent by a process on the same processor, the manager unblocks that process.

```
receive update(X, Val) from W →
    set write-lock on local copy of X;
    store Val in local copy of X;
    unlock local copy of X
    if W is a local process then
        unblock(W);
    fi;
```

This distributed update protocol basically provides the same semantics as the primary-copy update protocol with reliable multicast messages. Again, there is no total ordering of operations, but the protocol guarantees that all processors observe changes to shared objects in the same order. This is achieved by using the indivisibility property of multicast messages.

6.3.4 Summary

Above, we discussed the following design choices for replicating shared data-objects:

1. The strategy for replication (no replication, full replication, partial replication).
2. Invalidation of copies versus updating of copies.
3. The propagation of changes (send new value of the object or apply write operations to all copies of the object).
4. Primary-copy update protocols versus distributed update protocols.

We have discussed some of the advantages and disadvantages of each alternative. In Section 6.7 we will look at several existing implementations of the shared data-object model.

6.4 Management of processes

Besides management of shared data-objects, the Orca RTS also takes care of process management. Processes may be created by the user (through the **fork** statement) as well as by the RTS itself (as discussed above). The mapping of processes to processors is under full control of the programmer. The location of a process is determined when the process is created and is not changed thereafter.

Each incarnation of the RTS schedules the processes executing on its own machine. If a process on machine M_1 wants to fork off a new process on machine M_2, the incarnations of the RTS on M_1 and M_2 cooperate (through message passing) to create the new process.

For efficiency, it is important that processes are scheduled *pre-emptively*. In particular, messages sent to object managers should be handled as soon as possible. This means that the arrival of a message should pre-empt the currently executing user process. So, processes are best scheduled with a pre-emptive strategy that favours manager processes over user processes. However, processes should not be pre-empted while they are executing an operation on a shared data-object, otherwise the indivisibility of operations may be impaired.

One important task related to the management of data objects and processes is the deallocation of shared data-objects that are no longer accessible. The local data of a process (or procedure) are deallocated automatically when it terminates. The shared data-objects declared by a process P, however, may still be accessed by other processes after P has terminated.

In principle, delaying the termination of P until all its children have terminated would solve the problem, since no other process can access P's objects. This solution, however, requires the RTS to keep track of the descendants of each process. An alternative solution is to maintain a *reference count* with each shared object. Whenever an object is passed as shared parameter to a new process, the reference count is incremented. If a process sharing the object – either the process declaring the object or one of its descendants – terminates, the reference count is decremented. As soon as it drops to zero, the object (and all its copies) can no longer be accessed and is deallocated.

In summary, each incarnation of the RTS supports dynamic creation of local processes. Processes are scheduled pre-emptively and communicate through shared data. A remote process is created by sending a message to the RTS on the remote machine, asking it to create a local process. We assume the underlying operating system provides a primitive for creating local processes. The implementation of the RTS may either map Orca processes onto operating system processes or it can implement Orca processes in user space, as lightweight threads.

6.5 Management of data structures

The Orca RTS manipulates complex data structures, for example arrays, sets, and graphs. This is in contrast with, say, a C run-time system, which only needs to deal with unstructured data, such as integers, floating-point numbers, and pointers. The need for manipulating entire data structures arises in the following cases:

Marshalling
If a data structure is passed as a value parameter in a **fork** or operation invocation it has to be packed (*marshalled*) into a network packet, which usually is a linear sequence of bytes. Also, any structured values returned by a remote operation – either as result value or output parameter – have to be unmarshalled. Finally, if the RTS decides to create a copy of a shared data-object on a certain processor, the current value of the object has to be sent, which may also require marshalling.

Copying
If a structured variable is passed as a value parameter to a procedure or is used as right-hand side of an assignment statement, a copy of its entire structure must be created.

Comparing
If two structured variables are tested for equality, both data structures have to be traversed. For example, the equality test for arrays should compare the corresponding elements of the arrays.

Deallocation

Variables are deallocated automatically at the end of the procedure in which they are declared. If a variable contains a data structure, this entire structure has to be deallocated.

For data structures that are represented as contiguous memory blocks, the above tasks are simple. Unfortunately, data structures whose sizes can change dynamically (e.g. graphs, arrays, sets) are hard to implement efficiently using a single contiguous memory block. In general, complex data structures consist of multiple blocks of memory, linked together through pointers. The RTS therefore needs to have information about the representation of *structured variables* (i.e. variables of a structured type), in order to carry out each of the above tasks.

One way of representing this information is through procedures. In this case, the compiler generates four special routines for each complex user-defined type T, each doing one of the above tasks. A more efficient method is to store information about the types of structured variable in run-time *descriptors*. A descriptor for a structured variable contains information about the type of the variable and its components. With this approach, it suffices to have one general routine for each of the tasks described above.

Many different implementation schemes for storing type descriptions during run time are possible. Van Katwijk for example, describes several schemes that have been proposed for the Ada language [Van Katwijk, 1987]. Below, we will discuss one simple model for managing data structures, using run-time descriptors. We will first describe the general implementation model. In Section 6.5.2, we will look at the implementation of specific data structures, in particular graphs.

6.5.1   Descriptors

In our implementation model, we integrate the descriptor for a structured variable with the data stored in the variable. Each structured variable is represented as a pointer to a descriptor. (Scalar variables do not have descriptors.) The descriptor contains a pointer to the actual data of the variable and some descriptive information about the layout of these data. Most importantly, the type field of the descriptor specifies the type constructor of the variable; this field is either ARRAY, SET, BAG, RECORD, UNION, GRAPH, or OBJECT. The remaining fields of the descriptor depend on the type field and on the implementation of the model.

Figure 6.5 shows examples of descriptors for arrays and sets. The lower and upper bounds stored in the array descriptor are used for array bound checking during run time. (Note that the bounds may change during execution, as arrays can be re-assigned.) The EltSize field specifies the size of the array elements. By convention, a size of *zero* is used to denote elements that are themselves data structures; in this case, the elements are pointers to other descriptors. The array descriptor also con-

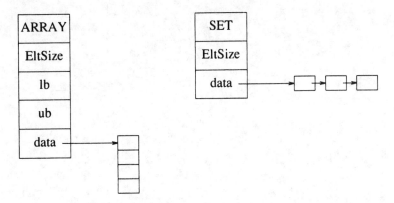

Figure 6.5 *Example representation of arrays and sets. The array descriptor contains the size of the elements, the lower and upper bound, and a pointer to the actual data. The set descriptor contains the size of the elements and a pointer to the elements (a linear list, in this example).*

tains a pointer to a table for the elements. This table consists of either pointers to other descriptors (if the `EltSize` field is zero) or the actual elements of the array.

A set descriptor contains the size of the elements and a pointer to a data structure storing the elements. In the example of Figure 6.5, the elements are stored in a linear list, but other (more efficient) schemes are also possible.

As an example of how structured variables are stored during run-time, consider the following type:

type T = **array**[integer 5..7] **of set of** integer;

Variables of this type are represented as shown in Figure 6.6. The leftmost box represents the entire array. The elements of this array are data structures (sets), represented as pointers to set descriptors. The elements of these sets are integers, which do not have descriptors.

The allocation of structured variables requires support from the compiler. For each declaration of a structured variable, the compiler generates code that dynamically builds the entire data structure, including the descriptors. In some simple cases, the descriptors or data can be allocated on the execution stack, but in general they have to be stored on the heap.

With this representation, the RTS is able to perform the four tasks described above – marshalling, copying, comparing, and deallocation. (As stated above, allocation of data structures is under control of the compiler rather than the RTS.) To deallocate a structured variable, for example, the RTS first looks at the `type` field of the variable. This field determines how the components of the data structure are stored (e.g. as a table or as a linear list). These components have to be deallocated too. If the `EltSize` field is zero, the components are themselves data structures, so the dealloca-

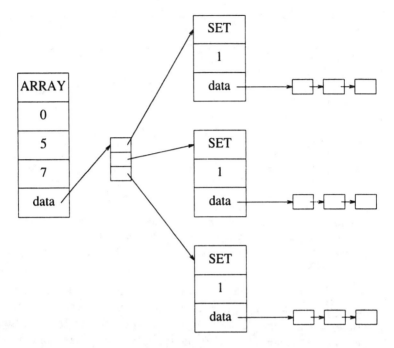

Figure 6.6 *The representation of an array of sets, using the descriptors shown in Figure 6.5.*

tion routine is applied recursively to each component. If the field is nonzero, the components are simply deallocated. Finally, the descriptor for the variable itself is deallocated.

The other tasks can be done in a similar, recursive way. So, for each of the four tasks, the RTS provides a single routine which operates on data structures of any complexity. The compiler generates calls to these run-time routines at the appropriate places in the executable code. For example, at the end of a procedure it generates calls to deallocate the local structured variables of the procedure. Likewise, if a structured variable is passed as a value parameter to a procedure, the compiler generates a call to a run-time routine that copies the variable.

For marshalling of data structures there is one subtle problem. If a data structure is passed as a value parameter in an operation invocation on a shared object, a copy of the data structure has to be created. Whether or not this copy has to be marshalled depends on *where* the operation is executed. If the operation is executed locally (i.e. on the processor of the invoking process) there is no need for marshalling the data structure, as it need not be sent over a network. As the compiler does not know where the operation is executed, however, it is unable to decide whether marshalling is necessary.

The same problem occurs when a data structure is passed as a value parameter in a **fork** statement. If the newly created process executes on the same processor as its parent, there is no need for marshalling the parameters. The compiler cannot always tell whether the parent and child will execute on the same processor.

Our solution to this problem is to let the RTS figure out whether to marshall parameters. For this purpose, the compiler generates a descriptor for every process and operation declared in the source program. These descriptors specify the number of parameters and their modes – input, output, or shared – and sizes. If an operation or process is to be executed remotely, the RTS examines the corresponding descriptor to see which parameters are data structures that have to be marshalled.

In summary, the RTS uses a descriptor for every process, operation, and structured variable. Descriptors for processes and operations are *static*: there is only one descriptor per declaration. Descriptors for variables are allocated dynamically, when the variable is created. These descriptors are used for manipulating entire data structures, but they are useful for other purposes as well. A process descriptor, for example, can be used to determine which parameters passed in a **fork** statement are shared objects. This enables the RTS to maintain the reference counts on shared objects discussed in the previous section.

6.5.2   Implementation of data structures

Most of the data-structuring capabilities of Orca are straightforward to implement. Arrays, records, and unions have a fairly simple representation, not much different from their counterparts in, say, Ada.

The set and bag type-constructors are more difficult to implement efficiently, as they are content-addressable structures. Many alternative ways exist for representing a set, such as a bit vector (if the elements are scalar), a linear list, a tree, or a hash table. In general, the most efficient representation depends on how the set is used. This problem has been studied extensively in the context of languages like SETL [Schwartz *et al.*, 1986] and ABC [Krijnen and Meertens, 1983], so we will not discuss it any further in this book.

The implementation of graphs, on the other hand, is a novel aspect of our RTS. In Section 5.4.4, we stated two requirements for graphs: they should be type secure and it should be possible to pass graphs as parameters to remote machines. Below, we discuss how an implementation can meet these requirements.

A type-secure implementation of graphs
Type security implies that any attempt to access a nonexisting node of a graph should be detected at run time. Making the error is easy. The trick is to detect it. In languages using pointers (e.g. Pascal), programmers usually have uncontrolled access to the allocation and deallocation of memory. This may easily result in unexpected program behaviour. Mechanisms for making pointers safe do exist (e.g. see [Lomet, 1985]), but these are rarely used by language implementors, mainly because they are expensive.

In Orca, access to dynamically allocated data (i.e. nodes of a graph) is completely controlled. The nodes of a graph are identified by nodename variables, which have a similar role to pointers in Pascal. In the implementation, however, a nodename variable N does not point directly to a node of the graph. Rather, it identifies an entry in a so-called *master table* associated with the graph, as shown below:

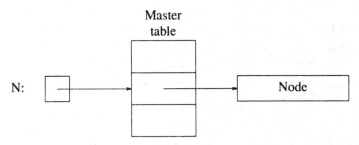

The master table entry contains a pointer to the node denoted by the nodename. The nodename itself may contain either a pointer to a table entry or an offset within the table.

If a node of a graph G is deallocated, the entry in the master table is set to a special value, **nil**, which indicates that the entry is now invalid. Whenever a node of a graph is accessed, the RTS checks if the master table entry is valid. If the entry is invalid (**nil**), a node that no longer exists is being accessed and a run-time error will be generated.

This basic idea has one problem, however. If a node is deleted from the graph, its table entry can no longer be used. Each node of the graph must be assigned a new entry. If nodes are added and deleted frequently, many table entries will be marked as invalid, so memory will be wasted. To solve this problem, an *age* field is added to every table entry and nodename variable, resulting in the following scheme:

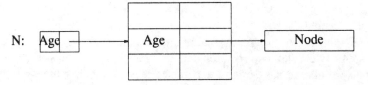

For an access to be valid, the age fields in the nodename and the table entry must be the same. If a node is added to the graph, the nodename returned by **addnode** includes the current age of the table entry used for the node. If the node is later deleted, the age of the table entry is incremented and the entry's pointer is set to **nil**. From then on, access to the node is invalid, since the age fields of the nodename and the corresponding table entry differ. So, if the node is accessed after being deleted, a run-time error will occur. The table entry can safely be reused for a new node, because its nodename will contain the new (incremented) age. (If the age field overflows, the entry will not be reused; with 32-bit integers, this will happen very rarely, however.)

If a node is added to a graph, the RTS tries to find an unused entry in the master table (i.e. an entry containing a **nil** pointer). If the number of nodes in the graph equals the length of the master table, however, all entries will be occupied. In this case, the RTS dynamically *extends* the master table. It allocates a new, larger table and copies the entries of the old table into the new one. To enable this operation, nodenames should not contain explicit pointers to master table entries, but should use *offsets* within the table.

The execution-time overhead of the master table mechanism is significant. A run-time check is required to determine the validity of access to the graph. Also, nodes are accessed indirectly through a table, rather than directly through a pointer. Part of the overhead can be optimized away, however, using dataflow analysis. As a simple example, in the following code:

```
t: BinTree;  # the types BinTree and node were
n: node;     # defined in Section 5.4.4
  ...

t[n].data +:= 10;  # increment node n's data by 10
WriteLine(t[n].data);  # print value of n's data
```

the second access to node n can be optimized, since the validity of the access has already been established by the first statement.

Distribution of graphs

The second requirement imposed on the implementation of graphs (besides type security) is the possibility of sending graphs to remote machines. To achieve this, the RTS should be able to determine the nodes that belong to a given graph. The master table mechanism described above allows this to be done easily, as we will show.

Graph variables are represented by graph descriptors during run time, as shown in Figure 6.7. A graph descriptor contains the current size of the master table and a pointer to the table itself. Each master table entry contains an age field and a pointer to a node. Entries that are currently not in use contain **nil** pointers.

The fields of a node are stored in the same way as the fields of a record, so a node is represented as a record descriptor. The first entry of the master table is reserved for the global fields of the graph, which are also stored in a record. As this entry is never deallocated, its age field always contains the same value.

The above representation contains all the information needed for transmitting entire graphs. The set of nodes that belong to a certain graph is fully determined by its master table. To transmit a graph variable G to a remote machine, the RTS traverses the master table pointed to by G's descriptor and marshalls each of its nodes. (In effect, the graph is physically a tree, not a graph.)

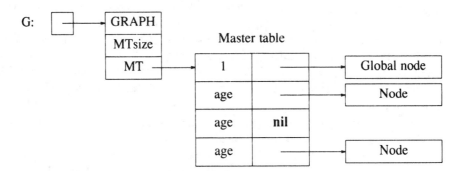

Figure 6.7 *Representation of graph variables.*

6.6 Implementation of the compiler

We will now switch our attention from general design issues to a more detailed description of the prototype implementations of Orca. Here, we will describe the implementation of the Orca compiler. In Section 6.7 we will look at implementations of the RTS.

The compiler does syntactic and semantic analysis of source programs written in Orca and translates legal programs to object code for a given target machine. The code produced by the compiler contains calls to subroutines of the RTS, which are usually linked together with the object code to produce an executable program (see Figure 6.1).

Although Orca is a distributed language, its compiler may very well benefit from existing compiler technology for sequential languages. We have built our compiler using the *Amsterdam Compiler Kit*, which is a toolkit for implementing portable compilers [Tanenbaum *et al.*, 1983]. So far, ACK has mainly been used for sequential languages like C and Pascal and for uniprocessor implementations of parallel (or pseudo-parallel) languages like Modula-2, occam, and Ada. As we will see, ACK is useful for distributed languages like Orca as well.

Below, we will first describe the structure of the Orca compiler. Next, we will look at the interface between the compiler and the RTS. This interface determines the code that has to be generated by the compiler. Subsequently, we will discuss the most interesting aspects of the compiler.

6.6.1 Structure of the Orca compiler

The compiler has basically the same structure as all other compilers implemented with ACK. It consists of a number of *phases*, as shown in Figure 6.8. A language-specific front end translates the source code into an intermediate code called EM, which is the assembly code of a virtual stack machine. The EM code is fed into several language- and machine-independent optimizers that improve the quality of the code [Tanenbaum *et al.*, 1982; Bal and Tanenbaum, 1986]. A machine-specific back end (or code generator) translates the optimized EM code to the assembly code for the target machine. Finally, the assembly code is assembled into object code.

Of these four phases, only the front end depends on the source language. Therefore, implementing an Orca compiler with ACK merely involves writing a front end that translates Orca programs into EM. The details of machine-code generation are taken care of by the other phases, which already exist. Moreover, the front end does not have to worry about standard optimizations like constant folding, common subexpression elimination, and so on, because these are already done by the existing optimizers. So, the front end only has to do optimizations that are specific to the source language.

6.6.2 Interface between the compiler and run-time system

The code to be produced by the compiler front end is largely determined by the definitions of the Orca language and the EM intermediate code. Simple **if** statements, for example, can be translated straightforwardly to EM code. However, the output code also contains calls to RTS routines that manage processes, objects, and data structures. Therefore, we have to define a clear *interface* between the compiler and the RTS. This interface specifies which routines are to be provided by an RTS and how they are to be invoked.

The interface must allow different implementations of the RTS on different hardware configurations. The compiler is to be retargetable, so the interface should hide the details of the underlying communications network. A similar policy is taken by EM for hiding properties of uniprocessor machines. For example, a compiler generating EM code does not have to know how many CPU registers the target machine has or whether it supports an 'increment' instruction.

The interface definition is an extension to the EM model. The compiler generates code for a *virtual Orca machine*, which supports the EM instructions and several new primitives tailored to Orca. The virtual Orca machine hides physical properties of the target system, such as the instruction set and addressing modes of the individual CPUs and the topology of the network that interconnects them. The extensions to the EM model fall into three classes:

1. Primitives for managing processes.
2. Primitives for managing data objects.
3. Primitives for managing complex data structures.

We will discuss these in turn. In principle, the primitives could be included in the EM instruction set. As this would require changes to several parts of ACK, however, our current prototype implementation treats the new primitives as library routines.

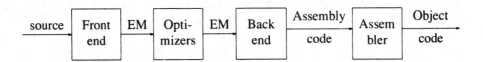

Figure 6.8 *Structure of the Orca compiler.*

Primitives for managing processes

The most important primitive for process management is the FORK routine, which creates a new process on a given CPU. This primitive is invoked as follows:

    FORK(cpu-number, process-descriptor, parameters ...);

The first argument specifies the CPU on which the new process is to be run. The second argument is a pointer to a process descriptor (see Section 6.5.1), which has the form shown in Figure 6.9. The descriptor specifies the code to be executed by the new process, the number of parameters taken by the process, and the sizes and modes – shared or input – of these parameters. The number of parameters passed as the remaining arguments of FORK must agree with the number given in the descriptor.

Obviously, the FORK primitive is intended for implementing the Orca **fork** statement. A source statement of the form

    fork child(parameters ..) **on**(cpu-number);

is translated directly into a call to FORK.

There is one other primitive related to process management: the routine NCPUS returns the total number of processors involved in the program. This primitive is used for implementing the standard Orca function with the same name.

Primitives for managing data objects

There is only one RTS primitive for managing data objects. This primitive, INVOKE, is used to invoke operations on objects. It is called as follows:

    INVOKE(object, operation-descriptor, parameters ...);

The first argument is the object to which the operation is applied. The second argument is the operation descriptor. Operation descriptors are more complicated than process descriptors, because operations may have several alternatives (guards).

The structure of operation descriptors is shown in Figure 6.10. The parameters of the operation are represented in a similar way as for processes, except that the modes are either input or output (but not shared). If the operation returns a result value, the compiler generates an extra output parameter for the operation; as far as the RTS is concerned, there is no difference between result values and output parameters of operations.

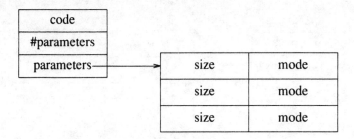

Figure 6.9 *Structure of a process descriptor.*

The code of an operation consists of several alternatives (guards). For efficiency reasons, the compiler distinguishes between the *read alternatives* (which do not modify the object's data) and *write alternatives* (which do modify the data) of an operation. This optimization and the `safe` attribute of write alternatives will be discussed further in Section 6.6.4.

Primitives for managing complex data structures

The third class of RTS primitives comprises routines for manipulating complex data structures. As discussed above, data structures are represented by descriptors during run time. The implementor of the RTS has the freedom to decide on the format of these descriptors. An array descriptor, for example, may either contain a lower and upper bound or a lower bound and the number of elements, whichever is preferred by the implementor. The compiler does not know the exact contents of these descriptors. We treat descriptors of data structures like abstract data types. The interface defines a set of operations (routines) that can be applied to descriptors, but it does not specify the actual data stored in the descriptors.

The interface defines some general primitives that can be applied to any data structure. For example, there is a primitive DCOPY that copies data structures of any complexity. Also, there are primitives specific to one type constructor. Arrays, for example, have primitives for storing and retrieving elements and for obtaining the current lower and upper bound.

6.6.3 The compiler front end

As stated before, we have implemented a prototype compiler front end for Orca. The primary goal of the prototype was to have a usable implementation of the language. Also, we wanted to experiment with certain language-dependent optimizations. The prototype compiler implements the full language, although not in an optimally efficient way. For example, all structured variables are allocated on the heap, since this simplifies storage management for dynamically growing data structures. As another example, generics are implemented in the simplest possible way – namely, by pure

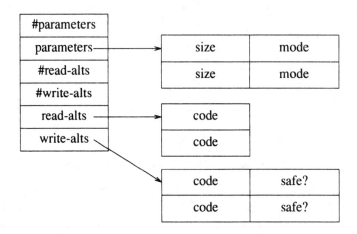

Figure 6.10 *Structure of an operation descriptor.*

textual substitution. A more advanced implementation would combine multiple instances of the same generic module to reduce the space overhead [Bray, 1983].

Instead of writing a new front end from scratch, we decided to use significant parts of the existing Modula-2 front end. For example, the code for symbol table management and most of the code for analyzing expressions and statements is adapted from the Modula-2 front end. As a minor disadvantage, the resulting front end is somewhat larger than necessary, because it contains code that will never be executed. (The symbol-table manager, for example, is capable of handling nested procedures and modules, even though these cannot occur in Orca programs.) We feel, however, that this disadvantage is more than compensated by the development time saved in reusing existing software.

Part of the differences between Orca and Modula-2 are purely syntactic. These differences present no implementation problems whatsoever, because the Modula-2 front end uses a sophisticated LL(1) parser generator (called *LLgen* [Grune and Jacobs, 1988]) for doing syntax analysis. Adapting the LLgen grammar to Orca turned out to be easy.

The more important differences between Orca and Modula-2 are related to the typing mechanisms of the languages. In contrast to Modula-2, Orca supports dynamic arrays, general sets, bags, and graphs. The semantic analysis phase of the Modula-2 front end therefore had to be changed significantly.

6.6.4   Compiler optimizations

Although the prototype compiler front end was not designed for generating production-quality code, it performs some interesting optimizations. These optimizations include the read/write analysis of operations, the test for 'safety' of operations, and the optimization of large value parameters.

Read-write analysis of operations

As discussed in Section 6.3, a distributed implementation of Orca greatly benefits from the distinction between operations that read the object's data and those that modify the data. An operation is marked as read-only if it does not change any local variables of the object it is applied to. An operation can only change a variable stored in an object by:

1. Using it as left-hand side in an assignment statement, or
2. Passing it as shared or output parameter to a (user-defined or built-in) procedure.

Both cases are recognized by the compiler.

In general, an operation consists of multiple alternatives (guards), some of which modify the object's data and some of which do not. Whether a given invocation of such an operation modifies its object depends on the alternative that is selected. As an example, suppose we want to extend the object type IntObject with an operation min:

```
operation min(v: integer);
```

that sets the current value of the shared integer to the minimum of the current value (stored in the variable x) and the parameter v. This operation can be implemented as follows:

```
operation min(v: integer);
begin
    guard v >= x do od;  # a read-only alternative
    guard v < x do x := v;   od;  # a write alternative
end
```

The operation potentially modifies its object, so it is not a read-only operation. However, if the value passed as actual parameter is greater than or equal to x, the operation has no effect. (Note, however, that the first alternative cannot be omitted, since that would cause the operation to block if v >= x.) In this case, a distributed RTS may apply the operation to a local copy of the object. In conclusion, distinguishing between the 'read' and 'write' alternatives of a single operation is more efficient than marking entire operations as 'read' or 'write'.

To implement this optimization, the compiler generates a separate procedure for each alternative. The min operation, for example, is compiled into the following two procedures:

```
function min_1(obj: shared SharedInt; v: integer): boolean;
begin
    if v >= obj.x then   # test first guard
        return true;   # body is empty, return immediately
    else
        return false;
    fi;
end;


function min_2(obj: shared SharedInt; v: integer): boolean;
begin
    if v < obj.x then   # test second guard
        obj.x := v;   # body of second alternative
        return true;
    else
        return false;
    fi;
end;
```

Each procedure returns 'true' only if its guard succeeds. All procedures generated for an operation are collected in the operation's descriptor. Such a descriptor contains separate tables for read alternatives and write alternatives, as shown in Figure 6.10. In a distributed implementation, the INVOKE primitive will first try to apply the read alternatives of the operation to a local copy of the object. The write alternatives will only be considered if all read alternatives fail.

Nested objects

The second important optimization done by the compiler is related to the problem of nested objects discussed in Section 5.4.3. Our solution to this problem implies that objects are copied before each operation invocation. In most cases, however, the compiler will be able to optimize away this need for copying. To be more specific, the object need not be copied if:

1. The operation does not modify the object, or
2. The operation does not perform any operations on subobjects that may block.

The compiler therefore determines which write alternatives of an operation contain blocking suboperations on nested objects. Such write alternatives are said to be *unsafe*. This information is stored in the operation's descriptor (see Figure 6.10). The RTS will only copy the object before trying an unsafe write alternative.

To implement this optimization, the compiler needs to have information about the implementation of nested objects. Therefore, it maintains a simple database with information about object implementations. Whenever an object implementation is compiled, the compiler adds one entry for each operation to this database, indicating whether the operation may block or may change its object. If the object type later is used for implementing another object type, the compiler consults the database to see which operations are safe. If an object implementation uses another object type whose implementation part has not yet been compiled, the compiler assumes all operations on the latter object type block and modify their object. Also, if the implementation part of an object type is changed, all other object definitions using it have to be recompiled.

Data structures as value parameters

A third optimization done by the compiler concerns the parameter mechanism. Whenever a data structure is passed as a value parameter to a procedure, it has to be copied. If the called procedure does not modify the copy, the overhead of copying can be avoided without changing the semantics. In our implementation, structured parameters are copied by the called procedure (rather than the calling procedure), so this optimization can be implemented easily.

In Pascal, this optimization frequently is done by the programmer rather than the compiler, by declaring parameters of mode **var**. We feel this is an abuse of Pascal's parameter mechanism, however. It is much cleaner to let the programmer specify the parameter mode required by the logic of the program and let the compiler worry about optimizations.

6.7   Implementations of the run-time system

A run-time system for Orca is responsible for managing processes, shared data-objects, and data structures. The first two tasks depend on the hardware and operating system on which the RTS is implemented. In particular, the best protocol for updating replicated objects depends on which message-passing primitives are available and on how expensive they are. We have experimented with three different implementations of the RTS, using two different hardware architectures.

The first implementation runs on a shared-memory multiprocessor. Because shared objects are kept in the shared memory, they need not be replicated. This RTS was mainly intended for obtaining a working prototype implementation of the language. Also, it allows us to compare the performance of Orca on shared-memory and distributed hardware. This implementation also runs on a uniprocessor under UNIX.

The second implementation is truly distributed. It replicates all objects on all processors and uses a distributed update protocol based on reliable multicast messages for keeping all copies up to date. It runs on the bare hardware, rather than on top of an operating system.

The third RTS is implemented on top of the Amoeba distributed operating system. It selectively replicates and migrates objects based on statistical information gathered during run time. It updates the replicas through a primary-copy protocol.

Table 6.1 *Comparison of the three Orca run-time systems*

	Shared-memory RTS	Multicast RTS	Amoeba RTS
General			
Runs on top of	Amoeba	hardware	Amoeba
Communication primitive	shared memory	multicast messages	Amoeba RPC
Object management			
Replication	none	full	partial (based on run-time statistics)
Update protocol	locking	distributed	primary copy
Process management			
Processes	in user space	OS threads	OS threads
Scheduling	nonpre-emptive	time-sliced	pre-emptive

The three RTSs cover a wide spectrum of design choices, as illustrated in Table 6.1. The systems also have some resemblances. The code for managing complex data structures, for example, is shared among all three RTSs.

Below, we will give brief descriptions of the three run-time systems. In Chapter 7, we will use these systems for measuring the performance of several Orca application programs.

6.7.1   The shared-memory run-time system

The run-time system described here currently runs on a multiprocessor consisting of several CPUs, each with local memory, and a shared memory that can be accessed through a bus. This RTS is much simpler than a distributed RTS, because it does not have to replicate objects. Instead, it simply puts shared objects in the shared memory and protects them with locks.

The shared-memory RTS runs on top of the Amoeba distributed operating system. However, the RTS uses the shared memory for interprocess communication, rather than Amoeba RPC. Therefore, the implementation is largely operating system independent.

Although this RTS is not useful for studying replication of objects, it still is worth discussing. The implementation addresses issues that any RTS – whether distributed or not – has to deal with, like process creation and condition synchronization. Also, it is quite conceivable to build large distributed systems by interconnecting multiple shared-memory multiprocessors. An implementation of Orca on such an architecture would certainly use parts of the shared-memory RTS. Below, we will discuss the two most interesting aspects of the shared-memory RTS, namely process management and object management.

Process management

Processes in the shared-memory RTS are implemented as lightweight threads in user space. All Orca processes on the same processor are mapped onto a single operating system (Amoeba) process. Each Orca process has its own stack, but processes share the text and data segment.

On each processor, there is one *scheduler* process, which is part of the run-time system. Processes are only rescheduled when they are blocked inside an operation, as discussed below. Context switching from one process to another is implemented by a simple assembly routine that changes the current stack pointer and program counter. Creating a new local process merely involves allocating a stack and doing a context switch, so process creation is cheap.

If a process wants to create a new process on a remote machine, it sends a message to that machine's scheduler, asking it to create a local process. Message passing between remote schedulers is implemented through message queues in shared memory.

Object management

Each shared data-object is put in the shared memory and is protected by a lock variable. Before doing an operation on a shared object, the invoking process must first acquire the object's lock. The lock is released as soon as either:

1. The operation is completed successfully, or
2. All the operation's alternatives have failed.

In the latter case, the invoking process suspends until some other process changes the object's data. This is implemented by keeping a *waiting list* for each object, containing those processes that are waiting for the object to be changed. Whenever the object is changed, all processes on its waiting list are made runnable again.

An outline of the implementation of INVOKE is given in Figure 6.11. It first tries all read alternatives of the operation. As soon as one alternative succeeds, it unlocks the object and returns. If all read alternatives fail, the write alternatives are tried. If one such alternative succeeds, the object has been changed by this alternative, so all processes waiting for the object to be changed have to be reactivated. To reactivate a remote process, a message is sent to the scheduler of the process's machine, asking it to make the process runnable.

If all alternatives fail, the object is unlocked and the current process is added to the waiting list of the object. Finally, the current process suspends, which means it is marked as 'not runnable' and does a context switch to the scheduler, which will pick a new process to run.

The actual implementation of INVOKE is slightly more complicated. If a write alternative is tried that is not safe, the object has to be copied before the alternative is tried (see Section 6.6.4). Also, the implementation can be configured to use a readers/writers locking scheme rather than exclusive locks. This makes locking and

```
INVOKE(obj, op, args)
    do # infinite loop; exit through return statement
        lock(obj); # acquire lock on object
        forall r ∈ ReadAlternatives(op) do
            if r(obj, args) then # try read alternative
                unlock(obj); # release the lock
                return;  # successful read alternative
            fi;
        od;
        forall w ∈ WriteAlternatives(op) do
            if w(obj, args) then # try write alternative
                # reactivate all waiting processes
                forall p ∈ waitinglist(obj) do
                    make p runnable;
                od;
                unlock(obj); # release the lock
                return;  # successful write alternative
            fi;
        od;
        # Here, all read and write alternatives have failed.
        add current process to waitinglist(obj);
        unlock(obj); # release the lock
        suspend current process;
    od;
```

Figure 6.11 *Shared-memory implementation of INVOKE.*

unlocking of objects more expensive, but allows more parallelism, since multiple read operations can be executed in parallel.

6.7.2   A distributed run-time system using reliable multicast

The second Orca run-time system, described in this subsection, is a distributed RTS that replicates objects and updates replicas using reliable multicast messages. The RTS contains protocols for implementing reliable multicast on top of an unreliable network.

The multicast RTS currently runs on two different parallel systems. First, it has been implemented on the shared-memory multiprocessor described above. This implementation uses the shared memory only for simulating an unreliable multicast network, with a user-specifiable error rate. Shared objects are *not* kept in the shared memory. Second, the RTS runs on a distributed system consisting of several CPUs connected through an Ethernet. This version uses the multicast capabilities of the Ethernet. Both prototypes run on the bare hardware.

Below, we briefly describe the current (experimental) status of the multicast RTS. We will first give an overview of its structure. Next, we will explain how it deals with process and object management. The RTS is discussed in more detail in [Bal *et al.*, 1989a]. The reliable multicast protocol and its implementation on top of an unreliable network are described in [Kaashoek *et al.*, 1989b].

Structure of the multicast RTS

The multicast RTS is best thought of as a new kind of operating system kernel designed specifically for parallel applications. It provides part of the functionality of traditional distributed operating systems, such as I/O, interprocess communication, and memory management. For example, it uses the Amoeba protocols [Mullender and Tanenbaum, 1986] to communicate with our local UNIX and Amoeba systems. In addition, it provides primitives specific to Orca, for process and object creation and operation invocations.

In the current prototype implementation, all user and system processes on a processor execute in a single address space. As Orca is a type-secure language, there is no danger of Orca user processes corrupting kernel data structures. Orca processes run in user mode, and the kernel in supervisor mode.

Shared data-objects are created and updated by the kernel. User processes can directly read local copies of objects, without using the kernel. If a user process applies a write operation to a shared object, the user process traps into the kernel; the local kernel multicasts the operation and its parameters to the kernels of all processors; each kernel then applies the operation to its local copy of the object.

Process management

Processes in the multicast RTS are created and scheduled by the kernel. Unlike in most other operating systems, processes contain little status information and are lightweight. Each kernel contains a scheduler that schedules local processes preemptively. In other words, Orca processes running on the same processor are time sliced. Processes are not rescheduled, however, while they are in the middle of an operation on a shared object.

Object management

The prototype system replicates all shared objects on all processors. The replicas are updated using the distributed update protocol described in Section 6.3.3. Updating is implemented by multicasting the write operation and its parameters to all processors. As the multicast primitive is reliable and indivisible, write operations are executed by all kernels in the same order.

The implementation of operation invocations is significantly different from the one in the shared-memory RTS shown in Figure 6.11. Write operations are implemented as system calls, rather than as user subroutines. Also, the multicast RTS does not use a centralized list of suspended processes (the 'waiting list') for each object. Instead, there is a local waiting list associated with each copy of the object. As write operations are executed everywhere, they will reactivate suspended processes on all processors. As a final difference with the shared-memory RTS, the multicast RTS needs to marshall the parameters of INVOKE.

6.7.3   A distributed run-time system on top of Amoeba

The third Orca run-time system runs on top of the Amoeba distributed operating system. The Amoeba RTS has been implemented on the same distributed hardware configuration as the multicast RTS (i.e. a collection of CPUs connected through an Ethernet). Whereas the multicast system runs on top of the bare hardware, the RTS described here uses the Amoeba primitives for process management and IPC.

As described in Section 2.2, Amoeba supports only point-to-point communication. The Amoeba RTS therefore uses the two-phase primary-copy update protocol described in Section 6.3.3. For each object, one processor contains the primary copy of the object and zero or more other processors contain secondary copies. Read operations are applied to the local copy, if available, and write operations are forwarded to the processor with the primary copy.

Updating replicas through point-to-point messages is more expensive than through multicast messages. Furthermore, the communication overhead with point-to-point messages grows linearly with the number of replicas. The Amoeba RTS therefore replicates objects *selectively*. A given processor only keeps a copy of an object if it frequently reads the object. Run-time statistics are maintained for deciding where to store the primary and secondary copies of each object.

Structure of the Amoeba RTS

The Amoeba RTS is structured as a set of cooperating lightweight processes (Amoeba tasks) sharing a common address space. There is one incarnation of the RTS on each processor. Each incarnation is a single Amoeba cluster. The RTS uses three different types of tasks: Orca tasks, listener tasks, and talker tasks. Each Orca task executes an Orca user process. Each incarnation of the RTS starts a number of *listener tasks* that wait for requests from remote machines. A request can be one of the following:

1. An update of a replicated object.
2. An operation to be performed on an object whose primary copy resides on this machine, on behalf of a remote machine.
3. A request to create a new Orca process.

When a message needs to be sent to another machine, the task wishing to send the message deposits it in a per-machine queue. For each queue – and thus for each remote machine – there is a *talker task* that handles the messages in the queue. A talker repeatedly waits for a message, sends it to the remote machine (using Amoeba RPC), and optionally returns a reply to the task that requested the message to be sent.

With this approach, the replicas of an object can be updated in parallel by depositing update messages in multiple queues. This programming model is similar to the *promises* model [Liskov and Shrira, 1988]. If each Orca process performed the RPC calls itself, parallel updating would not be possible, since RPC calls are blocking. As another advantage of our approach, multiple objects residing on the same machine can be updated in parallel.

Process management

In the RTS described here, processes are implemented as Amoeba tasks. So, creation and scheduling of processes are done by the underlying operating system. The Amoeba scheduler, however, is nonpre-emptive. In Chapter 2, we showed that this strategy causes severe problems for some parallel applications. Essentially the same problems strike again in the Amoeba implementation of the RTS.

For example, a CPU-bound user process can prevent listener processes from being scheduled, so the listeners will not be able to respond quickly to requests from remote talkers. As a result, updating all copies of a shared object may take a very long time. Our current prototype implementation of the RTS takes some ad hoc measures to solve this problem. It simulates pre-emptive scheduling by pre-empting user processes at certain points during their execution.

The problem will disappear in future implementations, however, since the next edition of Amoeba is going to support pre-emptive scheduling and task priorities. With these facilities, the listener and talker tasks can be assigned higher priorities than Orca user processes, so they will execute as soon as a request comes in.

Object management

The RTS is responsible for the distribution of shared objects and the execution of operations on objects. When a new object is created, the RTS puts the primary copy on the machine of the creating process. Other machines are not informed about the new object, so the object does not have secondary copies.

If an object is passed as **shared** parameter to a remote child process, the value actually passed is a *remote reference* to the object on the current processor. The remote reference is a network-wide unique name for the object. The RTS of the remote machine allocates a data structure (a descriptor) for the object, containing the remote reference and the location of the object. This data structure does *not* contain the object's local data.

If the child process later wants to apply an operation to the object, the RTS on its machine will notice that the object is located elsewhere. The RTS will marshall the parameters of the operation, do an RPC call to the machine holding the object, and unmarshall the return values.

If a certain machine holding a remote reference of an object frequently applies read-only operations to the object, the RTS may decide to send a replica (a secondary copy) of the object to that machine. In other words, the RTS automatically and selectively replicates objects on those processors that frequently read the objects. All these copies are updated using the two-phase update protocol, as mentioned above.

The processor containing the primary copy of an object keeps track of the number of remote read and write operations issued by each processor. The overhead of maintaining these statistics is negligible compared to the total costs of remote operations. As soon as the read/write ratio of a remote processor exceeds a certain threshold, the RTS creates a copy of the object on that processor.

Each processor having a secondary copy keeps track of the ratio of local read operations and (global) write operations. If the overhead in updating the copy exceeds the time saved in doing read operations locally, the RTS discards the local copy. From then on, all operations on the object will be done remotely.

With the primary-copy update protocols, all write operations are forwarded to the processor containing the primary copy of the object. If the RTS discovers that an object is written frequently by a machine different from the one containing the primary copy, the RTS may decide to *migrate* the primary copy to that machine. Again, statistics are used to determine the best location for an object. If an object is migrated, precautions are taken for dealing with machines that are unaware of the object's new location.

## CHAPTER 7

Example Programs
and Their Performance

The language implementations described in the previous chapter have been used for developing several Orca programs. Below, we will take a closer look at some of these programs and their performance. The intent of this chapter is to study the expressivity and performance of Orca, by implementing existing algorithms for important applications. We have not tried to design new algorithms for any of these applications.

As discussed in Chapter 1, we are mainly concerned with the implementation of parallel, high-performance applications on distributed systems. We will study five such applications in detail: matrix multiplication, the all-pairs shortest paths problem, branch-and-bound, game tree search, and successive overrelaxation. These applications are taken from different areas of mathematics and computer science (linear algebra, graph theory, operations research, artificial intelligence, and numerical analysis).

The applications differ widely in their complexity and communication requirements. Matrix multiplication is an example of 'easy parallelism' [Almasi and Gottlieb, 1989], since the problem can be split into subtasks that hardly do any communication. The other applications, however, have more complex communication patterns, as we will see. Some of the applications require logically shared data, but we will also discuss how a message-passing application (successive overrelaxation) can be implemented in Orca.

The algorithms we will describe illustrate several different styles of parallel programming. The first two algorithms use a fixed partitioning of work among the available processors, thus minimizing the overhead of work distribution. For branch-and-bound and game tree search, this method is less suitable, because the subtasks used by these algorithms have highly unpredictable execution times. For these two applications, we use the replicated worker style. Finally, the successive overrelaxation algorithm is an example of a parallel iterative algorithm.

The structure of this chapter is as follows. First, we will make some general remarks about how we measure the performance of Orca programs. Next, in Sections 7.2 through 7.6, we will discuss five applications in detail. In each subsection, we will describe the application and the algorithm used for implementing it, we will discuss the resulting Orca program, and we will give graphs showing the speedup of this program on the three run-time systems described in Section 6.7. The source code for the programs is given in Appendices A through E. More detailed performance figures are given in Appendix F. In Section 7.7 we will briefly discuss the largest application that has been implemented in Orca so far, a chess problem solver. Finally, in Section 7.8, we will present some conclusions.

7.1   Notes on the performance measurements

In this section, we will discuss how we have determined the performance of the Orca applications. We will first describe the hardware and software used for the measurements. Next, we will define how we compute the speedup of parallel Orca programs. Finally, we will present some details of the measurements.

7.1.1   The environments used for the measurements

The performance figures presented below are based on the prototype Orca compiler and run-time systems described in the previous chapter. We have used two different systems for our measurements:

- A shared-memory multiprocessor containing ten MC68020 CPUs and 8 MB shared memory, connected through a VME bus. Each CPU board contains 2 MB of local memory, used for storing programs and local data. Unlike in most commercial multiprocessors, the CPU boards do not contain snooping caches for the shared memory. Each access to shared memory goes over the VME bus. Local memory, on the other hand, can be accessed without using the VME bus, so ten local memory accesses can be performed in parallel. The CPU boards do not contain floating-point coprocessors.
- A distributed system containing 10 nodes that are connected by a 10 Mbit/s Ethernet. Each node consists of a CPU board, identical to the ones used in the multiprocessor, and an Ethernet controller board using the Lance chip.

The multiprocessor has only been used for measuring the performance of the shared-memory RTS; for the multicast RTS and Amoeba RTS, the distributed system has been used.

We conclude this subsection with some timing statistics of the communication protocols used by the distributed run-time systems. (A more detailed description of the performances of these protocols is given in [Bal *et al.*, 1989b].)

The Amoeba RTS uses the Amoeba RPC protocol, the performance of which is described in [Van Renesse *et al.*, 1988]. For the hardware configuration described above, a remote procedure call with a single integer argument costs approximately 1.4 ms.

The multicast RTS uses a highly efficient reliable multicast protocol, described in [Kaashoek *et al.*, 1989b]. The time needed for multicasting a short message reliably to two processors is 1.3 ms, which is faster than an Amoeba RPC. Each additional receiver adds approximately 25 µs to the elapsed time. So, with 10 receivers, a multicast takes 1.5 ms. The time also depends on the number of senders that are active simultaneously. If, for example, 7 processors are simultaneously sending a message to 10 processors, the average time per multicast is 4.6 ms.

7.1.2 Computing speedups

We compute the speedup of a parallel Orca program by taking the ratio of the execution times of the program on 1 CPU and N CPUs:

$$\text{Speedup with } N \text{ CPUs} \;=\; \frac{\text{time taken by parallel program with 1 CPU}}{\text{time taken by parallel program with } N \text{ CPUs}}$$

So, we will take the execution time of the parallel program on a single processor as a basis for comparison. Alternatives that we have considered but rejected are to use any of the following programs for comparison:

1. A sequential program written in Orca, using the same underlying algorithm as the parallel program.
2. A sequential program written in Orca, using the best possible sequential algorithm.
3. A sequential program written in the fastest language available and using the best possible sequential algorithm.

As we will discuss below, these choices are less appropriate.

Since the compiler and run-time systems used for our measurements are *prototypes*, it is not very meaningful to compare the performance of Orca with languages such as C and FORTRAN, which have highly optimized implementations. Our research has focused on the distributed aspects of the implementation. Many sequential parts of the language have been implemented in a preliminary, inefficient way. For example, accessing components of arrays, records, and graphs is more expensive than necessary. Furthermore, Orca does heavy run-time checking. Although this slows down execution, we feel the overhead is justified by the type security thus obtained. Orca programs that frequently use such data structures typically are three to five times slower than similar programs written in C.

Also, it is not significant to compare sequential Orca programs with parallel programs that run on one CPU. The parallel programs can only use objects (values of abstract data types) for communication. As our prototype implementations have not optimized abstract data types in any way, the execution-time overhead of an operation is substantial. A sequential Orca program would not have this overhead, since it can use regular (nonabstract) variables for communication. Most of the overhead of abstract data types can be eliminated, but our current prototype compiler does not do this optimization.

The underlying sequential algorithm certainly must be taken into account when analyzing speedups. Consider, for example, the minimax and alpha-beta algorithms for game tree search. It is almost trivial to implement an optimally parallel minimax tree search algorithm. Even if it achieves linear speedup, however, it may be slower than a sequential alpha-beta search algorithm, simply because alpha-beta is a vastly more efficient algorithm for game tree search than minimax. The point is, speedups alone do not tell much about the efficiency of a program. The efficiency of the underlying algorithm must be considered too. For many applications, slow algorithms are much easier to parallelize than fast algorithms. The algorithms described in this chapter are parallelizations of efficient sequential algorithms. Therefore, we will not look at alternative sequential algorithms.

The speedup of a given program is determined not only by the program itself, but also by the hardware and system sofware used to run the program and by the input of the program. These two factors will be discussed below.

One important pitfall, which is especially important to distributed systems, is the usage of slow hardware or software that masks communication overhead. As an illustrative example, consider a program in which each process repeatedly does N floating-point multiplications and then sends a message to some other process. Clearly, the more expensive the floating-point instructions are, the lower the relative communication overhead of the program will be. Thus, the program may achieve excellent speedups on systems that implement floating-point instructions in software, but may perform poorly with hardware floating units.

As our systems lack hardware floating-point units, we will avoid using floating-point arithmetic. Only one of the applications discussed below, successive overrelaxation, requires floating-point instructions (mainly additions). Nonetheless, the speedups reported below may still be somewhat over optimistic, since they are based on prototype implementations of Orca. If the sequential constructs of Orca are optimized, the relative communication overhead will be increased. Most of the applications we use, however, are not communication intensive, so the speedups will not degrade much in an optimized implementation.

Another factor that influences speedups is which inputs are used for each program. In particular, the *problem size* plays a key role. For many parallel programs, significant speedups are only obtained for sufficiently large input problems. Frequently, this restriction is not important, since one of the primary motivations for using parallelism is the potential for solving large problems. We will not study this relation between problem sizes and speedups. Instead, we will use input problems that are suitably large.

For some applications, the speedup depends not only on the size of the input problem, but also on the problem itself. For example, the branch-and-bound algorithm described in Section 7.4 uses heuristics for determining the order in which subproblems are solved. For some inputs these heuristics perform better than for others. (Even super linear speedups can be obtained with such algorithms, as we will see.)

We have solved this by using several randomly generated input sets for applications like these and computing the average speedups obtained over these inputs.

7.1.3   The measurements

We have measured the execution times of the programs using the Orca library routine `GetTime`, which returns the current time accurate to about a tenth of a second. For each program, `GetTime` is called twice; the difference between the two calls is taken as the elapsed computation time. The first call is executed as soon as the executable code has been downloaded into all processors and the main process, called `OrcaMain`, has been started. The second call is executed when the results have been computed.

So, the measured times include forking of slave processes, but exclude the I/O time for outputting data. Including I/O time would obscure the results, since the systems we use serialize all I/O. (Parallel I/O has been addressed, for example, by the designers of the Connection Machine [Tucker and Robertson, 1988]. This issue is outside the scope of this book, however.)

All measurements have been repeated several times, on otherwise idle systems. The figures presented below are based on the average values of these runs. The execution times varied very little between different runs of the same program. Nearly all measured values were within three per cent of the average value, but in most cases the differences were even less.

The performance measurements will be presented graphically. For each application we will give a graph showing the speedups obtained for the shared-memory RTS, the multicast RTS, and the Amoeba RTS. The measured average execution times are given in Appendix F.

In comparing the speedups, one should keep in mind that Orca is designed for programming *distributed* systems. Therefore, the performance of the two distributed RTSs is far more relevant than the performance of the shared-memory RTS. We will use the shared-memory RTS mainly for comparison. Of the two distributed RTSs, the multicast RTS can be expected to achieve to highest performance, since it uses multicast rather than point-to-point messages. Also, it runs on the bare hardware, so it is not burdened by operating system overhead.

The Amoeba operating system does not support profiling of user code. It is therefore difficult to obtain a time breakdown of the Orca programs. In several cases, profiles would have been useful for explaining some slight but obscure differences in execution times between the three systems.

7.2   Matrix multiplication

The first parallel Orca program we will consider multiplies two matrices and prints the result matrix. The algorithm used by this program is straightforward and well suited to distributed systems. Basically, each processor computes one or more rows of the result matrix. We assume the matrices are sufficiently large, so the number of rows of the result matrix exceeds the number of processors available.

7.2.1   Parallel matrix multiplication in Orca

The program (see Appendix A.3) uses two types of process: one *master* process and one or more *slave* processes. The single master process, OrcaMain, is invoked automatically by the run-time system when the program is started. It determines how many processors are available to the program and forks off one slave process on each processor. Each slave is assigned some portion of the rows of the result matrix.

Each slave process has a copy of the two matrices to be multiplied. These matrices are represented as two-dimensional arrays. For testing, the matrices are initialized to arbitrary values. After initialization, each slave process computes its part of the result matrix independently of all other slave processes. During the multiplication, the slaves do not need to communicate with each other. To print the result matrix, however, some coordination is needed among the slaves. To serialize printing, a shared object turn of type IntObject is used. (This object type has been discussed in Section 5.4.3; for completeness, the specification and implementation of the object type are also given in Appendices A.1 and A.2.) Before printing its results, a slave executes the statement

```
turn$AwaitValue(lb);
```

This statement suspends the slave until turn contains the number of the first row it is working on. After printing the results, turn is set to the row index of the next slave through the statement

```
turn$assign(ub+1);
```

The program of Appendix A.3 illustrates how variables of a structured type can be used in Orca. As explained in Chapter 5, structured variables can be manipulated (e.g. assigned, copied) in the same way as scalar variables. As an example, consider the way a slave process computes its part of the result matrix. A slave declares a two-dimensional array variable Result. The declaration only provides bounds for the first dimension of the array, so it allocates an array whose elements are empty arrays. The elements are assigned a value (an array of integer numbers) by the statement

```
Result[row] := ComputeRow(row, A, B);
```

Finally, it is worth noting that both DotProduct and ComputeRow are true mathematical functions that take some input parameters and deliver one or more result values.

7.2.2   Performance

The performance of the matrix multiplication program is shown in Figure 7.1. We have used 250 × 250 integer matrices for the measurements. As explained in Section 7.1.3, the time needed for printing the result matrix has been excluded from the timing. As the program does little interprocess communication, the speedups obtained for the three run-time systems do not differ very much. The shared-memory RTS is fastest.

The speedups achieved by the program are less than linear. This is easily explained. Before starting any real computations, each slave initializes its local copies of the matrices. Since each slave requires at least a copy of the entire B matrix, this initialization code takes $O(N^2)$ time, where N is the size of the matrices. The actual computation time per slave takes $O(N^3/P)$ time, where P is the number of processors used. The speedup obtained therefore is

$$O\left[\frac{N^2 + N^3}{N^2 + N^3/P}\right] = O\left[\frac{1+N}{1+N/P}\right]$$

The initialization code is a sequential part of the program. However, if the matrices are very large compared to the number of processors used (i.e. $N \gg P$), the speedup will be almost perfect. Therefore, the algorithm scales well, provided it is applied to a problem of sufficiently large size.

7.3   The all-pairs shortest paths problem

In the all-pairs shortest paths (ASP) problem it is desired to find the length of the shortest path from any node i to any other node j in a given graph. Sequential solutions to the ASP problem are given in several text books on algorithms and data structures [Aho *et al.*, 1974; Horowitz and Sahni, 1976]. We will first review the standard sequential algorithm, due to Floyd, for solving the ASP problem and then discuss how it can be implemented in a parallel way. The algorithm assumes that the nodes of the graph are numbered sequentially from 1 to N (the total number of nodes) and that each edge in the graph is assigned a positive length (or weight).

The standard sequential solution to the ASP problem uses an iterative algorithm. During iteration k it finds the shortest path from every node i in the graph to every node j that only visits intermediate nodes in the set {1..k}. During iteration k, the algorithm checks if the current best path from i to k concatenated with the current best path from k to j is shorter than the best path from i to j found so far (i.e. during the first $k-1$ iterations).

Before the first iteration, such a path only exists if the graph contains a direct edge from node i to node j. After the last iteration, the resulting path may visit any other node, as the set {1..k} includes all nodes if $k = N$. Therefore, after the last iteration the resulting path is the shortest path from node i to node j.

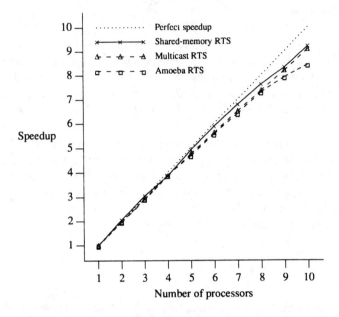

Figure 7.1 *Measured speedups for matrix multiplication, using 250 × 250 integer matrices.*

The standard algorithm uses a sequence of matrices for storing the lengths of all these paths. After iteration k, element $C^k[i,j]$ contains the length of the shortest path from i to j found so far (i.e. the best path visiting only nodes between 1 and k). During iteration k, the matrix C^{k-1} is transformed into a matrix C^k as follows:

$$C^k[i,j] = \text{MINIMUM}(\ C^{k-1}[i,j],\ C^{k-1}[i,k] + C^{k-1}[k,j])\quad (1 \le i,j \le N)$$

Note that the value of row k of matrix C^k is equal to row k of matrix C^{k-1}, because

$$C^k[k,j] =$$
$$\text{MINIMUM}(\ C^{k-1}[k,j],\ C^{k-1}[k,k] + C^{k-1}[k,j]) =$$
$$\text{MINIMUM}(\ C^{k-1}[k,j],\ C^{k-1}[k,j]) =$$
$$C^{k-1}[k,j]$$

7.3.1   Parallel ASP in Orca

This sequential algorithm can be transformed into a parallel algorithm by computing the rows of the matrices $C^k[i,j]$ in parallel. There are two ways for structuring such a parallel ASP algorithm. First, we can have a single master process that executes N iterations. During iteration k, the master forks one or more slave processes and passes part of the matrix C^{k-1} to each slave. A slave computes one or more rows of C^k, sends these values back to the master, and then terminates.

An alternative way for structuring the parallel algorithm is to let each slave execute an iterative algorithm. In this case, the master process forks a number of slave processes (just as in the matrix multiplication program of Appendix A) and then terminates. Each slave process performs N iterations and then outputs its results. The latter approach is more efficient, because it requires fewer **fork** statements. Also, it has more parallelism, because different slave processes may be working on different iterations.

We therefore use the second approach and structure the algorithm as a number of iterative slave processes. Each slave process computes a fixed number of rows of the C matrices. Unlike the matrix multiplication algorithm, however, the different rows of C^k cannot be computed independently of each other. Suppose a slave process wants to compute row i of matrix C^k. That is, it has to compute the values

$C^k[i,j]$, for all j between 1 and N

To compute the value $C^k[i,j]$, the values of $C^{k-1}[i,j]$, $C^{k-1}[i,k]$, and $C^{k-1}[k,j]$ are needed. The first two values have been computed by this process during the previous iteration. The value of $C^{k-1}[k,j]$, however, has been computed (during iteration k−1) by the process that takes care of row k. The above argument applies to any value of i and j between 1 and N. Therefore, during iteration k, each process needs to know the value of the entire row k of matrix C^{k-1}. So, after each iteration k, the process that computed the value of row k+1 of matrix C^k has to send this value to all other processes. Furthermore, a process should not continue computing its part of C^k until it has received row k of the previous iteration. Clearly, the processes must be *synchronized* to achieve this.

In conclusion, the ASP problem can be solved in parallel by letting each slave process taking care of some of the rows of the C matrices. Each process performs an iterative algorithm. During iteration k, a processor that is assigned rows lb up to ub computes the values

$C^k[i,j]$, for all i between lb and ub, and all j between 1 and N

A processor should not start working on iteration k until the value of row k of matrix C^{k-1} is available. Apart from this restriction, the processors do not depend on each other. In particular, they need not all be working on the same iteration.

The synchronization constraint described above is implemented through an object of type RowCollection, whose specification is shown in Appendix B.2. This object type defines two operations, AddRow and AwaitRow. Whenever a process has computed row k of matrix C^{k-1}, it executes the operation AddRow, passing the iteration number (k) and the value of the row (an array of integers) as parameters. Before a process starts working on iteration k, it first waits until the value of row k for this iteration is available. It does so by invoking AwaitRow(k).

The implementation of object type `RowCollection` is shown in Appendix B.3. The internal data of an object of this type consist of an array of rows. There is one row for each iteration of the algorithm. As different processes may be working on different iterations, all these rows are retained during the entire execution of the program. Initially, each entry of `tab` will contain an empty array, as the declaration of `tab` does not specify actual bounds for the rows. The `AddRow` operation assigns a nonempty array to a certain entry of the table. The `AwaitRow` operation blocks until the specified entry of the table is nonempty. (Recall that an empty array has a lower bound that is higher than its upper bound.)

The code for the ASP program itself is shown in Appendix B.4. It is structured in a similar way to the matrix multiplication program of Appendix A. The master process, `OrcaMain`, forks one slave process per processor. Each slave is assigned part of the initial C matrix. A slave initializes its part of the C matrix by calling the procedure `InitializeTable`. Each slave takes a shared object of type `RowCollection` as parameter. This object, called `RowkColl`, is used for synchronizing the slaves, as described above.

Conceptually, the slave processes compute a sequence of matrices $C^0, C^1, \ldots, C^N$. In the implementation, however, each slave simply uses a single array variable, which is modified in place. There is basically only a single C matrix, which is partitioned among all the slaves.

Each slave process executes N iterations (see the **for** statement in the function ComputeRows). At the beginning of iteration k, it first obtains the value of row k. This value may have been computed either by itself (if $lb \leq k \leq ub$) or by some other slave. In the first case, it sends the value to all other slaves, using the `AddRow` operation on `RowkColl`. In the second case, it obtains the value by invoking the `AwaitRow` operation, which blocks until the value is available. In either case, the slave process proceeds by updating the values of its rows.

As soon as a slave process has finished all N iterations, it is ready to print its results. The same synchronization mechanism as for matrix multiplication is used for serializing printing.

7.3.2   Performance

The performance of the ASP program for a graph with 200 nodes is shown in Figure 7.2. The speedups for the shared-memory and multicast run-time systems are only slightly less than perfect. In part, this is due to the same initialization problem that we saw for matrix multiplication. For ASP, the problem is less severe, since each processor needs only initialize part of the matrix, which takes $O(N^2/P)$ time.

Another reason why the speedup for ASP is less than perfect is the communication overhead. Before each iteration, the current value of row k must be transmitted from one processor to all the others. The shared-memory RTS implements this by putting the new value in the shared memory, where it can be read by all processors. The distributed RTSs, however, actually have to transmit the value across the Ethernet, which is more expensive.

Despite this overhead, the multicast RTS obtains good speedups. With 10 processors, the speedup is 9.17, which is almost as good as the speedup for the shared-memory RTS. In addition, this implementation seems to scale well, since the speedup increases with the number of processors. One of the main reasons for this good performance is the use of multicast messages for transferring the row to all processors.

The performance of the multicast implementation of ASP also compares favourably with the parallel ASP program described in [Jenq and Sahni, 1987]. Jenq and Sahni have implemented ASP on an NCUBE/7 hypercube, using a similar work distribution as ours. For a graph with 112 nodes they report speedups of approximately 6.5 with 8 processors and 10.5 with 16 processors. As the NCUBE/7 does not support multicast in hardware, they have used a binary tree transmission scheme for simulating multicast. The elapsed time for a simulated multicast message is proportional to the logarithm of the number of processors. In contrast, the protocol used in our multicast RTS typically only uses two messages per reliable multicast. The time needed for multicasting a message is almost independent of the number of receivers [Kaashoek *et al.*, 1989b].

The Amoeba RTS achieves a good speedup up to 8 processors. From then on, the performance severely degrades, because of the increased communication overhead. With 10 processors, for example, the total number of RPCs issued by all processors together was measured to be approximately 3600. (Each RPC requires several Ethernet packets.) For comparison, the multicast RTS sends approximately 250 multicast packets and 550 point-to-point packets over the Ethernet, if 10 processors are used.

The bends in the graphs for the shared-memory and multicast RTS of Figure 7.2 are caused by the slightly unbalanced work distribution. With 8 CPUs, for example, each processor manages exactly 25 rows of the distance matrix; with 9 CPUs, however, some processors will have 22 rows, but others will have 23 rows. As the elapsed computation time is determined by the processor that terminates last, the speedup with 9 processors cannot exceed $200/23 \approx 8.7$.

7.4 Branch-and-bound

Branch-and-bound algorithms were described in Section 2.3. In that section, we discussed the implementation of one example branch-and-bound algorithm, for the travelling salesman problem (TSP). The TSP algorithm has been implemented on top of an existing distributed operating system, Amoeba, using a sequential language (the C language) extended with library routines for process creation and communication.

In Amoeba, processes on different machines can only communicate through remote procedure calls; such processes cannot share any data. The branch-and-bound algorithm used for solving TSP, however, requires a global shared variable containing the length of the best path found so far. In the Amoeba implementation, this shared vari-

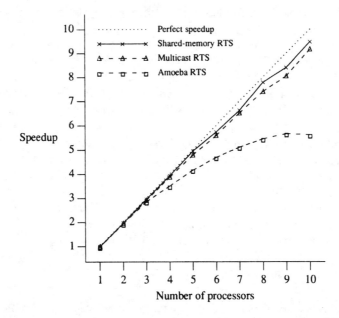

Figure 7.2 *Measured speedups for the all-pairs shortest paths problem, using an input graph with 200 nodes.*

able was simulated by replicating its value on every processor. Keeping the replicas up to date, however, turned out to be difficult.

7.4.1   Parallel branch-and-bound in Orca

In Orca, the shared variable can simply be stored in a shared data-object of type IntObject. The Orca run-time system takes care of replicating this object and updating the copies in a consistent way. Therefore, the Orca implementation of TSP is much simpler than the Amoeba version. Moreover, the object and its copies are updated as soon as a process finds a better route, so the new length is made known to all processes immediately. In the Amoeba implementation this is very hard to realize, because remote procedure calls cannot return intermediate results.

The distribution of work among processors is also simplified by the ability to use shared data-objects. Instead of using intermediate agent tasks, the Orca implementation of TSP is based on the replicated worker style. There is one *worker process*, similar to the subcontractor processes of Figure 2.4, on each processor. All these workers are identical. Each worker repeatedly takes work from a *job queue* and executes it. The jobs in the job queue are generated by a *manager process*, similar to the manager task of Figure 2.4. As in the Amoeba implementation, a job consists of a subtree that has to be searched.

The structure of the TSP program is shown in Figure 7.3. The job queue is a data object shared among the manager and the workers. The manager process adds jobs to the tail of the job queue. The workers fetch jobs from the head of the queue. The workers also share a data object minimum of type IntObject. Whenever a worker finds a full route of length less than minimum, it assigns the length of the new path to minimum.

The type definitions used by the TSP program are shown in Appendix C.1. The distances between the cities are stored in a two-dimensional array of type DistTab. The distances stored in this array are *sorted*. Entry [C, i] of the array contains the *i*th closest city to C and the distance from C to that city. With this representation, it is easy to implement the nearest-city-first heuristic discussed in Section 2.3.1.

Appendix C.1 also declares a type JobType, which defines the jobs to be executed by the workers. A job consists of an initial (partial) route for the salesman and the length of this partial route. The latter number is included for efficiency reasons only; it could also be derived from the path itself.

The job queue is a shared data-object encapsulating a queue of JobType items. The job queue data structure may be useful to many applications. We therefore define it as a *generic* object type. The specification part of the generic job queue type is given in Appendix C.2. The formal parameter T represents the type of the elements of the queue. For the TSP program, we will instantiate the generic object type with type JobType as actual parameter.

Three different operations are defined on job queues. The first operation, AddJob adds a new job to the tail of the queue. In the TSP program, this operation will only be invoked by the manager process. The operation NoMoreJobs is to be called when no more jobs will be added to the queue (i.e. when the manager has generated all the jobs). Finally, the operation GetJob tries to fetch a job from the head of the queue. If the queue is not empty, GetJob removes the first job from the queue and returns it through the **out** parameter job; the operation itself returns 'true' in this case. If the queue is empty and the operation NoMoreJobs has been applied to the queue, the operation fails and returns 'false'. If neither of these two conditions – queue not empty or NoMoreJobs invoked – holds, the operation blocks until one of them becomes true.

The implementation part of the generic job queue type is shown in Appendix C.3. Objects of this type contain two variables: a Boolean variable done and a variable Q of type queue. The latter type is defined as a **graph** with two global fields, identifying the first and last element of the queue. Each element contains the **nodename** of the next element in the queue and data of formal type T.

The implementation of AddJob uses straightforward list manipulation. The GetJob operation is more interesting. It contains two **guards**, reflecting the two conditions described above.

The Orca code for the TSP program itself is shown in Appendix C.4. The manager process is OrcaMain, which is the first process that executes. This process creates and initializes the shared object minimum, initializes the distance table, and forks one worker process on each processor except its own one. Subsequently, OrcaMain generates the jobs. When all jobs have been generated, the manager forks a worker pro-

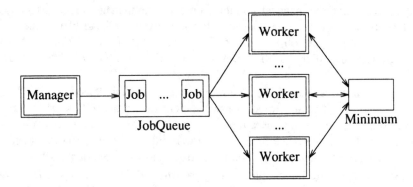

Figure 7.3 *Structure of the Orca implementation of TSP. The manager and workers are processes. The JobQueue is a data object shared among all these processes. Minimum is a data object of type IntObject; it is read and written by all workers.*

cess on its own processor and waits until all work has been done. In this way, job generation executes in parallel with most of the worker processes. The final worker process is not created until all jobs have been generated, so job generation will not be slowed down by a competing process on the same processor. When all worker processes have terminated, the manager prints the final value of minimum (i.e. the length of the optimal solution).

The jobs are generated through the recursive function distributor. In the implementation of Appendix C.4, a job contains an initial path with a fixed number of cities (MaxHops). Basically, the manager process traverses the top MaxHops − 1 levels of the search tree (see Figure 2.2 in Chapter 2), while the workers traverse the remaining levels. The manager process generates the jobs in 'nearest-city-first' order. It is important that the worker processes execute the jobs in the same order they were generated. This is the reason why we use an ordered queue rather than an unordered bag for storing the jobs.

Each worker process repeatedly fetches a job from the job queue and executes it by calling the function tsp. The tsp function generates all routes that start with a given initial route. If the initial route passed as parameter is longer than the current best route, tsp returns immediately, because such a partial route cannot lead to an optimal solution. If the route passed as parameter is a full route (visiting all cities), a new best route has been found, so the value of minimum should be updated. It is possible, however, that two or more worker processes simultaneously detect a route that is better than the current best route. Therefore, the value of minimum is updated through the indivisible operation min, which checks if the new value presented is actually less than the current value of the object.

If the job queue is empty and no more jobs will be generated, the operation GetJob will return 'false' and the workers will terminate. Before terminating, a worker process decrements the global counter WorkersActive. As soon as this counter drops to zero, the manager process knows that there are no more active workers, so it can print the result value.

7.4.2   Performance

We have determined the performance of the TSP program by measuring its execution time for solving three randomly generated input graphs with 12 cities each. The manager process searches 2 levels of the tree, so it generates 110 jobs, each of which solves a 10-city TSP problem. Figure 7.4 shows the average speedups obtained for these three problems.

The most striking aspects of Figure 7.4 are the poor performance of the shared-memory RTS and the remarkably high performance of the two distributed RTSs. The multicast RTS achieves perfect speedup. The speedup of the Amoeba RTS is slightly lower. In absolute speed, the multicast RTS is 12 to 18 per cent faster than the Amoeba RTS, because operations in the Amoeba RTS have a higher overhead.

With fewer than five processors, the shared memory and distributed implementations are equally fast. With five or more processors, however, the distributed systems are far more efficient. Although surprising at first sight, this behaviour is easy to explain. In the distributed RTSs, each processor will have its own local copy of the shared object minimum. (The multicast RTS replicates all objects; the Amoeba RTS will dynamically replicate minimum, since it has a high read/write ratio.) Thus, all processors can simultaneously read their copies. In the shared-memory RTS, on the other hand, the object is put in the shared memory and protected by locks, so it becomes a sequential bottleneck. In our prototype implementation of the RTS, the situation is particularly bad, because of the following:

1. Operations are implemented inefficiently and thus are expensive. The value operation, which is used to read the current value of minimum, takes about 40 µs.
2. Exclusive locks – rather than readers/writer locking – are used.
3. The hardware we use (i.e. the VME bus) allows only one processor at a time to access the shared memory.

As the value operation is executed very frequently (over a million times in total), it will often have to wait for the lock to be free. Undoubtedly, the contention problem would be less severe in a well-tuned shared-memory implementation on more advanced hardware. Still, it is not clear whether the problem can be eliminated entirely in this way, without using local copies of objects.

The distributed Orca implementations of TSP also have a much better performance than the C/Amoeba version of TSP described in Section 2.3. The main reason for this difference is the high search overhead of the C/Amoeba version. In Section 2.3.3 we discussed the near impossibility of keeping the bound variable minimum up to date

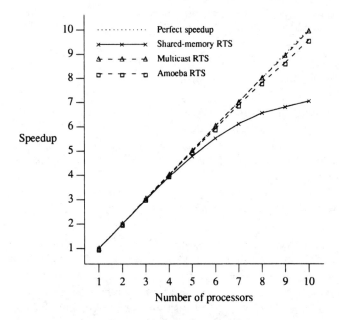

Figure 7.4 *Measured speedups for the travelling salesman problem, averaged over three randomly generated graphs with 12 cities each.*

using Amoeba's RPC. Because processors do not have the most recent value of this bound, they sometimes will search parts of the tree that the sequential algorithm cuts off. This search overhead may become quite significant. For one of the input graphs we obtained the following statistics:

Total number of nodes in the tree	108 505 112
Nodes searched by sequential C version	1 272 076
Nodes searched by 10-CPU C/Amoeba version	1 763 552
Nodes searched by 10-CPU Orca multicast version	1 149 270

In this example, the C/Amoeba version of TSP searches 39 per cent more nodes than the sequential algorithm. The Orca version running on the multicast RTS, on the other hand, searches 10 per cent *fewer* nodes. It achieves superlinear speedup in this case (a speedup of 10.75 with 10 processors). Such anomalous behaviour of parallel branch-and-bound programs has also been reported by other authors [Lai and Sahni, 1983]. It is due to the fact that one processor quickly finds a near-optimal solution, which other processors use for pruning parts of their trees. However, if we were to make a large number of runs with different input data, we would not see a superlinear effect on the average.

The different versions of the TSP program also give us some indication of the efficiency of the current Orca implementation. The sequential C program takes 132 seconds to solve the first problem. The parallel Orca program, if run on a single processor using the multicast RTS, takes 576.5 seconds, which is 4.4 times slower. With 10 processors, the Orca version takes 53.7 seconds, which is 2.5 times faster than sequential C.

The application discussed in this subsection is a good example of when our approach is most effective. The TSP program uses a shared object with a high read/write ratio. As this object is replicated and the copies are updated immediately after each change, the application is very efficient. In the RPC model used by Amoeba, this replication is hard to express adequately by the programmer. In the shared data-object model, it is taken care of automatically by the run-time system.

7.5 Game tree search

Game tree search was introduced in Section 2.4, where we described the implementation of a parallel alpha-beta program in C on top of Amoeba. Here, we will discuss how parallel alpha-beta search can be implemented in Orca.

7.5.1 Parallel game tree search in Orca

We have implemented a parallel alpha-beta search algorithm in Orca, using a similar approach as the travelling salesman problem. The program is structured as a single manager process that generates jobs for one or more worker processes (see Figure 7.5).

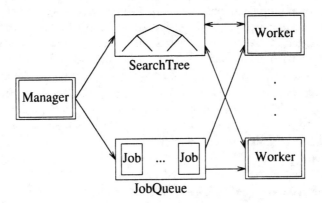

Figure 7.5 *Structure of the Orca implementation of alpha-beta search. The manager and workers are processes. The JobQueue is a data object shared among all these processes. SearchTree is an object containing the top part of the search tree. It is built by the manager and manipulated by the workers.*

In Section 2.4.1, we showed that parallel alpha-beta search differs from parallel TSP, in that alpha-beta uses an explicit search tree for storing alpha and beta values. In our C/Amoeba implementation of alpha-beta, the top part of this tree is managed by the root processor (see Figure 2.7) and is accessed by subcontractors (slave processors) through remote procedure calls.

In our Orca implementation of alpha-beta, the top part of the tree is stored in a data object that is shared among all processes. The tree is initially built by the manager process and is subsequently used for communication among worker processes. (As in the C/Amoeba version, the worker processes do not build explicit data structures for the subtrees.) After the entire search has been completed, the root of the tree will contain the result value to be computed by the program.

The job queue used by alpha-beta is similar to the one used for TSP, except that the job descriptions are different. For alpha-beta, a job consists of evaluating a subtree rooted at one of the leaves of the top part of the tree. The job queue type used by alpha-beta is an instantiation of the generic job queue type of Appendix C.2. In principle, our alpha-beta program could also use an unordered data structure – such as a bag – for storing the jobs, since it does not order the jobs.

The search tree supports operations for adding nodes, reading the contents of existing nodes, reading the value of the root node, and propagating intermediate result values (see Appendix D.1). In addition to these operations, the specification part declares a type `Node` and a function `NullNode`. The type identifies nodes of the search tree; it is an opaque type, which means only its name but not its representation is visible. The function `NullNode` returns a value of type `Node` corresponding to NIL.

The manager uses the operation `AddNode` for building the tree and the operation `RootValue` for printing the final result of the program. Worker processes invoke `ReadNode` to obtain the contents of a specific node, consisting of a board position and alpha and beta values. After a worker has evaluated a subtree, it invokes `PropagateResult` to update the alpha and beta values of other nodes in the tree. Propagation of result values was already discussed in Section 2.4.2 (see Figure 2.8 in Chapter 2).

The implementation of object type `SearchTree` is shown in Appendix D.2. The search tree is represented as a graph. Each node of the graph contains the nodename of its parent and of a fixed number of children. Also, each node stores a board position, alpha and beta values, and a counter specifying how many children of the node still have to be evaluated. The latter number is used for determining when the subtree rooted at the node has been fully searched.

Most of the code of Appendix D.2 is straightforward, except for the propagation of result values by `PropagateResult`. The implementation of this operation uses the auxiliary functions `ImproveAlpha`, `ImproveBeta`, `UpdateAlpha`, `UpdateBeta`, and `propagate`. This code is explained further by several comments in the program.

The code for the manager and worker processes is shown in Appendix D.3. The manager process, `OrcaMain`, declares the search tree and job queue objects described above. The manager first generates the top of the search tree, together with the jobs to be executed by the workers. Next, it forks off one worker process for each available processor and waits until all workers have finished. Finally, it prints the result value, which is the alpha value of the root of the tree.

The worker processes are not started until the top part of the search tree has been built. If worker processes were allowed to proceed in parallel with search tree and job generation, more synchronization between the manager and worker processes would be needed. Although tree generation is done sequentially, it will in general not become a performance bottleneck, because the time needed for building the top part of the tree is only a very small part of the total search time.

The search tree is built by the recursive procedure `GenerateTopOfTree`. This procedure builds the tree up to a certain number of levels (specified by the constant `SplitLevel`). For each leaf of this tree it also adds a job to the shared job queue.

The code for the worker processes is also shown in Appendix D.3. Each worker repeatedly takes a job from the job queue and executes it. A job description identifies a leaf node of the top part of the search tree. After obtaining a job, a worker fetches the board position and current alpha and beta values of the node. This is more efficient than storing these values in the job descriptor, because the alpha and beta values of the node may have been improved after the job was generated; by retrieving the values from the tree the worker uses the most recent alpha and beta values. Subsequently, the worker executes the job by calling a sequential alpha-beta routine. The search depth of this sequential routine is the constant `WorkerLevels`, which is the difference between the total search depth and the search depth of the manager. Finally, the worker updates the shared search tree through the operation `PropagateResult`.

7.5.2 Performance

The speedups obtained for parallel alpha-beta search are shown in Figure 7.6. We have used three different game trees for our measurements and computed the average speedup. The trees are identical to the ones used in the C/Amoeba implementation (see Section 2.4.3). So, the fanout of each tree (i.e. the constant `Nsons` in the specification of the module `Game`) is 38 and the depth of the trees is 6 plies. The nodes of the tree contain integer values (i.e. the type `board` imported from the module `Game` is the standard `integer` type).

The speedup of the parallel alpha-beta program depends on the size of the jobs generated by the manager process. If the constant `SplitLevel` is set to a high value, the manager will search many levels of the tree, and it will generate many small jobs for the slaves. As a disadvantage, managing the job queue will then be expensive, due to communication overhead. If, on the other hand, `SplitLevel` is set to a low value, the manager will generate a few large jobs. In this case, the communication overhead will be lower, but the search overhead will be increased [Bal *et al.*, 1987].

We have measured the speedup of alpha-beta for several different values of `SplitLevel`. It turns out that, for all three run-time systems, the best absolute performance is obtained by letting the manager traverse only a single level of the tree.

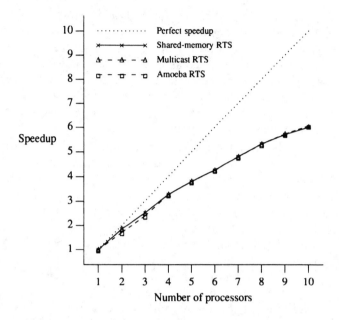

Figure 7.6 *Measured speedups for alpha-beta search, averaged over three randomly generated game trees with fanout 38 and depth 6.*

Thus, the manager generates 38 jobs, each containing a 5-ply deep search tree. With this arrangement, the communication overhead is very low, which explains why all three implementations achieve the same performance. The search overhead is approximately 40 per cent in this case.

The alpha-beta program spends most of its time in the recursive procedure `AlphaBeta`, which does not use any data structures. As a result, the program does not suffer from the overhead of data structures incurred by the prototype implementations. The absolute speed of the Orca program therefore is comparable to that of the C/Amoeba version.

The speedup achieved by the Orca implementations is only slightly better than the speedup of the Amoeba implementation of Section 2.4. In contrast to TSP, the Orca and Amoeba implementations of alpha-beta have the same search overhead. In the parallel alpha-beta algorithm, worker processes cannot return any intermediate results. Each worker must search an entire subtree and then return the value of its root node.

The speedup obtained by alpha-beta search is far from linear. This is not surprising, since the algorithm is hard to parallelize. The speedup is comparable to those reported by other authors, summarized in [Bal and Van Renesse, 1986].

7.6   Successive overrelaxation

Successive overrelaxation (SOR) is an iterative method for solving discretized Laplace equations on a grid [Stoer and Bulirsch, 1983]. The sequential SOR algorithm works as follows. During each iteration, the algorithm considers all nonboundary points of the grid. For each point, SOR first computes the average value of its four neighbours. Next, it determines the new value of the point through the following correction:

$$Gnew[r,c] = G[r,c] + \omega \times (av - G[r,c])$$

where *av* is the average value of the four neighbours and ω is the so-called *relaxation parameter* [Stoer and Bulirsch, 1983]. The entire process terminates if, during the current iteration, no single point has been changed by more than a certain quantity.

Parallel implementations of SOR have been described in several research papers [Butler *et al.*, 1986; Chase *et al.*, 1989]. The SOR program described below is based on the parallel Red/Black SOR algorithm used for the Amber system [Chase *et al.*, 1989]. This algorithm treats the grid as a draughtboard and alternately updates all black points and all red points. As each point only has neighbours of the opposite colour, each update phase can easily be parallelized. The grid can be partitioned among the available processors, which can all update different points of the same colour in parallel.

7.6.1   Parallel SOR in Orca

As explained in the Amber paper, the distribution of the grid among the processors is of vital importance to the performance of parallel SOR. We have used a similar distribution scheme as in the Amber implementation. The grid is partitioned into regions, each containing several rows of the grid. Each region is assigned to a separate processor. Alternative distribution schemes of the grid would be less efficient. Putting the entire grid in a single shared object would create a severe bottleneck, since the grid is read and written very frequently. The other extreme, putting each point of the grid in a separate shared object, is also inefficient, since it would introduce a very high communication overhead.

With the above distribution scheme, all processors repeatedly compute new values for the points in their region, based on the current value of the point and its four neighbours. For a point on the upper or lower boundary of a region, however, one of the neighbours is stored on a remote processor. The processors, therefore, have to exchange the values of their boundary points before each iteration. This is illustrated in Figure 7.7.

The program (see Appendix E.6) uses one *slave* process per processor. The slaves execute a number of iterations. Each iteration consists of two phases, one for the black points and one for the red points of the grid. Before each phase, a slave sends

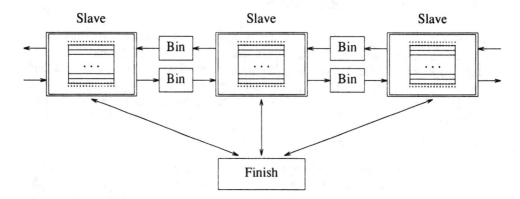

Figure 7.7 *Structure of the Orca implementation of successive overrelaxation. Each slave process maintains some portion of the rows of the grid. The dotted boxes are copies of the last row of the left neighbour and the first row of the right neighbour. These rows are transferred through shared 'bin' objects. The processes also communicate through a shared object 'finish' of type 'PollSequence', to decide when the convergence criterion has been reached.*

its first row to its left neighbour and its last row to its right neighbour. Next, it waits for the last row of its left neighbour and the first row of its right neighbour. Subsequently, it updates those points in its regions that have the right colour.

The exchange of the rows is implemented through shared objects of type RowBin, which is an instantiation of the generic type GenericBin (see Appendix E.1). Basically, a bin object is a message buffer capable of holding a single message, in this case a row of the grid. The put operation on a bin blocks while the bin is full; the get operation blocks while the bin is empty.

As mentioned above, the SOR program should continue updating points until each point has reached a stable value, approximately the average value of its four neighbours. Each slave process therefore keeps track of the maximum change of all points in its region. If, at the end of an iteration, the slaves agree that no point has changed by more than a certain value (the constant stopdiff), the program terminates.

Distributed agreement is obtained through an object of type PollSequence (see Appendix E.3). This object mimics a sequence of polls. Every process participating in the polls may bring out one vote per iteration. If all processes vote 'yes', the result of a poll is 'yes'; a 'no' vote, on the other hand, is regarded as a veto, so the result of the poll is negative. It is assumed that a successful poll terminates the entire sequence.

All slave processes share an object finish of type PollSequence. This object is used as follows. After each iteration, a slave determines if any point in its own region has changed by more than the value stopdiff. If so, it votes 'no', else it votes 'yes.' Subsequently, the slave waits until a global decision has been made. The outcome of the poll for the current iteration is available as soon as either one slave has voted 'no' or all slaves have voted 'yes'. In the first case, the slave continues with the next iteration. In the second case, each slave prints the final value of its local region and then terminates. This type of synchronization is similar to barrier synchronization [Almasi and Gottlieb, 1989].

7.6.2 Performance

The SOR program described above is a difficult one for Orca, since it mainly uses point-to-point message-passing communication. Apart from the termination protocol, each processor only communicates with its left and right neighbour. The multicast RTS therefore is at clear disadvantage, since it uses multicast messages throughout.

The Amoeba RTS initially stores all bin objects on the processor that executes OrcaMain, since this process created the objects. The objects will not be replicated, because they only have write operations. The RTS will soon detect that each of these objects is only being used by two processors, so it will migrate the object to one of them. From then on, the program behaves very much as if it were implemented using straight message-passing. It achieves a speedup of almost 9 on 10 processors (see Figure 7.8).

The multicast RTS, on the other hand, replicates all shared objects on all processors. If, for example, one processor wants to send a row to its left neighbour, all processors will receive the put operation and apply it to their local copies of the bin. Despite this inefficiency, the multicast RTS still achieves a remarkably good performance, due to the highly efficient multicast protocol being used. The speedup on 10 processors is approximately 8.5. The speedup is comparable to that of the Amber implementation, which runs on a collection of Firefly multiprocessor workstations [Chase *et al.*, 1989].

7.7 A chess problem solver

The largest application that has been implemented so far in Orca is a chess problem solver, called Oracol [Elias, 1989]. The program consists of approximately 2500 lines of code.

Oracle is capable of solving two kinds of chess problem: mate combinations and tactical wins. In the first case, it does an exhaustive search, ignoring possible material gains, and terminates only after finding a mate combination. In the second case, it is less greedy and simply tries to find any combination that wins material. In principle, the program could also be used as a chess tournament program, except that its evaluation function is heavily biased towards material gains. For example, it does not look at positional characteristics, such as open lines and pawn structures.

The search algorithm of Oracol is based on alpha-beta with iterative deepening and the quiescence search heuristic [Marsland, 1986]. It starts with a 1-ply deep search. If it does not find a winning combination within 1 ply, it continues with a 3-ply deep search, using the results of the 1-ply search for ordering the moves. If the 3-ply

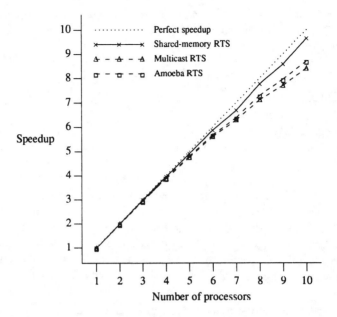

Figure 7.8 *Measured speedups for successive overrelaxation, using a grid with 80 columns and 242 rows.*

search fails too, the next iteration will search 5 plies, using the results of the 3-ply search as move-ordering heuristic, and so on. The program terminates as soon as it finds a mate combination or a material win – whatever it was looking for – or if the search depth exceeds a certain threshold.

Parallelism in Oracol is based on tree splitting, so different processors may search different parts of the tree in parallel. Unlike the parallel tree search program of Section 7.5, however, the distribution of the tree among the processors is done dynamically. Rather than splitting the tree at a fixed depth, Oracol decides at run time which parts of the tree will be searched in parallel. It uses several heuristics for this decision. For example, it restricts the number of tree splittings at the top level. Since the search tree is ordered, it is unlikely that the best move will be found in the rightmost subtrees. Thus, it does not pay off to search these trees in parallel.

Oracol uses two important heuristics for decreasing the number of nodes that have to be searched: the *killer table* and the *transposition table* [Marsland, 1986]. The killer table contains so-called *killer moves*, which are moves that cause a cutoff in the tree. The underlying idea is that if a move causes a cutoff in a certain position on level N of the tree, it is likely to cause cutoffs in other positions on level N too. Therefore, it is fruitful to try killer moves first.

The second shared data structure is the transposition table. This table is used as follows. During the search, the same board position may be encountered several times, since different sequences of moves can lead to the same position. Therefore, it sometimes is useful to store the result of a subtree evaluation in a table. If the same board position is encountered again later during the search, the value of that position can simply be looked up in the table, without doing any search. The time saved depends on the depth of the subtree and on how many times the table entry can be reused. To be effective, the time saved must exceed the overhead of managing the table.

In a parallel chess program like Oracle, the killer and transposition table can either be implemented as local tables or as shared data structures. With local tables, each processor has its own table. Unfortunately, local tables are not very effective, because, for example, a processor may evaluate positions that other processors already have analyzed and stored in their local transposition tables.

The alternative is to use global tables implemented as shared objects. Global tables will cause a higher reduction of the search overhead than local tables. On the other hand, they will also be more expensive to manage, since extra interprocess communication will be needed. Whether or not global tables are superior to local tables therefore depends on the costs of shared data. For Oracol, we have determined that, especially for the killer heuristic, global tables are more efficient than local tables [Elias, 1989].

7.8   Discussion

We have described several Orca applications that achieve significant speedups on a distributed system. For matrix multiplication, the all-pairs shortest paths problem, branch-and-bound, and successive overrelaxation, the multicast RTS achieves a speedup between 8 and 10 on a 10-processor system. As expected, for game tree search and chess problem solving the speedups are lower. Such applications are hard to parallelize efficiently, because of the high search overheads.

It is difficult to make a fair comparison between the relative efficiency of Orca and other languages, since we do not have distributed implementations of any other languages. For two applications, branch-and-bound and alpha-beta search, we have compared the speedup of the Orca program with a similar C program implemented directly on top of Amoeba. The Amoeba programs use RPC, which is the basic communication primitive of many languages for distributed programming described in Chapter 4. For branch-and-bound, the Orca implementation is more efficient, mainly because the RPC model makes it very difficult for processes to share data. The Amoeba and Orca implementations of alpha-beta search achieve comparable speedups. The Amoeba version is slightly less efficient.

The usefulness of shared objects for obtaining efficient programs has been demonstrated by at least three of the applications. ASP uses a shared object for transmitting rows of the distance matrix from one processor to all the others. TSP is an extreme example, since it uses a shared object that is read many times and changed only a few times. The chess problem solver uses two heuristics, the killer table and transposition table, that are most effective if they use shared data structures.

CHAPTER 8
_____

Conclusions

Distributed computing systems consisting of many autonomous computers, each with their own private memory, are becoming commonplace due to their good price/performance ratio. The issue of how to program a single application that uses many such machines is still open. In the preceding chapters we have studied this issue carefully. We have discussed distributed programming using only support from the operating system and we have surveyed the state of the art in languages for distributed programming. We have made a contribution to the latter area by presenting a new model and language for distributed programming and by studying the implementation, usage, and performance of the language.

As explained in the introduction, the goal of our research has been to ease the implementation of distributed applications. More specifically, we have tried to design a language that is expressive, type secure, reasonably efficient, and portable, that has simple semantics, and leads to readable programs. Below, we will evaluate these issues, draw some conclusions, and look at topics for future research.

8.1 Evaluation of the research goals

In Section 1.5.1, we described several goals for our research. In this section, we will discuss to what extent these goals have been met.

8.1.1 Expressiveness

The most important requirement for our language was the support for a high-level model that eased the expression of parallelism, communication, and synchronization. We will look at these issues in turn.

Parallelism in Orca is based on explicit process creation. At least for the programs discussed in Chapter 7, this mechanism is adequate. Most programs use one master process for distributing work and one slave process per processor for doing the work.

The work distribution can either be determined before creating the slave processes (as in the matrix multiplication, ASP, and SOR programs) or dynamically, using the replicated worker style (as in the TSP and alpha-beta programs). So, large-grain parallelism is easy to express in Orca. For applications with fine-grain parallelism, the process model is less suitable.

Orca hides the physical communication of the distributed hardware by presenting a communication model based on logically shared data. Processes do not communicate with each other directly, but interact through shared objects. For many applications, this model is easier to use than message passing. In addition, programs using logically shared data frequently have good performance, even on systems without physical shared memory.

The best example supporting these claims is parallel branch-and-bound, which is hard to implement efficiently using message passing, but almost trivial to implement using logically shared data. For one parallel branch-and-bound application, the travelling salesman problem, the distributed Orca program is almost 10 times faster on 10 CPUs as on one CPU. Another good example is the chess problem solver Oracol, which uses several shared data structures. The availability of logically shared data makes an efficient implementation of these shared data structures easy.

The support for logically shared data is, of course, not needed for every application. For some applications, message passing will still be the best fit. If required, however, message passing can be simulated with objects, as shown by the SOR program.

Condition synchronization is expressed through operations that block. This mechanism has been used in several examples of Chapter 7 (e.g. in the RowCollection objects for ASP, in the GenericJobQueue object for branch-and-bound and alpha-beta search, and in the GenericBin and PollSequence objects for SOR). In our experience, the mechanism is very easy to use. A PollSequence object, for example, essentially implements a barrier synchronization, without the users being aware of how it is implemented. The users invoke simple operations like vote and AwaitDecision, and the implementation of the object type takes care of synchronization.

Mutual exclusion synchronization in our language is hidden from the programmer, by executing operations indivisibly. In other words, locking of (logically) shared data is done implicitly, at the object level. Since users can write their own operations, arbitrary indivisible actions on a single object can easily be defined. We feel this is a higher level of abstraction than that supported by most other mutual exclusion mechanisms.

Perhaps the most controversial design decision regarding expressiveness is the lack of support for indivisible operations on multiple shared objects. Our experiences so far indicate this decision can be justified. None of the applications we have studied need such operations. The design and implementation of the language would be greatly complicated by adding them and it is doubtful whether the same efficiency could be obtained at all. Moreover, applications that do need indivisible multi-object operations can obtain this behaviour by constructing locks for sequences of operations.

8.1.2   Simple semantics

In general, we feel that the semantics of Orca are very simple. The effects of operations are well defined. Although the underlying implementations do a lot of trickery and may replicate or migrate objects on their own initiative, this is not reflected in the semantics. In contrast, systems such as the problem-oriented shared memory make replication visible to the programmers and leave it up to them to worry about the semantics.

The sequential and distributed constructs of Orca are integrated in a clean way. For example, similar mechanisms are used for passing parameters locally to procedures and remotely to processes and operations. In particular, complex data structures can be transmitted to remote machines without any programming overhead. No restrictions exist on the kind of data structure that may be passed.

The principle of orthogonality has been used with care. For example, Orca supports a single mechanism for abstract data typing, which can be used for creating shared as well as nonshared objects. On the other hand, we have deviated from the principle whenever we felt justified. The three parameter mechanisms mentioned above, for example, are similar but not identical. Restrictions are imposed on the parameters of processes – no output parameters or return value – and operations – no shared parameters. Removing these restrictions would improve orthogonality, but would complicate the language and its implementation.

8.1.3   Type security

The importance of having a type secure language has been emphasized several times in this book. For sequential programs, insecure constructs, such as unchecked array references or explicit deallocation of memory, frequently lead to subtle bugs that are very hard to find. For distributed programs, security is even more important, since testing and debugging of such programs is more difficult than for sequential programs.

All data types used in Orca are secure. All references to the elements of arrays and the fields of unions are checked at run time. Memory management in Orca is also done in a controlled way. Complex data structures are not built out of chunks of memory connected through pointers, as in many other languages. Rather, Orca has a graph type for defining such data structures. Graphs can be expanded or shrunk dynamically, by adding or deleting nodes. Both operations are type secure and referencing a node that has just been deleted will always result in a run-time error.

Undoubtedly, security has its price. The run-time checks will increase the access costs of data structures. At least part of this overhead can be removed by an optimizer. If an array variable is traversed using a **for** loop, for example, its bounds need not be checked before each access. In this case, the overhead can be reduced to some simple tests before the loop. It remains to be seen how expensive security is after such optimizations have been implemented.

8.1.4 Efficiency

The applications described in Chapter 7 show significant speedups. For most programs, the multicast RTS is highly efficient, even though it uses a very simple replication strategy. This shows that, at least for some applications, our approach is successful. The multicast RTS could be improved further to deal more efficiently with applications that only use point-to-point messages. For successive overrelaxation, for example, the selective replication scheme of the Amoeba RTS is more efficient.

Most (but not all) Orca programs are slower than equivalent programs written in C. There are two reasons for this difference. First, Orca does extensive run-time checking, as discussed above. Second, the current Orca implementations are prototypes that still can be improved substantially. Despite these deficiencies, absolute speedups over sequential C programs have been obtained with a relatively low number of processors.

8.1.5 Readability

Readability is very much a subjective issue. Still, we feel that Orca encourages the development of readable programs, because of its highly modular structure. Orca programs consist of collections of modules and abstract data type definitions. Each such unit consists of a specification part and an implementation part. Their users only deal with the specification part and need not worry about implementation details.

Modularization makes programs easy to understand. For example, the declaration of an identifier used in a given procedure can easily be located. It is either declared in the current procedure or declared or imported at the beginning of the current module. Also, modularization encourages the development of modules that can be reused in other programs. The job queue object type, for example, has been used in several Orca programs. The possibility of defining generic modules or object types even further increases reusability.

8.1.6 Portability

We have described three implementations of Orca on two different systems. Orca is most suitable for distributed systems that support multicast. The implementation on top of Amoeba, which is based on point-to-point communication, achieves a good performance for some applications. For other applications (e.g. ASP), it is far less efficient than the multicast implementation. Thus far, we do not have experience in porting the language to other types of distributed systems, such as hypercubes or Transputer grids.

Although Orca has not been designed for shared-memory multiprocessors, it is easy enough to implement the language on such architectures. For many applications, the efficiency of the shared memory implementation is quite satisfactory. Our experience with parallel branch-and-bound, however, indicates that the implementation still can be improved substantially. Also, for some fine-grained parallel applications, the locking mechanism used by the shared-memory RTS will be too coarse.

8.2   Conclusions and future research

The final judgement of a new programming language should be left to its users rather than its designers. Nonetheless, we believe most of the research goals stated in Chapter 1 have been met. Orca has turned out to be an expressive yet simple language, and it is useful for implementing a broad range of parallel applications on at least one type of distributed system.

The distributed system that we have used to substantiate the latter claim consists of multiple processors connected through a broadcast network. This type of system is somewhat outside the main stream of research on parallel and distributed computing. Almasi and Gottlieb, for example, state that 'communication in such systems is currently too slow to allow close cooperation on one job' [Almasi and Gottlieb, 1989]. We dispute this statement. As we (and others) have shown, many interesting problems can be solved in parallel on such systems.

In the future, we intend to continue our research in several areas. We will first work on new applications. We already have done some initial work on numerical algorithms (e.g. fast fourier transformation) and on an implementation of Finkel and Manber's DIB package [Finkel and Manber, 1987]. We will also look at other classes of distributed applications besides parallel ones.

Based on our experiences in using Orca, we will further evaluate the language. One issue that needs more attention is I/O, which currently is present in only rudimentary form. This issue is not very crucial for the parallel applications we have discussed, but for other classes of distributed applications it may be more important. Another language issue that we may look into is the typing mechanism (e.g. the usage of polymorphism instead of generic types).

A fault-tolerant implementation of Orca is another topic for future research. One can envision using replicated objects for increasing fault tolerance as well as decreasing the access costs of shared objects. A major implementation problem still left open, however, is how to restart processes after processor failures.

Another topic for future research is optimization of Orca programs. The issue of optimization is very important, because of our design principle to keep the language simple and rely on optimizations for obtaining efficiency. We have identified several areas in which the implementations can be improved, such as run-time checking, abstract data types, and storage management. Also, the replication and migration algorithms used in the implementations will need further attention.

Finally, we will do more comparisons between our approach and those of other languages discussed in the book. A very large number of models and languages for distributed programming have emerged during the past decades. We have experiences in using some of these languages, but we plan to do a more thorough comparison. We intend to implement a number of distributed applications in several languages, based on different models, and determine the advantages and disadvantages of each model.

Matrix Multiplication

A.1 Specification of object type IntObject

```
object specification IntObject;
    operation value(): integer;          # return value
    operation assign(v: integer);        # assign new value
    operation min(v: integer);           # value := min(value, v)
    operation inc();                      # indivisibly increment value
    operation dec();                      # indivisibly decrement value
    operation AwaitValue(v: integer);    # wait for certain value
end;
```

A.2 Implementation of object type IntObject

```
object implementation IntObject;
    x: integer; # internal data

    operation value(): integer;
    begin
        return x;     # return current value
    end;

    operation assign(v: integer);
    begin
        x := v;      # assign new value
    end;

    operation min(v: integer);
    begin
        guard v < x do     # if new value is lower, assign it to x
```

```
            x := v;
        od;
        guard v >= x do      # else do nothing
        od;
    end;

    operation inc();
    begin
        x +:= 1;    # increment
    end;

    operation dec();
    begin
        x -:= 1;    # decrement
    end;

    operation AwaitValue(v: integer);
    begin
        guard x = v do od;  # block until value equals v
    end;
begin
    x := 0; # initialize objects to zero
end;
```

A.3   Implementation of module MatrixMult

```
module implementation MatrixMult;
    import IntObject;

    const N = 250;  # size of the matrices
    type RowType = array [integer] of integer;
    type matrix = array[integer] of RowType;


    function DotProduct(row, col: integer; A, B: matrix): integer;
        i : integer;
        sum: integer;
    begin   # Compute the dot product of a row of A and a column of B.
        sum := 0;
        for i in 1 .. N do
            sum +:= A[row][i] * B[i][col];
        od;
        return sum;
    end;


    function ComputeRow(row: integer; A, B: matrix): RowType;
        col: integer;
        R: RowType[1..N];
```

```
begin   # Compute one row of the result matrix
    for col in 1 .. N do
        R[col] := DotProduct(row, col, A, B);
    od;
    return R;
end;


function InitMatrices(A, B: out matrix[1..N][1..N]);
    r, c: integer;
begin
    # Initialize A and B matrices.
    # We use arbitrary values for testing the program
    for r in 1.. N do
        for c in 1..N do
            A[r][c] := r+c;
            B[r][c] := r-c;
        od;
    od;
end;


# Description of slave processes
process slave(lb, ub: integer; turn: shared IntObject);
    row, col: integer;
    A, B: matrix;              # the matrices to be multiplied
    Result: matrix[lb..ub]; # part of result matrix
begin
    InitMatrices(A,B);  # initialize A and B
    for row in lb .. ub do
        Result[row] := ComputeRow(row, A, B);
    od;
    turn$AwaitValue(lb);     # Wait until it's my turn to print results
    for row in lb .. ub do
        for col in 1 .. N do
            Write(" ", Result[row][col]);
        od;
        WriteLine();
    od;
    turn$assign(ub+1);  # Allow next slave to print
end;


# Description of master process; this is the first process to be run
process OrcaMain();
    turn: IntObject;    # used to coordinate printing
    nslaves: integer;   # number of slaves
    i, lb, ub: integer;
begin
    nslaves := NCPUS(); # determine number of processors
    turn$assign(1);     # initialize turn object
    if nslaves > N then nslaves := N; fi;
        # useless to have more than N processors
    lb := 1;    # Distribute the work among the slaves. Take into
                # account that N need not be a multiple of nslaves.
```

```
    for i in 0 .. nslaves-1 do
            # The size of the next job is the number of rows left (N-lb+1)
            # divided by the number of slaves left (nslaves-i).
            ub := lb + (N-lb+1) / (nslaves-i) - 1;
            fork slave(lb, ub, turn)  on (i);          # start slave on CPU i
            lb := ub+1;
        od;
    end;
end;
```

The All-pairs Shortest Paths Problem

B.1 Specification of module AspTypes

```
module specification AspTypes;
    const N = 200;  # number of nodes in the graph
    type RowType = array[integer] of integer;
end;
```

B.2 Specification of object type RowCollection

```
object specification RowCollection;
    from AspTypes import RowType;

    # Object used to exchange row k before each iteration
    operation AddRow(iter: integer; R: RowType);
        # Add the row for the given iteration number
    operation AwaitRow(iter: integer): RowType;
        # Wait until the row for the given iteration is available,
        # then return it.
end;
```

B.3 Implementation of object type RowCollection

```
object implementation RowCollection;
    from AspTypes import N, RowType; # N is the number of nodes in the graph

    # The local data of objects of type RowCollection consist
    # of an array of rows, one row per iteration. Initially,
```

```
# each row is an empty array.

type collection = array[integer 1..N] of RowType;
tab: collection;      # the local data of RowCollection objects

operation AddRow(iter: integer; R: RowType);
begin
    tab[iter] := R; # fill in the row for given iteration
end;


operation AwaitRow(iter: integer): RowType;
begin
    # wait until row "iter" is defined, i.e. tab[iter] is non-empty.
    guard lb(tab[iter]) < ub(tab[iter]) do
        return tab[iter];     # return the requested row
    od;
end;
end;
```

B.4 Implementation of module asp

```
module implementation asp;
    import RowCollection;
    from AspTypes import N, RowType; # N is the number of nodes in the graph
    import IntObject;    # The IntObject type is shown in Appendix A.1

    type DistTab = array[integer] of RowType;  # table with distances


    function DoIteration(C: shared DistTab; RowK: RowType; lb, ub, k: integer);
        i, j, tmp: integer;
    begin  # update the values of rows C[lb] .. C[ub] for iteration k.
        for i in lb .. ub do
            if i /= k then  # Skip C[k], as it won't change.
                for j in 1 .. N do
                    # See if path i->k->j is better than  current path i->j.
                    tmp := C[i][k] + RowK[j];   # i->k + k->j
                    if tmp < C[i][j] then
                        C[i][j] := tmp;
                    fi;
                od;
            fi;
        od;
    end;


    function ComputeRows(
```

```
        C: shared DistTab;        # Table with distances
        RowkColl: shared RowCollection; # used for transmitting row k
        lb, ub: integer);         # lower and upper bound of my rows

    k: integer;
    RowK: RowType;

begin
    for k in 1 .. N do  # do N iterations
        if (k >= lb) and (k <= ub) then
            # I have row k; add it to shared object RowkColl.
            RowK := C[k];
            RowkColl$AddRow(k, RowK);
        else
            # Someone else is computing row k; wait for it.
            RowK := RowkColl$AwaitRow(k);
        fi;
        DoIteration(C, RowK, lb, ub, k); # execute iteration k
    od;
end;


function InitializeTable(lb, ub: integer; C: out DistTab[lb..ub][1..N]);
    i, j: integer;
begin
    # For testing, initialize distances matrix with arbitrary values.
    for i in lb .. ub do
        for j in 1..N do
            if i = j then
                C[i][j] := 0;
            else
                C[i][j] := i+j;
            fi;
        od;
    od;
end;


# Description of slave processes.
process slave(
        RowkColl : shared RowCollection;# used for transmitting row k.
        lb, ub: integer;              # handle rows between lb and ub
        turn: shared IntObject);      # used for synchronizing output

    C: DistTab;        # table with distances between nodes
    i,j: integer;
begin
    InitializeTable(lb, ub, C); # initialize distances table
    ComputeRows(C, RowkColl, lb, ub); # do real work
    turn$AwaitValue(lb);  # Wait until it's my turn to print results
    for i in lb .. ub do
        for j in 1 .. N do
```

```
                Write(C[i][j], "  ");
            od;
            WriteLine();
        od;
        turn$assign(ub+1);   # Allow next slave to print
    end;


    # Description of master process
    process OrcaMain();
        RowkColl: RowCollection; # shared object for sending row k
        i: integer;
        nslaves: integer;    # number of slave processors
        lb, ub: integer;     # lower and upper bound
        turn: IntObject;     # shared object used to coordinate printing
    begin
        turn$assign(1);      # initialize turn
        nslaves := NCPUS();  # number of CPUs available
        if nslaves > N then nslaves := N; fi;
            # useless to have more than N processors
        lb := 1;    # distribute work among slave processors:
        for i in 0 .. nslaves-1 do
            ub := lb + (N-lb+1) / (nslaves-i) - 1;
            # Fork one slave process on each available CPU
            fork slave(RowkColl, lb, ub, turn) on(i);
            lb := ub+1;
        od;
    end;
end;
```

APPENDIX C

The Travelling Salesman Problem

C.1 Specification of module TspTypes

```
module specification TspTypes;
    # distance table, sorted by nearest-city-first heuristic
    type pair =
        record
            ToCity: integer;   # to which city
            dist: integer;     # distance to that city
        end;
    type DistArray = array[integer] of pair;
    type DistTab = array[integer] of DistArray;

    # job type:
    type PathType = array[integer] of integer;
    type JobType =
        record
            len: integer;   # length of partial route
            path: PathType; # the partial route itself
        end;
end;
```

C.2 Specification of generic object type GenericJobQueue

```
generic (type T)
object specification GenericJobQueue;
    operation AddJob(job: T);    # add a job to the tail of the queue
    operation NoMoreJobs();      # invoked when no more jobs will be added
    operation GetJob(job: out T): boolean;
        # Fetch a job from the head of the queue. This operation
        # fails if the queue is empty and NoMoreJobs has been invoked.
```

```
end generic;
```

C.3   Implementation of generic object type GenericJobQueue

```
generic
object implementation GenericJobQueue;
    type ItemName = nodename of queue;
    type queue =
        graph  # a queue is represented as a linear list
            first, last: ItemName;  # first/last element of queue
        nodes
            next: ItemName;         # next element in queue
            data: T;                # data contained by this element
        end;

    done: boolean;  # set to true if NoMoreJobs has been invoked.
    Q: queue;       # the queue itself

    operation AddJob(job: T);
        p: ItemName;
    begin  # add a job to the tail of the queue
        p := addnode(Q);       # add a new node to Q, return its name in p
        Q[p].data := job;      # fill in data field of the new node
        if Q.first = NIL then  # Is it the first node?
            Q.first := p;      # yes; assign it to global data field
        else
            Q[Q.last].next := p;  # no; set its next field
        fi;
        Q.last := p;           # Assign to 'last' global data field
    end;

    operation NoMoreJobs();
    begin   # Invoked to indicate that no more jobs will be added
        done := true;
    end;

    operation GetJob(job: out T): boolean;
        p: ItemName;
    begin   # Try to fetch a job from the queue
        guard Q.first /= NIL do   # A job is available
            p := Q.first;         # Remove it from the queue
            Q.first := Q[p].next;
            if Q.first = NIL then Q.last := NIL; fi;
            job := Q[p].data;     # assign to output parameter
            deletenode(Q,p);      # delete the node from the queue
            return true;          # succeeded in fetching a job
        od;
        guard done and (Q.first = NIL) do
            return false;         # All jobs have been done
```

```
        od;
    end;


begin    # Initialization code for JobQueues ; executed on object creation.
    done := false;  # initialize done to false
end generic;
```

C.4   Implementation of module tsp

```
module implementation tsp;
    from TspTypes import DistTab, DistArray, pair, PathType, JobType;
    import IntObject;
        # Instantiate the GenericJobQueue type:
    object TspQueue = new GenericJobQueue(JobType);

    const NrTowns = 12;  # number of towns
    const MaxHops = 3;   # search depth of manager

    function present(city, hops: integer; path: PathType): boolean;
        i: integer;
    begin    # See if a given city is present on a given path
        for i in 1..hops do
            if path[i] = city then return true; fi;
        od;
        return false;
    end;

    function tsp(
                hops: integer;               # number of cities in route so far
                len: integer;                # length of route so far
                path: shared PathType;       # route so far
                minimum: shared IntObject;   # length of best path
                distance: DistTab);          # table with distances

        city, dist, me, i: integer;
    begin
        # Search a TSP subtree that starts with initial route 'path'.
        # If partial route is longer than current best full route
        # then forget about this partial route.
        if len >= minimum$value() then return; fi;      # cut-off
        if hops = NrTowns then
            # We found a full route better than current best route.
            # Update minimum, using indivisible 'min' operation.
            minimum$min(len);
        else
            # 'path' really is a partial route.  Call tsp recursively
            # for each subtree. Try all cities that are not on the initial
            # path,  in 'nearest-city-first' order.
            me := path[hops];  # Last city of path
```

```
        for i in 1.. NrTowns do
            city := distance[me][i].ToCity;
            if not present(city, hops, path) then
                # 'city' not yet on current path
                path[hops+1] := city;
                dist := distance[me][i].dist;
                tsp(hops+1, len+dist, path, minimum, distance);
            fi;
        od;
    fi;
end;


function distributor(
        hops: integer;          # number of cities in route so far
        len: integer;           # length of route so far
        path: shared PathType;  # route so far
        q: shared TspQueue;     # shared job queue
        distance: DistTab);     # table with distances

    city, dist, me, i: integer;
begin
    # Generate all jobs for the workers.  A job is an initial path of
    # 'MaxHops' hops.  Also keep track of length of the initial path.
    if hops = MaxHops then
        q$AddJob(JobType:{len, path}); # send this path to workers
    else
        me := path[hops];
        for i in 1.. NrTowns do
            city := distance[me][i].ToCity;
            if not present(city, hops, path) then
                path[hops+1] := city;
                dist := distance[me][i].dist;
                distributor(hops+1, len+dist, path, q, distance);
            fi;
        od;
    fi;
end;


function GenerateJobs(q: shared TspQueue; distance: DistTab);
    path: PathType[1..NrTowns];
begin
    path[1] := 1;   # start with city 1
    distributor(1, 0, path, q, distance);       # generate jobs
    q$NoMoreJobs(); # all jobs have been generated now
end;


function InitDistance(distance: out DistTab);
begin
    # initialize distance table
    # DistTab :=  ...
end;
```

```
# Description of the worker processes.
process worker(
        minimum: shared IntObject;          # length current best path
        q: shared TspQueue;                 # job queue
        distance: DistTab;                  # distances between cities
        WorkersActive: shared IntObject);   # used for termination


    job: JobType;
begin
    while q$GetJob(job) do   # while there are jobs to do:
        tsp(MaxHops, job.len, job.path, minimum, distance);
    od;
    WorkersActive$dec();    # this worker becomes inactive
end;



# Description of the manager process
process OrcaMain();
    minimum: IntObject;      # length of current best path (shared object)
    q: TspQueue;             # the job queue (shared object)
    i: integer;
    distance: DistTab;           # table with distances between cities
    WorkersActive: IntObject;    # number of active workers (shared object)
begin
    minimum$assign(MAX(integer));       # initialize minimum to infinity
    WorkersActive$assign(NCPUS());      # initialize number of workers
    InitDistance(distance);             # initialize distance table
    for i in 1.. NCPUS() - 1 do
        # fork one worker per processor, except current processor
        fork worker(minimum, q, distance, WorkersActive) on(i);
    od;
    GenerateJobs(q, distance); # main thread generates the jobs
    fork worker(minimum, q, distance, WorkersActive) on(0);
        # jobs have been generated; fork a worker on this cpu too
    WorkersActive$AwaitValue(0);    # wait until workers have finished
    WriteLine("minimum = ", minimum$value());  # length of shortest path
    end;
end;
```

Alpha-Beta Search

D.1 Specification of object type SearchTree

```
object specification SearchTree;
    from Game import board; # representation of a board position

    type Node;  # Opaque type; the actual type is defined in impl. part
    function NullNode(): Node;  # returns NIL node
    operation ReadNode(n: Node; b: out board; alpha, beta: out integer);
        # Fetch information stored in the given node
    operation AddNode(
            parent: Node; b: board; WhichSon: integer;
            nsons: integer): Node;
        # Add a new node to the tree with the given parent and board.
        # Its alpha and beta are initialized to -Infinity and +Infinity.
    operation PropagateResult(n: Node; score: integer);
        # Propagate the value computed for a leaf node to
        # other nodes of the tree.
    operation RootValue(): integer;
        # Fetch the alpha value of the root node.
end;
```

D.2 Implementation of object type SearchTree

```
object implementation SearchTree;
    from Game import board, Nsons;   # Nsons is the fan-out of the tree

    const Inf = 1000000000;          # Infinity
    type Node = nodename of tree;    # implementation of opaque type 'Node'
```

```
type tree =
  graph
    root: Node;  # root node of the search tree
  nodes
    b:  board;         # the board position
    alpha, beta,       # alpha and beta values of this position
    nsons: integer;    # number of children still to be analyzed
    parent: Node;      # The parent of this node
    sons:   array[integer 1.. Nsons] of Node;   # The children
  end;

t: tree;    # The internal data of objects of type SearchTree


function NullNode(): Node;
begin
    return NIL;
end;


operation ReadNode(n: Node; b: out board; alpha, beta: out integer);
begin    # Return the contents of a given node
    b := t[n].b;           # board position
    alpha := t[n].alpha;   # alpha
    beta := t[n].beta;     # beta
end;


operation AddNode(
        parent: Node;        # parent of the new node
        b: board;            # board position of the new node
        WhichSon: integer;   # new node is WhichSon'th son of parent
        nsons: integer): Node;  # number of sons of new node
    n: Node;
begin    # Add a new node with the given contents to the tree
    n := addnode(t);    # add a new node to the tree
    t[n].b := b; t[n].parent := parent;
    t[n].alpha := -Inf; t[n].beta := Inf;
    t[n].nsons := nsons;
    if parent = NIL then
        t.root := n;    # this is the root node of the tree
    else
        t[parent].sons[WhichSon] := n;
    fi;
    return n;          # return newly created node
end;


function ImproveAlpha(t: shared tree; n: Node; newalpha: integer): boolean;
begin    # Try to improve the alpha value of node n
    if (t[n].alpha < t[n].beta) and (newalpha > t[n].alpha) then
        t[n].alpha := newalpha;
```

```
            return true;      # alpha has been improved
    else
            return false;     # alpha has not been improved
    fi;
end;


function ImproveBeta(t: shared tree; n: Node; newbeta: integer): boolean;
begin       # Try to improve the beta value of node n
    if (t[n].alpha < t[n].beta) and (newbeta < t[n].beta) then
            t[n].beta := newbeta;
            return true;      # beta has been improved
    else
            return false;     # beta has not been improved
    fi;
end;



function UpdateAlpha(t: shared tree; parent: Node; newalpha: integer);
    s: Node;
    i: integer;
begin       # Propagate a new alpha value downwards in the tree
    for i in 1 .. Nsons do
            s := t[parent].sons[i]; # s is the i'th son of parent
            # If the alpha of s can be improved and s has children that
            # still have to be analyzed, then propagate a new beta.
            if (s /= NIL) and (ImproveAlpha(t,s,newalpha)) and
               (t[s].nsons > 0)
            then
                UpdateBeta(t, s, -newalpha);    # go one level deeper
            fi;
    od;
end;



function UpdateBeta(t: shared tree; parent: Node; newbeta: integer);
    s: Node;
    i: integer;
begin       # Propagate a new beta value downwards in the tree
    for i in 1 .. Nsons do
            s := t[parent].sons[i];
            # If the beta of s can be improved and s has children that
            # still have to be analyzed, then propagate a new alpha.
            if (s /= NIL) and (ImproveBeta(t,s,newbeta)) and
               (t[s].nsons > 0)
            then
                UpdateAlpha(t, s, -newbeta);    # go one level deeper
            fi;
    od;
end;



function propagate(
```

```
              t: shared tree;      # The top part of the search tree
              n: Node;             # A node that has been evaluated by a worker
              score: integer);     # The score of that node

        parent: Node;
        AlphaImproved, LastSon: boolean;
    begin    # Propagate the result of node n to other nodes in the tree
        parent := t[n].parent;
        if parent /= NIL then     # if n is not the root node:
            t[parent].nsons -:= 1;  # decrement #sons to be evaluated
            LastSon := (t[parent].nsons = 0);
            AlphaImproved := ImproveAlpha(t, parent, -score);
            if AlphaImproved then
                # Update all descendents of n's parent
                UpdateBeta(t, parent, score);
            fi;

            # The result is sent to the grandparent of n if:
            # (1) n is the last son of his parent, and his parent
            #      still hasn't been pruned, or
            # (2) n's parent has just been pruned by n, as a
            #      result of improving alpha.
            # One subtle point is that ImproveAlpha(t,x,sc) always
            # fails if x has been pruned.
            if t[parent].alpha < t[parent].beta then
                if LastSon then
                    propagate(t,parent,t[parent].alpha);   # 1st case
                fi;
            elsif AlphaImproved then
                propagate(t,parent, -score);     # 2nd case
            fi;
        fi;
    end;


    operation PropagateResult(n: Node; score: integer);
    begin
        propagate(t, n, score);
    end;


    operation RootValue(): integer;
    begin    # Return alpha value of the root
        return t[t.root].alpha;
    end;
end;
```

D.3 Implementation of module ab

```
module implementation ab;
    import SearchTree;    # import operations of SearchTree
    from SearchTree import Node, NullNode;  # and its other identifiers
    from Game import board, Nsons, DoMove, StaticEvaluation;
        # The 'Game' module contains game-specific information.
    import IntObject;


    object abqueue = new GenericJobQueue(Node);
        # instantiation of generic object type defined in Appendix C.2.


    const Depth = 6;        # Total depth of the search tree
    const SplitLevel = 1;   # Number of levels to be searched by the manager.
    const WorkerLevels = Depth - SplitLevel;
        # Number of levels to be searched by the workers


    function AlphaBeta(b: board; depth, alpha, beta: integer): integer;
        i, tmp: integer;
    begin     # Do sequential alpha-beta search on a given board position
        if depth = 0 then return StaticEvaluation(b); fi; # leaf node
        for i in 1 .. Nsons do
            tmp := -AlphaBeta(DoMove(b,i), depth-1, -beta, -alpha);
            if tmp > alpha then
                alpha := tmp;   # improve alpha value
                if alpha >= beta then return alpha; fi;    # pruning
            fi;
        od;
        return alpha;
    end;


    process worker(
            t: shared SearchTree;    # shared top-part of the search tree
            q: shared abqueue;       # shared job queue
            WorkersActive: shared IntObject);      # used for termination

        n: Node;
        b: board;
        alpha, beta: integer;
        score: integer;
    begin
        while q$GetJob(n) do
            # A job identifies a node of the top part of the tree
            t$ReadNode(n, b, alpha, beta);  # read the node's info
            if alpha < beta then # pruning?
                # no; do the job by calling sequential alpha-beta
                score := AlphaBeta(b,WorkerLevels,alpha,beta);
```

```
                    t$PropagateResult(n, score);    # update rest of tree
            fi;
        od;
        WorkersActive$dec();    # this worker becomes inactive
    end;

    function GenerateTopOfTree(
            t: shared SearchTree;    # shared top-part of the search tree
            q: shared abqueue;       # job queue to store jobs in
            level: integer;          # level of current node
            b: board;                # board position of current node
            WhichSon: integer;       # current node is WhichSon'th son
            parent: Node);           # parent of current node

        n: Node;
        i: integer;
    begin
        # Generate the top part of the search tree.
        # For each leaf node, add a job to the jobqueue.
        if level < SplitLevel then
            # Interior node; add node and generate its sons recursively
            n := t$AddNode(parent, b, WhichSon, Nsons);
            for i in 1 .. Nsons do
                GenerateTopOfTree(t, q, level+1, DoMove(b,i), i, n);
            od;
        else
            # Leaf node; add node without children to the tree.
            # Also add a job to the job queue.
            n := t$AddNode(parent, b, WhichSon, 0);
            q$AddJob(n);    # generate job for leaf node
        fi;
    end;


    process OrcaMain();
        t: SearchTree;  # The top part of the search tree
        q: abqueue;     # The jobqueue
        WorkersActive: IntObject;  # Used for termination
        i: integer;
    begin
        WorkersActive$assign(NCPUS());       # Initialize number of workers
        GenerateTopOfTree(t, q, 0, 0, 0, NullNode());
        q$NoMoreJobs(); # job generation is completed now.
        for i in 0 .. NCPUS() - 1 do
            # Fork one worker per processor
            fork worker(t, q, WorkersActive) on (i);
        od;
        WorkersActive$AwaitValue(0);  # Wait until workers have finished
        WriteLine("Result = ", t$RootValue() );
            # Result is final value of the root of the tree
    end;
end;
```

Successive Overrelaxation

E.1 Specification of generic object type GenericBin

generic (**type** T)
object specification GenericBin;
   # A 'bin' is a buffer capable of holding a single item of type T.

   operation put(e: T);   # put item in the bin; block while bin is full
   operation get(e: **out** T); # fetch item from bin; block while bin is empty

end generic;

E.2 Implementation of generic object type GenericBin

generic
object implementation GenericBin;
   bin: T;   # the buffer containing the item
   empty: boolean; # indicates whether there's an item in the buffer now

   operation put(e: T);
   begin
      guard empty **do** # wait until bin is empty
         bin := e;   # put item in bin
         empty := false; # bin is no longer empty
      od;
   end;

   operation get(e: **out** T);
   begin

```
        guard not empty do   # wait until there's an item in the bin
            e := bin;         # fetch the item
            empty := true;    # bin is now empty
        od;
    end;

begin
    empty := true;   # initialization code, invoked when bin object is created
end generic;
```

E.3   Specification of object type PollSequence

```
object specification PollSequence;
    # Gallup poll consisting of a sequence of simple polls
    # If all voters say yes, the result of a simple poll is yes.
    # if anyone votes no, the result of the simple poll is 'no'

    operation init(n: integer);
        # initialize PollSequence; n is number of voters
    operation vote(iter: integer; YesOrNo: boolean);
        # bring out vote for given iteration
    operation AwaitDecision(iter: integer): boolean;
        # wait until the decision for the given iteration is available
end;
```

E.4   Implementation of object type PollSequence

```
object implementation PollSequence;

    cleared: integer;   # all polls up till 'cleared' return 'no'
    FinalIter: integer; # poll 'FinalIter' (if > 0) returns 'yes'
    votes: integer;     # number of 'yes' votes for this iteration
    nvoters: integer;   # total number of voters

    operation init(n: integer);
    begin
        nvoters := n;   # number of voters
        cleared := 0;   # no polls cleared yet
        votes := 0;     # no votes for current iteration yet
        FinalIter:= 0;  # poll has not yet been finished
    end;

    operation vote(iter: integer; YesOrNo: boolean);
    begin
        # First check if this is a vote for the current iteration. If it's
        # a vote for a previous iteration that has already been cleared,
        # ignore this vote, since it won't change the decision.
```

```
        if iter = cleared+1 then
            if YesOrNo then   # a 'yes' vote
                votes +:= 1;
                if votes = nvoters then
                    # Everyone voted 'yes'. This terminates the
                    # entire poll sequence.
                    FinalIter := iter;  # this is the final iteration
                fi;
            else  # A 'no' vote; this means a veto
                cleared +:= 1;   # this iteration is cleared now
                votes := 0;      # initialize votes for next iteration
            fi;
        fi;
    end;


    operation AwaitDecision(iter: integer): boolean;
    begin   # Wait until global decision has been reached for given iteration
        guard FinalIter = iter do
            return true;  # everyone voted 'yes' for given iteration
        od;

        guard cleared >= iter do
            return false;    # someone voted 'no' for given iteration
        od;
    end;
end;
```

E.5   Specification of module sor

```
module specification sor;

    type RowType = array[integer] of real;
    process OrcaMain();
end;
```

E.6   Implementation of module sor

```
module implementation sor;
    import PollSequence, IntObject;

    object RowBin = new GenericBin(RowType);

    const NCOL=80;    # number of columns of the grid
    const NROW=242;   # number of rows of the grid

    # We use a tolerance of 0.001
```

```
# omega and stopdiff are defined by the following equations:
#     r = 0.5 * (cos(pi/NCOL) + cos(pi/NROW));
#     om = 2 / (1 + sqrt(1-r*r));
#     stopdiff = 0.001/(2 - om);
const omega = 1.943179;      # the relaxation parameter
const stopdiff = 0.017599;   # stop criterion

const MAXCPU = 10;

type grid = array[integer] of RowType;

function NewValue(G: grid; r,c: integer): real;
begin    # compute the average value if the four neighbours
    return (G[r-1][c] + G[r+1][c] + G[r][c-1] + G[r][c+1])/4.0;
end;

function abs(x: real): real;
begin
    if x > 0.0 then
        return x;
    else
        return -x;
    fi;
end;

function DoPhase(
    G: shared grid;              # the local region of the grid
    lb, ub: integer;             # bounds of extended region
    colour: integer;                # colour of current phase
    maxdif: shared real);        # keep track of maximum change

    r, c: integer;
    Gnew, diff: real;
begin    # Update all points with the given colour in this region
    for r in lb+1 .. ub-1 do
        c := 1 + (r+colour)%2;  # start in column 1 or 2
        while c < NCOL-1 do
            Gnew := NewValue(G,r,c);
            diff := abs(Gnew-G[r][c]);  # average of neighbours
            if diff > maxdif then
                maxdif := diff;
            fi;
            G[r][c] := G[r][c] + omega*(Gnew-G[r][c]); # update point
            c +:= 2;    # move 2 columns to the right
        od;
    od;
end;

function InitLocalSection(lb, ub: integer;
            G: out grid[lb-1..ub+1][0..NCOL-1]);
    r, c: integer;
begin    # Initialize local region. Also reserve space for one extra
```

```
        # row (from neighbours) at the beginning and end of this region.
        # Points on the boundary of the (whole) grid are initialized
        # to an arbitrary value. Internal points are initialized to zero.
    for r in lb-1 .. ub+1 do
        for c in 0..NCOL-1 do
            if r = 0 then
                G[r][c] := 4.56;
            elsif r = NROW-1 then
                G[r][c] := 9.85;
            elsif c = 0 then
                G[r][c] := 7.32;
            elsif c = NCOL-1 then
                G[r][c] := 6.88;
            else
                G[r][c] := 0.0;
            fi;
        od;
    od;
end;


function PrintGrid(G: grid; lb, ub: integer);
    r,c: integer;
begin
    for r in lb..ub do
        for c in 0 .. NCOL-1 do
            Write(G[r][c], " ");
        od;
        WriteLine();
    od;
end;



process slave(
        lb, ub: integer;              # bounds of extended region
        ToLeft,
        ToRight: shared RowBin;       # bins for sending rows to neighbours
        FromLeft,
        FromRight: shared RowBin;     # bins for receiving rows
        finished: shared PollSequence;  # used for distributed termination
        WorkersActive: shared IntObject);

    section: grid;            # Current slave's part (region) of grid
    leftok, rightok: boolean;  # Leftmost/rightmost processors are special
    maxdif: real;             # Maximum change of any point in region
    colour, iter: integer;
begin
    InitLocalSection(lb, ub, section); # Initialize my region
    leftok := (lb > 0); # Do I have a left neighbour ?
    rightok := (ub < NROW-1);   # Do I have a right neighbour ?
    iter := 0;
    repeat
        iter +:= 1;
```

```
            maxdif := 0.0;
            # Each iteration has two phases, for Red/Black points
            for colour in 0..1 do
                # Send first and last row to neighbours
                if leftok  then ToLeft$put(section[lb+1]);fi;
                if rightok then ToRight$put(section[ub-1]);fi;
                # Obtain rows from neighbours
                if leftok  then FromLeft$get(section[lb]); fi;
                if rightok then FromRight$get(section[ub]);fi;
                # Do real computation
                DoPhase(section, lb, ub, colour, maxdif);
            od;
            # Bring out vote. Use veto if some points have changed too much
            finished$vote(iter, maxdif <= stopdiff);
        until finished$AwaitDecision(iter);  # Until all slaves want to quit
        PrintGrid(section, lb+1, ub-1);
            # Should actually synchronize output, as in MatrixMult and asp
        WorkersActive$dec();
    end;


    process OrcaMain();
        i, p, grain, lb: integer;
        UpperBins, LowerBins: array[integer 0 .. MAXCPU] of RowBin;
            # the shared bin objects
        finished: PollSequence; # Used for distributed termination
        WorkersActive: IntObject;
    begin
        p := NCPUS();
        if p > (NROW - 2) then p := NROW - 2; fi;
            # useless to have more than (NROW - 2) processors
        finished$init(p);   # Initialize PollSequence object
        lb := 0;
        WorkersActive$assign(p);
        for i in 0 .. p-1 do # fork slave processes
            grain := (NROW-2-lb) / (p-i);
            fork slave(lb, lb+grain+1,
                    UpperBins[i], LowerBins[i+1],
                    LowerBins[i], UpperBins[i+1],
                    finished, WorkersActive)  on(i);
            lb +:= grain;
        od;
        WorkersActive$AwaitValue(0);
    end;
end;
```

Performance of the Orca Programs

This appendix gives more detailed information on the performance measurements described in Chapter 7. For each program, we give the elapsed computation time (in seconds) and speedups on 1 to 10 processors, averaged over three runs. For the travelling salesman program and alpha-beta search we will present data for three different input sets (each of which was run three times).

Matrix multiplication

	Shared-memory RTS		Multicast RTS		Amoeba RTS	
#CPUs	Time (s)	Speedup	Time (s)	Speedup	Time (s)	Speedup
1	820.0	1.00	810.3	1.00	780.1	1.00
2	396.3	2.07	410.6	1.97	392.9	1.99
3	268.6	3.05	279.1	2.90	265.8	2.93
4	212.3	3.86	209.8	3.86	200.0	3.90
5	166.0	4.94	169.9	4.77	166.0	4.70
6	139.3	5.89	143.8	5.63	139.8	5.58
7	120.6	6.80	124.2	6.52	121.6	6.42
8	107.3	7.64	109.8	7.38	106.5	7.32
9	98.3	8.34	98.7	8.21	98.2	7.94
10	89.0	9.21	89.1	9.09	92.3	8.45

The travelling salesman problem

	Shared-memory RTS		Multicast RTS		Amoeba RTS	
	First problem					
#CPUs	Time (s)	Speedup	Time (s)	Speedup	Time (s)	Speedup
1	550.6	1.00	576.5	1.00	649.7	1.00
2	269.0	2.05	279.2	2.06	314.7	2.06
3	181.0	3.04	186.9	3.08	211.2	3.08
4	137.0	4.02	139.9	4.12	158.7	4.09
5	113.6	4.85	112.6	5.12	128.4	5.06
6	97.3	5.66	92.5	6.23	106.1	6.12
7	87.3	6.31	79.0	7.30	90.5	7.18
8	81.3	6.77	68.3	8.44	79.2	8.20
9	77.6	7.10	60.4	9.54	70.8	9.18
10	74.0	7.44	53.7	10.74	63.8	10.18

	Shared-memory RTS		Multicast RTS		Amoeba RTS	
	Second problem					
#CPUs	Time (s)	Speedup	Time (s)	Speedup	Time (s)	Speedup
1	319.6	1.00	334.2	1.00	376.6	1.00
2	161.0	1.99	168.2	1.99	189.1	1.99
3	109.3	2.92	112.7	2.97	127.7	2.95
4	83.6	3.82	85.3	3.92	97.4	3.87
5	68.3	4.68	68.0	4.91	77.2	4.88
6	59.3	5.39	56.7	5.89	65.4	5.76
7	54.0	5.92	48.9	6.83	56.0	6.73
8	50.0	6.39	43.1	7.75	49.8	7.56
9	49.0	6.52	38.9	8.59	45.7	8.24
10	47.6	6.71	35.1	9.52	41.0	9.19

	Shared-memory RTS		Multicast RTS		Amoeba RTS	
	Third problem					
#CPUs	Time (s)	Speedup	Time (s)	Speedup	Time (s)	Speedup
1	814.0	1.00	852.3	1.00	956.1	1.00
2	411.0	1.98	427.6	1.99	479.3	1.99
3	270.0	3.01	278.2	3.06	312.3	3.06
4	205.0	3.97	209.0	4.08	236.4	4.04
5	169.0	4.82	169.3	5.03	191.2	5.00
6	147.0	5.54	142.8	5.97	162.4	5.89
7	133.0	6.12	123.2	6.92	140.4	6.81
8	125.0	6.51	108.3	7.87	124.2	7.70
9	119.6	6.81	98.1	8.69	111.9	8.54
10	115.6	7.04	88.5	9.63	102.2	9.36

Alpha-beta search

First problem

#CPUs	Shared-memory RTS		Multicast RTS		Amoeba RTS	
	Time (s)	*Speedup*	*Time (s)*	*Speedup*	*Time (s)*	*Speedup*
1	2058.6	1.00	2052.9	1.00	2069.5	1.00
2	1087.3	1.89	1084.2	1.89	1235.0	1.68
3	804.3	2.56	802.4	2.56	808.9	2.56
4	612.3	3.36	610.9	3.36	615.7	3.36
5	522.3	3.94	521.5	3.94	525.5	3.94
6	469.0	4.39	468.4	4.38	472.1	4.38
7	404.3	5.09	403.4	5.09	406.4	5.09
8	369.3	5.57	369.0	5.56	372.0	5.56
9	344.6	5.97	344.8	5.95	347.4	5.96
10	321.6	6.40	321.4	6.39	323.8	6.39

Second problem

#CPUs	Shared-memory RTS		Multicast RTS		Amoeba RTS	
	Time (s)	*Speedup*	*Time (s)*	*Speedup*	*Time (s)*	*Speedup*
1	2032.0	1.00	2026.6	1.00	2042.7	1.00
2	1139.0	1.78	1136.3	1.78	1209.6	1.69
3	804.3	2.53	802.7	2.52	808.7	2.53
4	613.6	3.31	612.4	3.31	617.3	3.31
5	528.0	3.85	527.2	3.84	531.4	3.84
6	458.3	4.43	458.0	4.42	461.1	4.43
7	393.0	5.17	392.4	5.16	395.4	5.17
8	366.3	5.55	366.3	5.53	369.2	5.53
9	331.3	6.13	331.1	6.12	333.7	6.12
10	311.0	6.53	310.5	6.53	312.9	6.53

Third problem

#CPUs	Shared-memory RTS		Multicast RTS		Amoeba RTS	
	Time (s)	*Speedup*	*Time (s)*	*Speedup*	*Time (s)*	*Speedup*
1	1329.0	1.00	1325.0	1.00	1336.0	1.00
2	698.0	1.90	695.8	1.90	746.4	1.79
3	536.3	2.48	535.2	2.48	640.2	2.09
4	419.6	3.17	419.1	3.16	422.5	3.16
5	364.3	3.65	363.6	3.64	366.6	3.64
6	330.3	4.02	329.2	4.02	332.2	4.02
7	318.0	4.18	317.2	4.18	319.8	4.18
8	273.3	4.86	272.7	4.86	275.0	4.86
9	263.6	5.04	259.0	5.12	261.1	5.12
10	261.0	5.09	257.4	5.15	253.0	5.28

The all-pairs shortest paths problem

#CPUs	Shared-memory RTS		Multicast RTS		Amoeba RTS	
	Time (s)	Speedup	Time (s)	Speedup	Time (s)	Speedup
1	398.0	1.00	432.1	1.00	400.0	1.00
2	200.6	1.98	218.9	1.97	204.7	1.95
3	134.3	2.96	148.0	2.92	140.0	2.86
4	101.0	3.94	111.4	3.88	114.1	3.51
5	80.3	4.96	90.0	4.80	95.9	4.17
6	69.3	5.74	77.1	5.60	85.1	4.70
7	60.0	6.63	66.3	6.52	78.2	5.12
8	51.0	7.80	58.2	7.42	73.2	5.46
9	47.3	8.41	53.6	8.06	70.5	5.67
10	42.0	9.48	47.1	9.17	71.2	5.62

Successive overrelaxation

#CPUs	Shared-memory RTS		Multicast RTS		Amoeba RTS	
	Time (s)	Speedup	Time (s)	Speedup	Time (s)	Speedup
1	3032.6	1.00	3051.6	1.00	3071.4	1.00
2	1517.3	2.00	1531.3	1.99	1545.1	1.99
3	1016.3	2.98	1032.7	2.95	1039.8	2.95
4	766.3	3.96	785.5	3.88	788.5	3.90
5	616.6	4.92	639.5	4.77	639.1	4.81
6	516.0	5.88	543.3	5.62	540.8	5.68
7	453.3	6.69	485.4	6.29	480.4	6.39
8	390.0	7.78	427.9	7.13	420.4	7.31
9	353.0	8.59	395.3	7.72	385.3	7.97
10	314.6	9.64	362.5	8.42	352.6	8.71

Performance of the C Programs

This appendix gives the execution times (in seconds) of the two C/Amoeba programs described in Chapter 2. Both programs use one master processor and one or more slave processors, so the number of CPUs used varies between 2 and 10. Each program has been tested with the same three input problems as used for the Orca programs.

The travelling salesman problem

#Slaves	First problem		Second problem		Third problem	
	Time (s)	Speedup	Time (s)	Speedup	Time (s)	Speedup
1	141.3	1.00	83.0	1.00	212.6	1.00
2	74.0	1.91	44.3	1.87	108.6	1.96
3	53.6	2.64	30.6	2.71	72.3	2.94
4	43.0	3.29	25.0	3.32	56.6	3.76
5	38.0	3.72	20.3	4.09	47.0	4.52
6	34.3	4.12	18.3	4.54	40.3	5.28
7	32.0	4.42	16.3	5.09	37.0	5.75
8	30.6	4.62	15.6	5.32	34.3	6.20
9	27.3	5.18	14.6	5.68	31.6	6.73

Alpha-beta search

#Slaves	First problem		Second problem		Third problem	
	Time (s)	*Speedup*	*Time (s)*	*Speedup*	*Time (s)*	*Speedup*
1	2067.0	1.00	2040.0	1.00	1333.3	1.00
2	1091.3	1.89	1143.6	1.78	700.6	1.90
3	808.0	2.56	808.0	2.52	539.0	2.47
4	615.3	3.36	617.0	3.31	424.3	3.14
5	524.6	3.94	532.0	3.83	368.3	3.62
6	473.0	4.37	465.0	4.39	335.6	3.97
7	409.0	5.05	403.0	5.06	319.3	4.18
8	373.3	5.54	374.6	5.45	279.0	4.78
9	351.3	5.88	335.0	6.09	271.3	4.91

References

Abramsky, S. and Bornat, R., (1983), 'Pascal-m: a Language for Loosely Coupled Distributed Systems', pp. 163-189, in *Distributed Computing Systems*, ed. Y. Paker and J.-P. Verjus, Academic Press, London.

Ackerman, W. B., (Feb. 1982), 'Data Flow Languages', *IEEE Computer*, Vol. 15, No. 2, pp. 15-25.

Adamo, J-M., (Oct. 1982), 'Pascal+CSP, Merging Pascal and CSP in a Parallel Processing Oriented Language', *Proc. 3rd Int. Conf. on Distributed Computing Systems*, pp. 542-547, Miami/Ft. Lauderdale, FL.

Agha, G., (Oct. 1986), 'An Overview of Actor Languages', *SIGPLAN Notices*, Vol. 21, No. 10, pp. 58-67.

Aho, A. V., Hopcroft, J. E., and Ullman, J. D., (1974), 'The Design and Analysis of Computer Algorithms', Addison-Wesley, Reading, MA.

Ahuja, S., Carriero, N., and Gelernter, D., (Aug. 1986), 'Linda and Friends', *IEEE Computer*, Vol. 19, No. 8, pp. 26-34.

Ahuja, S., Carriero, N., Gelernter, D., and Krishnaswamy, V., (Aug. 1988), 'Matching Language and Hardware for Parallel Computation in the Linda Machine', *IEEE Trans. Computers*, Vol. C-37, No. 8, pp. 921-29.

Akl, S. G., Barnard, D. T., and Doran, R. J., (Apr. 1980), 'Design, Analysis, and Implementation of a Parallel Alpha-Beta Algorithm', Report 80-98, Kingston, Canada.

Aksit, M. and Tripathi, A., (Nov. 1988), 'Data Abstraction Mechanisms in SINA/st', *SIGPLAN Notices (Proc. Object-Oriented Programming Systems, Languages and Applications 1988)*, Vol. 23, No. 11, pp. 267-75, San Diego, CA.

Almasi, G. S. and Gottlieb, A., (1989), 'Highly Parallel Computing', The Benjamin/Cummings Publishing Company, Redwood City, CA.

Almes, G. T., (May 1986), 'The Impact of Language and System on Remote Procedure Call Design', *Proc. 6th Int. Conf. on Distributed Computing Systems*, pp. 414-21, Cambridge, MA.

Almes, G. T., Black, A. P., Lazowska, E. D., and Noe, J. D., (Jan. 1985), 'The Eden System: A Technical Review', *IEEE Trans. Softw. Eng.*, Vol. SE-11, pp. 43-59.

Ambler, A. L., Good, D. I., Browne, J. C., Burger, W. F., Cohen, R. M., Hoch, C. G., and Wells, R. E., (Mar. 1977), 'GYPSY: A Language for Specification and Implementation of Verifiable Programs', *SIGPLAN Notices*, Vol. 12, No. 3, pp. 1-10.

America, P., (1987), 'POOL-T: A Parallel Object-Oriented Language', pp. 199-220, in *Object-Oriented Concurrent Programming*, ed. A. Yonezawa and M. Tokoro, MIT Press, Cambridge, MA.

America, P., (May 1988), 'Rationale for the design of POOL2', Doc. No. 393, Philips Research Laboratories, Eindhoven, The Netherlands.

251

Andrews, G. R., (Oct. 1981), 'Synchronizing Resources', *ACM Trans. Program. Lang. Syst.*, Vol. 3, No. 4, pp. 405-30.

Andrews, G. R., (Aug. 1982), 'The Distributed Programming Language SR - Mechanisms, Design and Implementation', *Softw. Prac. Exper.*, Vol. 12, No. 8, pp. 719-53.

Andrews, G. R. and Olsson, R. A., (July 1986), 'The Evolution of the SR Programming Language', *Distributed Computing*, Vol. 1, pp. 133-49.

Andrews, G. R., Olsson, R. A., Coffin, M., Elshoff, I., Nilsen, K., Purdin, T., and Townsend, G., (Jan. 1988), 'An Overview of the SR Language and Implementation', *ACM Trans. Program. Lang. Syst.*, Vol. 10, No. 1, pp. 51-86.

Andrews, G. R. and Schneider, F. B., (Mar. 1983), 'Concepts and Notations for Concurrent Programming', *ACM Computing Surveys*, Vol. 15, No. 1, pp. 3-43.

Arvind and Nikhil, R. S., (June 1988), 'Executing a Program on the MIT Tagged-Token Dataflow Architecture', Computation Structures Group Memo 271, MIT, Cambridge, MA.

Athas, W. C. and Seitz, C. L., (Aug. 1988), 'Multicomputers: Message-Passing Concurrent Computers', *IEEE Computer*, Vol. 21, No. 8, pp. 9-24.

Baalbergen, E. H., (Spring 1988), 'Design and Implementation of Parallel Make', *Computing Systems*, Vol. 1, No. 2, pp. 135-58.

Backus, J., (Aug. 1978), 'Can Programming Be Liberated from the von Neumann Style? A Functional Style and Its Algebra of Programs', *Commun. ACM*, Vol. 21, No. 8, pp. 613-41.

Bagrodia, R. and Chandy, K. M., (May 1985), 'A Micro-kernel for Distributed Applications', *Proc. 5th Int. Conf. on Distributed Computing Systems*, pp. 140-49, Denver, CO.

Baiardi, F., Ricci, L., and Vanneschi, M., (June 1984), 'Static Type Checking of Interprocess Communication in ECSP', *SIGPLAN Notices (Proc. SIGPLAN 84 Symp. on Compiler Construction)*, Vol. 19, No. 6, pp. 290-99.

Bal, H. E., Kaashoek, M. F., and Tanenbaum, A. S., (Oct. 1989a), 'A Distributed Implementation of the Shared Data-object Model', *USENIX Workshop on Experiences with Building Distributed and Multiprocessor Systems*, pp. 1-19, Ft. Lauderdale, FL.

Bal, H. E., Kaashoek, M. F., Tanenbaum, A. S., and Jansen, J., (Oct. 1989b), 'Replication Techniques for Speeding up Parallel Applications on Distributed Systems', Report IR-202, Vrije Universiteit, Amsterdam, The Netherlands.

Bal, H. E., Steiner, J. G., and Tanenbaum, A. S., (Sep. 1989c), 'Programming Languages for Distributed Computing Systems', *ACM Computing Surveys*, Vol. 21, No. 3, pp. 261-322.

Bal, H. E. and Tanenbaum, A. S., (1986), 'Language- and Machine-independent Global Optimization on Intermediate Code', *Computer Languages*, Vol. 11, No. 2, pp. 105-21.

Bal, H. E. and Tanenbaum, A. S., (Oct. 1988), 'Distributed Programming with Shared Data', *Proc. IEEE CS 1988 Int. Conf. on Computer Languages*, pp. 82-91, Miami, FL.

Bal, H. E. and Van Renesse, R., (Sep. 1986), 'A Summary of Parallel Alpha-Beta Search Results', *Int. Computer Chess Assoc. Journal*, Vol. 9, No. 3, pp. 146-49.

Bal, H. E., Van Renesse, R., and Tanenbaum, A. S., (June 1987), 'Implementing Distributed Algorithms Using Remote Procedure Calls', *Proc. AFIPS Nat. Computer Conf.*, Vol. 56, pp. 499-506, AFIPS Press, Chicago, IL.

Ball, J. E., Williams, G. J., and Low, J. R., (Sep. 1979), 'Preliminary ZENO Language Description', *SIGPLAN Notices*, Vol. 14, No. 9, pp. 17-34.

Bennett, J. K., (Dec. 1987), 'The Design and Implementation of Distributed Smalltalk', *SIGPLAN Notices (Proc. Object-Oriented Programming Systems, Languages and Applications 1987)*, Vol. 22, No. 12, pp. 318-330, Orlando, FL.

Berglund, E. J., (Aug. 1986), 'An Introduction to the V-system', *IEEE Micro*, Vol. 6, No. 4, pp. 35-52.

Berglund, E. J. and Cheriton, D. R., (May 1984), 'Amaze: A Distributed Multi-Player Game Program using the Distributed V Kernel', *Proc. 4th Int. Conf. on Distributed Computing Systems*, pp. 248-53, San Francisco, CA.

Bernstein, A. J., (Apr. 1980), 'Output Guards and Nondeterminism in Communicating Sequential Processes', *ACM Trans. Program. Lang. Syst.*, Vol. 2, No. 2, pp. 234-238.

Bernstein, P. A. and Goodman, N., (June 1981), 'Concurrency Control in Distributed Database Systems', *ACM Computing Surveys*, Vol. 13, No. 2, pp. 185-221.

Birman, K. P. and Joseph, T. A., (Feb. 1987), 'Reliable Communication in the Presence of Failures', *ACM Trans. Comp. Syst.*, Vol. 5, No. 1, pp. 47-76.

Birrell, A. D. and Nelson, B. J., (Feb. 1984), 'Implementing Remote Procedure Calls', *ACM Trans. Comp. Syst.*, Vol. 2, No. 1, pp. 39-59.

Bisiani, R. and Forin, A., (Oct. 1987), 'Architectural Support for Multilanguage Parallel Programming on Heterogenous systems', *Proc. 2nd Int. Conf. on Architectural Support for Programming Languages and Operating Systems*, pp. 21-30, Palo Alto, CA.

Bjornson, R., Carriero, N., and Gelernter, D., (Mar. 1989), 'The Implementation and Performance of Hypercube Linda', Report RR-690, Yale University, New Haven, CT.

Bjornson, R., Carriero, N., Gelernter, D., and Leichter, J., (Jan. 1988), 'Linda, the Portable Parallel', Research Report 520, Yale University, New Haven, CT.

Black, A., Hutchinson, N., Jul, E., and Levy, H., (Nov. 1986), 'Object Structure in the Emerald System', *SIGPLAN Notices (Proc. Object-Oriented Programming Systems, Languages and Applications 1986)*, Vol. 21, No. 11, pp. 78-86, Portland, OR.

Black, A., Hutchinson, N., Jul, E., Levy, H., and Carter, L., (Jan. 1987), 'Distribution and Abstract Types in Emerald', *IEEE Trans. Softw. Eng.*, Vol. SE-13, No. 1, pp. 65-76.

Black, A. P., Hutchinson, N. C., McCord, B. C., and Raj, R. K., (June 1984), 'EPL Programmer's Guide', University of Washington, Seattle, WA.

Bloch, J. J., (May 1988), 'The Camelot Library', pp. 29-62, in *Guide to the Camelot Distributed Transaction Facility: Release 1*, ed. A. Z. Spector and K. R. Swedlow, Carnegie-Mellon University, Pittsburgh, PA.

Bloom, T., (Dec. 1979), 'Evaluating Synchronization Mechanisms', *Proc. 7th Symp. Operating Systems Principles*, pp. 24-32, ACM SIGOPS, Pacific Grove, CA.

Borg, A., Baumback, J., and Glazer, S., (Oct. 1983), 'A Message System Supporting Fault Tolerance', *Proc. 9th Symp. Operating Systems Principles*, pp. 90-99, ACM SIGOPS, Bretton Woods, NH.

Bray, G., (Sep. 1983), 'Implementation Implications of Ada Generics', *ACM Ada Letters*, Vol. 3, No. 2, pp. 62-71.

Brinch Hansen, P., (1973), 'Operating System Principles', Prentice-Hall, Englewood Cliffs, NJ.

Brinch Hansen, P., (June 1975), 'The Programming Language Concurrent Pascal', *IEEE Trans. Softw. Eng.*, Vol. SE-1, No. 2, pp. 199-207.

Brinch Hansen, P., (Nov. 1978), 'Distributed Processes: A Concurrent Programming Concept', *Commun. ACM*, Vol. 21, No. 11, pp. 934-41.

Brinch Hansen, P., (Jan. 1987), 'Joyce - A Programming Language for Distributed Systems', *Softw. Prac. Exper.*, Vol. 17, No. 1, pp. 29-50.

Browne, J. C., Azam, M., and Sobek, S., (July 1989), 'CODE: A Unified Approach to Parallel Programming', *IEEE Software*, Vol. 6, No. 4, pp. 10-18.

Burns, A., (1988), 'Programming in occam 2', Addison-Wesley, Wokingham, England.

Burns, A. and Davies, G., (Jan. 1988), 'Pascal-FC: A Language for Teaching Concurrent Programming', *SIGPLAN Notices*, Vol. 23, No. 1, pp. 58-66.

Burns, A., Lister, A. M., and Welling, A. J., (1987), 'A Review of Ada Tasking', in *Lecture Notes in Computer Science 262*, Springer-Verlag, Berlin.

Burton, F. W., (Apr. 1984), 'Annotations to Control Parallelism and Reduction Order in the Distributed Evaluation of Functional Programs', *ACM Trans. Program. Lang. Syst.*, Vol. 6, No. 2, pp. 159-74.

Butler, R., Lusk, E., McCune, W., and Overbeek, R., (July 1986), 'Parallel Logic Programming for Numeric Applications', *Proc. 3rd Int. Conf. on Logic Programming*, pp. 375-88, London.

Callahan, C. D., Cooper, K. D., Hood, R. T., Kennedy, K., and Torczon, L., (Winter 1988), 'ParaScope: A Parallel Programming Environment', *Int. J. of Supercomputer Applications*, Vol. 2, No. 4, pp. 84-99.

Cardelli, L. and Wegner, P., (Dec. 1985), 'On Understanding Types, Data Abstraction, and Polymorphism', *ACM Computing Surveys*, Vol. 17, No. 4, pp. 471-522.

Carpenter, B. E. and Cailliau, R., (Sep. 1984), 'Experience with Remote Procedure Calls in a Real-time Control System', *Softw. Prac. Exper.*, Vol. 14, No. 9, pp. 901-7.

Carriero, N., (Dec. 1987), 'The Implementation of Tuple Space Machines', Research Report 567 (Ph.D. dissertation), Yale University, New Haven, CT.

Carriero, N. and Gelernter, D., (May 1986), 'The S/Net's Linda Kernel', *ACM Trans. Comp. Syst.*, Vol. 4, No. 2, pp. 110-29.

Carriero, N. and Gelernter, D., (Apr. 1989), 'Linda in Context', *Commun. ACM*, Vol. 32, No. 4, pp. 444-58.

Carriero, N., Gelernter, D., and Leichter, J., (Jan. 1986), 'Distributed Data Structures in Linda', *Proc. 13th ACM Symp. Princ. Progr. Lang.*, pp. 236-42, St. Petersburg, FL.

Chandy, K. M. and Misra, J., (1988), 'Parallel Programming Design - A Foundation', Addison-Wesley, Reading, MA.

Chase, J. S., Amador, F. G., Lazowska, E. D., Levy, H. M., and Littlefield, R. J., (Apr. 1989), 'The Amber System: Parallel Programming on a Network of Multiprocessors', Report 89-04-01, University of Washington, Seattle, WA.

Cheriton, D. R., (Oct. 1985), 'Preliminary Thoughts on Problem-oriented Shared Memory: A Decentralized Approach to Distributed Systems', *Oper. Syst. Rev.*, Vol. 19, No. 4, pp. 26-33.

Cheriton, D. R., Slavenburg, G. A., and Boyle, P. D., (June 1986), 'Software-Controlled Caches in the VMP Multiprocessor', *13th Symp. on Computer Architecture*.

Clark, K. L., (Dec. 1988), 'PARLOG and Its Applications', *IEEE Trans. Softw. Eng.*, Vol. SE-14, No. 12, pp. 1792-804.

Clark, K. L. and Gregory, S., (Oct. 1981), 'A Relational Language for Parallel Programming', *Proc. 1981 ACM Conf. on Funct. Progr. Lang. and Comp. Arch.*, pp. 171-8, Portsmouth, NH.

Clark, K. L. and Gregory, S., (Apr. 1985), 'Notes on the Implementation of PARLOG', *The Journal of Logic Programming*, Vol. 2, No. 1, pp. 17-42.

Clark, K. L. and Gregory, S., (Jan. 1986), 'PARLOG: Parallel Programming in Logic', *ACM Trans. Program. Lang. Syst.*, Vol. 8, No. 1, pp. 1-49.

Clark, K. L., McCabe, F. G., and Gregory, S., (1982), 'IC-PROLOG Language Features', pp. 253-66, in *Logic Programming*, ed. K. L. Clark and S.-A. Tarnlund, Academic Press, London.

Clarke, L. A., Wileden, J. C., and Wolf, A. L., (Nov. 1980), 'Nesting in Ada is for the Birds', *SIGPLAN Notices (Proc. Symp. on the Ada Programming Language)*, Vol. 15, No. 11, pp. 139-45, Boston, MA.

Cmelik, R. F., Gehani, N. H., and Roome, W. D., (1987), 'Fault Tolerant Concurrent C: A Tool for Writing Fault Tolerant Distributed Programs', AT&T Bell Laboratories, Murray Hill, NJ.

Cmelik, R. F., Gehani, N. H., and Roome, W. D., (1988), 'Experience with Distributed Versions of Concurrent C', AT&T Bell Laboratories, Murray Hill, NJ.

Codish, M. and Shapiro, E., (July 1986), 'Compiling OR-Parallelism into AND-Parallelism', *Proc. 3rd Int. Conf. on Logic Programming*, pp. 283-97, London.

Cohen, J., (Sep. 1981), 'Garbage Collection of Linked Data Structures', *ACM Computing Surveys*, Vol. 13, No. 3, pp. 341-67.

Cook, R. P., (Nov. 1980), '*MOD-A Language for Distributed Programming', *IEEE Trans. Softw. Eng.*, Vol. SE-6, No. 6, pp. 563-71.

Cooper, E. C., (Dec. 1985), 'Replicated Distributed Programs', *Proc. 10th Symp. Operating Systems Principles*, pp. 63-78, ACM SIGOPS, Rosario Resort Orcas Island, WA.

Cooper, R. C. B. and Hamilton, K. G., (Feb. 1988), 'Preserving Abstraction in Concurrent Programming', *IEEE Trans. Softw. Eng.*, Vol. SE-14, No. 2, pp. 258-63.

Crookes, D. and Elder, J. W. G., (Oct. 1984), 'An Experiment in Language Design for Distributed Systems', *Softw. Prac. Exper.*, Vol. 14, No. 10, pp. 957-71.

Dannenberg, R. B., (Mar. 1981), 'AMPL: Design, Implementation and Evaluation of a Multiprocessing Language', Carnegie-Mellon University, Pittsburgh, PA.

Davis, A. L. and Robison, S. V., (Aug. 1985), 'The Architecture of the FAIM-1 Symbolic Multiprocessing System', *Proc. 9th Int. Joint Conf. on Artificial Intelligence*, pp. 32-8, Los Angeles, CA.

Day, M. S., (Apr. 1987), 'Replication and Reconfiguration in a Distributed Mail Repository', Report TR-376, MIT, Cambridge, MA.

Detlefs, D. L., Herlihy, M. P., and Wing, J. M., (Dec. 1988), 'Inheritance of Synchronization and Recovery Properties in Avalon/C++', *IEEE Computer*, Vol. 21, No. 12, pp. 57-69.

Dijkstra, E. W., (Aug. 1975), 'Guarded Commands, Nondeterminacy, and Formal Derivation of Programs', *Commun. ACM*, Vol. 18, No. 8, pp. 453-7.

Douglis, F. and Ousterhout, J., (Sep. 1987), 'Process Migration in the Sprite Operating System', *Proc. 7th Int. Conf. on Distributed Computing Systems*, pp. 18-23, Berlin.

Eichholz, S., (Aug. 1987), 'Parallel Programming with ParMod', *Proc. 1987 Int. Conf. Parallel Processing*, pp. 377-80, St. Charles, IL.

El-Dessouki, O. I. and Darwish, N., (May 1984), 'Distributed Search on Game Trees', *Proc. 4th Int. Conf. on Distributed Computing Systems*, pp. 183-91, San Francisco, CA.

El-Dessouki, O. I. and Huen, W. H., (Sep. 1980), 'Distributed Enumeration on Between Computers', *IEEE Trans. Computers*, Vol. C-29, No. 9, pp. 818-825.

Elias, R-J., (July 1989), 'Oracol, A Chess Problem Solver in Orca', Master thesis, Vrije Universiteit, Amsterdam, The Netherlands.

Elrad, T. and Maymir-Ducharme, F., (Aug. 1986), 'Distributed Languages Design: Constructs for Controlling Preferences', *Proc. 1986 Int. Conf. Parallel Processing*, pp. 176-83, St. Charles, IL.

Ericson, L. W., (Oct. 1982), 'DPL-82: A Language for Distributed Processing', *Proc. 3rd Int. Conf. on Distributed Computing Systems*, pp. 526-31, Miami/Ft. Lauderdale, FL.

Eswaran, K. P., Gray, J. N., Lorie, R. A., and Traiger, I. L., (Nov. 1976), 'The Notions of Consistency and Predicate Locks in a Database System', *Commun. ACM*, Vol. 19, No. 11, pp. 624-33.

Feldman, J. A., (June 1979), 'High Level Programming for Distributed Computing', *Commun. ACM*, Vol. 22, No. 6, pp. 353-68.

Felten, E. W. and Otto, S. W., (Nov. 1988), 'A Highly Parallel Chess Program', *Proc. of the Int. Conf. on Fifth Generation Computer Systems 1988*, pp. 1001-9, Tokyo.

Finkel, R., Anantharaman, A. P., Dasgupta, S., Goradia, T. S., Kaikini, P., Ng, C., Subbarao, M., Venkatesh, G. A., Verma, S., and Vora, K. A., (Feb. 1986), 'Experience with Crystal, Charlotte, and Lynx', Report TR-630, University of Wisconsin at Madison.

Finkel, R. A. and Fishburn, J. P., (1982), 'Parallelism in Alpha-Beta Search', *Artificial Intelligence*, Vol. 19, pp. 89-106.

Finkel, R. A. and Fishburn, J. P., (Jan. 1983), 'Improved Speedup Bounds for Parallel Alpha-Beta Search', *IEEE Trans. on Pattern Analysis and Machine Intelligence*, Vol. PAMI-5, No. 1, pp. 89-92.

Finkel, R. and Manber, U., (Apr. 1987), 'DIB - A Distributed Implementation of Backtracking', *ACM Trans. Program. Lang. Syst.*, Vol. 9, No. 2, pp. 235-56.

Fisher, A. J., (Oct. 1986), 'A Multi-processor Implementation of occam', *Softw. Prac. Exper.*, Vol. 16, No. 10, pp. 875-92.

Flynn, M. J., (1972), 'Some Computer Organizations and Their Effectiveness', *IEEE Trans. Computers*, Vol. C-21, pp. 948-60.

Forman, I. R., (Oct. 1986), 'On the Design of Large Distributed Systems', *Proc. IEEE CS 1986 Int. Conf. on Computer Languages*, pp. 84-95, Miami, FL.

Foster, I., (Aug. 1988), 'Parallel Implementation of PARLOG', *Proc. 1988 Int. Conf. Parallel Processing (Vol. II)*, pp. 9-16, St. Charles, IL.

Foster, I., Gregory, S., Ringwood, G., and Satoh, K., (July 1986), 'A Sequential Implementation of PARLOG', *Proc. 3rd Int. Conf. on Logic Programming*, pp. 149-56, London.

Gabriel, R. P. and McCarthy, J., (1984), 'Queue-based Multi-processing Lisp', *1984 ACM Symp. Lisp and Funct. Progr.*, pp. 25-43, Austin, TX.

Gammage, N. D., Kamel, R. F., and Casey, L. M., (Oct. 1987), 'Remote Rendezvous', *Softw. Prac. Exper.*, Vol. 17, No. 10, pp. 741-55.

Ganapathi, M., Fischer, C. N., and Hennessy, J. L., (Dec. 1982), 'Retargetable Compiler Code Generation', *ACM Computing Surveys*, Vol. 14, No. 4, pp. 573-92.

Gehani, N. H., (1984a), 'Ada: Concurrent Programming', Prentice-Hall, Englewood Cliffs, NJ.

Gehani, N. H., (July 1984b), 'Broadcasting Sequential Processes (BSP)', *IEEE Trans. Softw. Eng.*, Vol. SE-10, No. 4, pp. 343-51.

Gehani, N. H., (1987), 'Message Passing: Synchronous versus Asynchronous', AT&T Bell Laboratories, Murray Hill, NJ.

Gehani, N. H. and Cargill, T. A., (May 1984), 'Concurrent Programming in the Ada Language: The Polling Bias', *Softw. Prac. Exper.*, Vol. 14, No. 5, pp. 413-27.

Gehani, N. H. and Roome, W. D., (Sep. 1986), 'Concurrent C', *Softw. Prac. Exper.*, Vol. 16, No. 9, pp. 821-44.

Gehani, N. H. and Roome, W. D., (Nov. 1988), 'Rendezvous Facilities: Concurrent C and the Ada Language', *IEEE Trans. Softw. Eng.*, Vol. SE-14, No. 11, pp. 1546-53.

Gehani, N. and Roome, W. D., (1989), 'The Concurrent C Programming Language', Silicon Press, Summit, NJ.

Gelernter, D., (1984), 'A Note on Systems Programming in Concurrent Prolog', *Proc. Int. Symp. on Logic Programming*, pp. 76-82, Atlantic City, NJ.

Gelernter, D., (Jan. 1985), 'Generative Communication in Linda', *ACM Trans. Program. Lang. Syst.*, Vol. 7, No. 1, pp. 80-112.

Gelernter, D. and Carriero, N., (1986), 'Linda on Hypercube Multicomputers', *Proc. 1985 SIAM Conference*, pp. 45-55, Knoxville, TN.

Gelernter, D. and Carriero, N., (Sep. 1988), 'Applications Experience with Linda', *SIGPLAN Notices (Proc. PPEALS 1988)*, Vol. 23, No. 9, pp. 173-87.

Gelernter, D., Jagannathan, S., and London, T., (Jan. 1987a), 'Environments as First Class Objects', *Proc. 14th ACM Symp. Princ. Progr. Lang.*, Munich.

Gelernter, D., Jagannathan, S., and London, T., (July 1987b), 'Parallelism, Persistence and Meta-Cleanliness in the Symmetric Lisp Interpreter', *SIGPLAN Notices (Proc. Symp. Interpreters and Interpretive Techniques)*, Vol. 22, No. 7, pp. 274-82.

Geschke, C. M., Morris Jr., J. H., and Satterthwaite, E. H., (Aug. 1977), 'Early Experience with Mesa', *Commun. ACM*, Vol. 20, No. 8, pp. 540-553.

Ghezzi, C. and Jazayeri, M., (1982), 'Programming Language Concepts', John Wiley, New York, NY.

Gifford, D. K., (Dec. 1979), 'Weighted Voting for Replicated Data', *Proc. 7th Symp. Operating Systems Principles*, pp. 150-62, ACM SIGOPS, Pacific Grove, CA.

Goldberg, B. and Hudak, P., (Oct. 1986), 'Alfalfa: Distributed Graph Reduction on a Hypercube Multiprocessor', pp. 94-113, in *Lecture Notes in Computer Science 279 (Proc. Santa Fe Graph Reduction Workshop)*, Springer-Verlag, Berlin.

Goldberg, A. and Robson, D., (1983), 'Smalltalk-80: the Language and its Implementation', Addison-Wesley, Reading, MA.

Goldman, R. and Gabriel, R. P., (July 1989), 'Qlisp: Parallel Processing in Lisp', *IEEE Software*, Vol. 6, No. 4, pp. 51-9.

Graham, P. C. J., (Feb. 1985), 'Using BINS for Inter-Process Communication', *SIGPLAN Notices*, Vol. 20, No. 2, pp. 32-41.

Gregory, S., (1987), 'Parallel Logic Programming in PARLOG', Addison-Wesley, Wokingham, England.

Greif, I., Seliger, R., and Weihl, W., (Jan. 1986), 'Atomic Data Abstractions in a Distributed Collaborative Editing System', *Proc. 13th ACM Symp. Princ. Progr. Lang.*, pp. 160-72, St. Petersburg, FL.

Grimshaw, A. S. and Liu, J. W. S., (Dec. 1987), 'Mentat: An Object-Oriented Macro Data Flow System', *SIGPLAN Notices (Proc. Object-Oriented Programming Systems, Languages and Applications 1987)*, Vol. 22, No. 12, pp. 35-47, Orlando, FL.

Grune, D. and Jacobs, C. J. H., (Jan. 1988), 'A Programmer-friendly LL(1) Parser Generator', *Softw. Prac. Exper.*, Vol. 18, No. 1, pp. 29-38.

Guttag, J. V., (June 1977), 'Abstract Data Types and the Development of Data Structures', *Commun. ACM*, Vol. 20, No. 6, pp. 396-404.

Halstead, Jr., R. H., (Oct. 1985), 'Multilisp: A Language for Concurrent Symbolic Computation', *ACM Trans. Program. Lang. Syst.*, Vol. 7, No. 4, pp. 501-38.

Hamilton, K. G., (Dec. 1984), 'A Remote Procedure Call System', Report TR 70 (Ph.D. dissertation), University of Cambridge, Cambridge, UK.

Herlihy, M. and Liskov, B., (Oct. 1982), 'A Value Transmission Method for Abstract Data Types', *ACM Trans. Program. Lang. Syst.*, Vol. 4, No. 4, pp. 527-51.

Hewitt, C., (June 1977), 'Viewing Control Structures as Patterns of Passing Messages', *Artificial Intelligence*, Vol. 8, No. 3, pp. 323-64.

Hoare, C. A. R., (Oct. 1974), 'Monitors: An Operating System Structuring Concept', *Commun. ACM*, Vol. 17, No. 10, pp. 549-57.

Hoare, C. A. R., (Aug. 1978), 'Communicating Sequential Processes', *Commun. ACM*, Vol. 21, No. 8, pp. 666-677.

Hoare, C. A. R., (Feb. 1981), 'The Emperor's Old Clothes', *Commun. ACM*, Vol. 24, No. 2, pp. 75-83.

Hoare, C. A. R., (1985), 'Communicating Sequential Processes', Prentice-Hall, Englewood Cliffs, NJ.

Holt, R. C., (May 1982), 'A Short Introduction to Concurrent Euclid', *SIGPLAN Notices*, Vol. 17, No. 5, pp. 60-79.

Horiguchi, S. and Shigei, Y., (May 1986), 'A Parallel Sorting Algorithm for a Linearly Connected Multiprocessor System', *Proc. 6th Int. Conf. on Distributed Computing Systems*, pp. 111-18, Cambridge, MA.

Horowitz, E. and Sahni, S., (1976), 'Fundamentals of Data Structures', Pitman Publishing, London.

Houri, A. and Shapiro, E., (July 1986), 'A Sequential Abstract Machine for Flat Concurrent Prolog', Report CS86-20, The Weizmann Institute of Science, Rehovot, Israel.

Hudak, P., (Aug. 1986), 'Para-Functional Programming', *IEEE Computer*, Vol. 19, No. 8, pp. 60-70.

Hudak, P., (Jan. 1988), 'Exploring Parafunctional Programming: Separating the What from the How', *IEEE Software*, Vol. 5, No. 1, pp. 54-61.

Hudak, P. and Smith, L., (Jan. 1986), 'Para-Functional Programming: A Paradigm for Programming Multiprocessor systems', *Proc. 13th ACM Symp. Princ. Progr. Lang.*, pp. 243-54, St. Petersburg, FL.

Hull, M. E. C. and Donnan, G., (Sep. 1986), 'Contextually Communicating Sequential Processes - a Software Engineering Approach', *Softw. Prac. Exper.*, Vol. 16, No. 9, pp. 845-64.

Hummel, S. F., (Dec. 1988), 'SMARTS—Shared-memory Multiprocessor Ada Run Time Supervisor', Ph.D. thesis, New York University, New York, NY.

Hunt, J. G., (Jan. 1979), 'Messages in Typed Languages', *SIGPLAN Notices*, Vol. 14, No. 1, pp. 27-45.

Hur, J. H. and Chon, K., (June 1987), 'Overview of a Parallel Object-Oriented Language CLIX', pp. 265-73, in *Lecture Notes in Computer Science 276 (Proc. European Conference on Object-Oriented Programming)*, Springer-Verlag, Berlin.

Hutchinson, N. C., (Jan. 1987), 'Emerald: An Object-Based Language for Distributed Programming', Report TR 87-01-01 (Ph.D. dissertation), University of Washington, Seattle, WA.

Inmos Ltd., (1984), 'Occam Programming Manual', Prentice-Hall, Englewood Cliffs, NJ.

Ishikawa, Y. and Tokoro, M., (1987), 'Orient84/K: An Object-Oriented Concurrent Programming Language for Knowledge Representation', pp. 159-98, in *Object-Oriented Concurrent Programming*, ed. A. Yonezawa and M. Tokoro, MIT Press, Cambridge, MA.

Jazayeri, M., Ghezzi, C., Hoffman, D., Middleton, D., and Smotherman, M., (Sep. 1980), 'CSP/80: A Language for Communicating Sequential Processes', *IEEE COMPCON Fall 1980*, pp. 736-40, New York, NY.

Jenq, J.-F. and Sahni, S., (Aug. 1987), 'All Pairs Shortest Paths on a Hypercube Multiprocessor', *Proc. 1987 Int. Conf. Parallel Processing*, pp. 713-16, St. Charles, IL.

Jones, A. K. and Schwarz, P., (June 1980), 'Experience Using Multiprocessor Systems- A Status Report', *ACM Computing Surveys*, Vol. 12, No. 2, pp. 121-65.

Joseph, T. A. and Birman, K. P., (Feb. 1986), 'Low Cost Management of Replicated Data in Fault-Tolerant Distributed Systems', *ACM Trans. Comp. Syst.*, Vol. 4, No. 1, pp. 54-70.

Jouvelot, P. and Gifford, D. K., (Oct. 1988), 'The FX-87 Interpreter', *Proc. IEEE CS 1988 Int. Conf. on Computer Languages*, pp. 65-72, Miami, FL.

Jul, E., (Dec. 1988), 'Object Mobility in a Distributed Object-Oriented System', Report TR 88-12-06 (Ph.D. dissertation), University of Washington, Seattle, WA.

Jul, E., Levy, H., Hutchinson, N., and Black, A., (Feb. 1988), 'Fine-Grained Mobility in the Emerald System', *ACM Trans. Comp. Syst.*, Vol. 6, No. 1, pp. 109-33.

Kaashoek, M. F., Bal, H. E., and Tanenbaum, A. S., (Oct. 1989a), 'Experience with the Distributed Data Structure Paradigm in Linda', *USENIX Workshop on Experiences with Building Distributed and Multiprocessor Systems*, pp. 175-191, Ft. Lauderdale, FL.

Kaashoek, M. F., Tanenbaum, A. S., Flynn Hummel, S., and Bal, H. E., (July 1989b), 'An Efficient Reliable Broadcast Protocol', Report IR-195, Vrije Universiteit, Amsterdam, The Netherlands.

Kahn, K., Tribble, E. D., Miller, M. S., and Bobrow, D. G., (Nov. 1986), 'Objects in Concurrent Logic Programming Languages', *SIGPLAN Notices (Proc. Object-Oriented Programming Systems, Languages and Applications 1986)*, Vol. 21, No. 11, pp. 242-57, Portland, OR.

Kernighan, B. W. and Ritchie, D. M., (1978), 'The C Programming Language', Prentice-Hall, Englewood Cliffs, NJ.

Kerridge, J. and Simpson, D., (Jan. 1986), 'Communicating Parallel Processes', *Softw. Prac. Exper.*, Vol. 16, No. 1, pp. 63-86.

Kieburtz, R. A. and Silberschatz, A., (Oct. 1979), 'Comments on Communicating Sequential Processes', *ACM Trans. Program. Lang. Syst.*, Vol. 1, No. 2, pp. 218-25.

Koch, A. and Maibaum, T. S. E., (Oct. 1982), 'A Message Oriented Language for System Applications', *Proc. 3rd Int. Conf. on Distributed Computing Systems*, pp. 824-32, Ft. Lauderdale, FL.

Kramer, J. and Magee, J., (Apr. 1985), 'Dynamic Configuration for Distributed Systems', *IEEE Trans. Softw. Eng.*, Vol. SE-11, No. 4, pp. 424-36.

Krijnen, T. and Meertens, L. G. L. T., (Feb. 1983), 'Making B-Trees work for B', Report IW-219/83, Mathematisch Centrum, Amsterdam, The Netherlands.

Kruatrachue, B. and Lewis, T., (Jan. 1988), 'Grain Size Determination for Parallel Processing', *IEEE Software*, Vol. 5, No. 1, pp. 23-32.

Kung, H. T., (1982), 'Why Systolic Architectures?', *IEEE Computer*, Vol. 15, No. 1, pp. 37-46.

Lai, N. and Miller, B. P., (Aug. 1986), 'The Traveling Salesman Problem: The Development of a Distributed Computation', *Proc. 1986 Int. Conf. Parallel Processing*, pp. 417-20, St. Charles, IL.

Lai, T. H. and Sahni, S., (Aug. 1983), 'Anomalies in Parallel Branch-and-Bound Algorithms', *Proc. 1983 Int. Conf. Parallel Processing*, pp. 183-90.

Lai, T. H. and Sprague, A., (Oct. 1985), 'Performance of Parallel Branch-and-Bound Algorithms', *IEEE Trans. Computers*, Vol. C-34, No. 10, pp. 962-4.

Lamport, L., (July 1978), 'Time, Clocks, and the Ordering of Events in a Distributed System', *Commun. ACM*, Vol. 21, No. 7, pp. 558-65.

Lampson, B. W., (1981), 'Atomic Transactions', pp. 246-65, in *Distributed Systems - Architecture and Implementation*, ed. B. W. Lampson, Springer-Verlag, Berlin.

Lampson, B. W. and Redell, D. D., (Feb. 1980), 'Experience with Processes and Monitors in Mesa', *Commun. ACM*, Vol. 23, No. 2, pp. 105-17.

Lawler, E. L. and Wood, D. E., (July 1966), 'Branch-and-bound Methods: a Survey', *Operations Research*, Vol. 14, No. 4, pp. 699-719.

LeBlanc, T. J. and Cook, P., (June 1983), 'An Analysis of Language Models for High-Performance Communication in Local-Area Networks', *SIGPLAN Notices*, Vol. 18, No. 6, pp. 65-72.

LeBlanc, R. J. and Maccabe, A. B., (Oct. 1982), 'The Design of a Programming Language Based on Connectivity Networks', *Proc. 3rd Int. Conf. on Distributed Computing Systems*, pp. 532-41, Ft. Lauderdale, FL.

LeBlanc, R. J. and Wilkes, T., (May 1985), 'Systems Programming with Objects and Actions', *Proc. 5th Int. Conf. on Distributed Computing Systems*, pp. 132-9, Denver, CO.

Lesser, V., Serrain, D., and Bonar, J., (Oct. 1979), 'PCL - A Process Oriented Job Control Language', *Proc. 1st Int. Conf. on Distributed Computing Systems*, pp. 315-29, Huntsvillle, AL.

Leverett, B. W., G Cattell, R. G., Hobbs, S. O., Newcomer, J. M., Reiner, A. H., Schatz, B. R., and Wulf, W. A., (Aug. 1980), 'An Overview of the Production-Quality Compiler-Compiler Project', *IEEE Computer*, Vol. 13, No. 8, pp. 38-49.

Li, K., (Sep. 1986), 'Shared Virtual Memory on Loosely Coupled Multiprocessors', Research Report 492 (Ph.D. dissertation), Yale University, New Haven, CT.

Li, C., (Apr. 1988a), 'Concurrent Programming Language Lisptalk', *SIGPLAN Notices*, Vol. 23, No. 4, pp. 71-80.

Li, K., (Aug. 1988b), 'IVY: A Shared Virtual Memory System for Parallel Computing', *Proc. 1988 Int. Conf. Parallel Processing (Vol. II)*, pp. 94-101, St. Charles, IL.

Li, K. and Hudak, P., (Aug. 1986), 'Memory Coherence in Shared Virtual Memory Systems', *Proc. 5th Ann. ACM Symp. on Princ. of Distr. Computing*, pp. 229-39, Calgary, Canada.

Li, C.-M. and Liu, M. T., (Apr. 1981), 'Dislang: A Distributed Programming Language/System', *Proc. 2nd Int. Conf. on Distributed Computing Systems*, pp. 162-72, Paris.

Lieberman, H., (1987), 'Concurrent Object-Oriented Programming in Act 1', pp. 9-36, in *Object-Oriented Concurrent Programming*, ed. A. Yonezawa and M. Tokoro, MIT Press, Cambridge, MA.

Liskov, B., (Dec. 1979), 'Primitives for Distributed Computing', *Proc. 7th Symp. Operating Systems Principles*, pp. 33-42, ACM SIGOPS, Pacific Grove, CA.

Liskov, B., (May 1982), 'On Linguistic Support for Distributed Programs', *IEEE Trans. Softw. Eng.*, Vol. SE-8, No. 3, pp. 203-10.

Liskov, B., (Feb. 1984), 'Overview of the Argus Language and System', MIT Programming Methodology Group Memo 40, Cambridge, MA.

Liskov, B., (Mar. 1988), 'Distributed Programming in Argus', *Commun. ACM*, Vol. 31, No. 3, pp. 300-12.

Liskov, B., Curtis, D., Johnson, P., and Scheifler, R., (Nov. 1987), 'Implementation of Argus', *Proc. 11th Symp. Operating Systems Principles*, pp. 111-22, ACM SIGOPS, Austin, TX.

Liskov, B. and Scheifler, R., (July 1983), 'Guardians and Actions: Linguistic Support for Robust, Distributed Programs', *ACM Trans. Program. Lang. Syst.*, Vol. 5, No. 3, pp. 381-404.

Liskov, B. and Shrira, L., (June 1988), 'Promises: Linguistic Support for Efficient Asynchronous Procedure Calls in Distributed Systems', *Proc. of the SIGPLAN 88 Conf. on Progr. Lang. Design and Impl.*, pp. 260-7, Atlanta, GA.

Liskov, B., Snyder, A., Atkinson, R., and Schaffert, C., (Aug. 1977), 'Abstraction Mechanisms in CLU', *Commun. ACM*, Vol. 20, No. 8, pp. 564-76.

Lomet, D. B., (Jan. 1985), 'Making Pointers Safe in System Programming Languages', *IEEE Trans. Softw. Eng.*, Vol. SE-11, No. 1, pp. 87-96.

Lucco, S. E., (1987a), 'A Heuristic Linda Kernel for Hypercube Multiprocessors', *Conf. on Hypercube Multiprocessors*, pp. 32-8.

Lucco, S. E., (Dec. 1987b), 'Parallel Programming in a Virtual Object Space', *SIGPLAN Notices (Proc. Object-Oriented Programming Systems, Languages and Applications 1987)*, Vol. 22, No. 12, pp. 26-34, Orlando, FL.

Lujun, S. and Zhongxiu, S., (Aug. 1987), 'An Object-Oriented Programming Language for Developing Distributed Software', *SIGPLAN Notices*, Vol. 22, No. 8, pp. 51-6.

Maekawa, M., Oldehoeft, A. E., and Oldehoeft, R. R., (1987), 'Operating Systems—Advanced Concepts', The Benjamin/Cummings Publishing Company, Menlo Park, CA.

Marsland, T. A., (Mar. 1986), 'A Review of Game-Tree Pruning', *Int. Computer Chess Assoc. Journal*, Vol. 9, No. 1, pp. 3-19.

Marsland, T. A. and Campbell, M., (Dec. 1982), 'Parallel Search of Strongly Ordered Game Trees', *ACM Computing Surveys*, Vol. 14, No. 4, pp. 533-51.

Matsuoka, S. and Kawai, S., (Nov. 1988), 'Using Tuple Space Communication in Distributed Object-Oriented Languages', *SIGPLAN Notices (Proc. Object-Oriented Programming Systems, Languages and Applications 1988)*, Vol. 23, No. 11, pp. 276-84, San Diego, CA.

May, D., (Apr. 1983), 'Occam', *SIGPLAN Notices*, Vol. 18, No. 4, pp. 69-79.

May, D. and Shepherd, R., (Nov. 1984), 'The Transputer Implementation of occam', *Proc. Int. Conf. on Fifth Generation Computer Systems 1984*, pp. 533-41, Tokyo.

Mehrotra, P. and Van Rosendale, J., (Nov. 1987), 'The Blaze Language: A Parallel Language for Scientific Programming', *Parallel Computing*, Vol. 5, No. 3, pp. 339-61.

Mierowsky, C., Taylor, S., Shapiro, E., Levy, J., and Safra, M., (July 1985), 'The Design and Implementation of Flat Concurrent Prolog', Report CS85-09, The Weizmann Institute of Science, Rehovot, Israel.

Milewski, J., (Sep. 1984), 'Loglan Implementation of the AMPL Message-passing System', *SIGPLAN Notices*, Vol. 19, No. 9, pp. 21-9.

Moss, J. E. B., (1981), 'Nested Transactions: An Approach to Reliable Distributed Computing', Report TR-260 (Ph.D. dissertation), MIT, Cambridge, MA.

Mullender, S. J. and Tanenbaum, A. S., (Aug. 1986), 'Design of a Capability-Based Distributed Operating System', *Computer J.*, Vol. 29, No. 4, pp. 289-99.

Mundie, D. A. and Fisher, D. A., (Aug. 1986), 'Parallel Processing in Ada', *IEEE Computer*, Vol. 19, No. 8, pp. 20-5.

Myers, W., (Mar. 1987), 'Ada: First Users—Pleased; Prospective Users—Still Hesitant', *IEEE Computer*, Vol. 20, No. 3, pp. 68-73.

Needham, R. M. and Herbert, A. J., (1982), 'The Cambridge Distributed Computing System', Addison-Wesley, Reading, MA.

Nehmer, J., Haban, D., Mattern, F., Wybranietz, D., and Rombach, H. D., (Aug. 1987), 'Key Concepts in the INCAS Multicomputer Project', *IEEE Trans. Softw. Eng.*, Vol. SE-13, No. 8, pp. 913-23.

Nelson, B. J., (May 1981), 'Remote Procedure Call', Report CMU-CS-81-119, Carnegie-Mellon University, Pittsburgh, PA.

Ng, K.-W. and Li, W., (May 1984), 'GDPL - A Generalized Distributed Programming Language', *Proc. 4th Int. Conf. on Distributed Computing Systems*, pp. 69-78, San Francisco, CA.

Nierstrasz, O. M., (Dec. 1987), 'Active Objects in Hybrid', *SIGPLAN Notices (Proc. Object-Oriented Programming Systems, Languages and Applications 1987)*, Vol. 22, No. 12, pp. 243-53, Orlando, FL.

Nikhil, R. S., (Aug. 1988), 'ID Reference Manual, Version 88.1', Computation Structures Group Memo 284, MIT, Cambridge, MA.

Ogihara, T., Kajihara, Y., Nagano, S., and Arisawa, M., (1986), 'Concurrency Introduction to an Object-Oriented Language System Ondine', *3rd National Conference Record A-5-1*, Japan Society for Softw. Science and Technology.

Ohki, M., Takeuchi, A., and Furukawa, K., (May 1987), 'An Object-oriented Programming Language Based on the Parallel Logic Programming Language KL1', *Proc. 4th Int. Conf. on Logic Programming*, pp. 894-909, Melbourne, Australia.

Ousterhout, J. K., (Oct. 1982), 'Scheduling Techniques for Concurrent Systems', *Proc. 3rd Int. Conf. on Distributed Computing Systems*, pp. 22-30, Ft. Lauderdale, FL.

Padua, D. A. and Wolfe, M. J., (Dec. 1986), 'Advanced Compiler Optimizations for Supercomputers', *Commun. ACM*, Vol. 29, No. 12, pp. 1184-201.

Papert, S., (1981), 'Mindstorms: Children, Computers and Powerful Ideas', Basic Books, New York, NY.

Patniak, L. M. and Badrinath, B. R., (1984), 'Implementation of CSP-S for Description of Distributed Algorithms', *Computer Languages*, Vol. 9, No. 3, pp. 193-202.

Pereira, L. M., Monteiro, L., Cunha, J., and Aparicio, J. N., (July 1986), 'Delta Prolog: a Distributed Backtracking Extension with Events', *Proc. 3rd Int. Conf. on Logic Programming*, pp. 69-83, London.

Powell, M. L. and Miller, B. P., (Oct. 1983), 'Process Migration in DEMOS/MP', *Proc. 9th Symp. Operating Systems Principles*, pp. 110-19, ACM SIGOPS, Bretton Woods, NH.

Powell, M. L. and Presotto, D. L., (Oct. 1983), 'Publishing: A Reliable Broadcast Communication Mechanism', *Proc. 9th Symp. Operating Systems Principles*, pp. 100-9, ACM SIGOPS, Bretton Woods, NH.

Ranka, S., Won, Y., and Sahni, S., (Sep. 1988), 'Programming a Hypercube Multicomputer', *IEEE Software*, Vol. 5, No. 5, pp. 69-77.

Rashid, R. F. and Robertson, G. G., (Dec. 1981), 'Accent: A Communication Oriented Network Operating System Kernel', *Proc. 8th Symp. Operating Systems Principles*, pp. 64-75, Pacific Grove, CA.

Reppy, J. H., (June 1988), 'Synchronous Operations as First-class Values', *Proc. of the SIGPLAN 88 Conf. on Progr. Lang. Design and Impl.*, pp. 250-9, Atlanta, GA.

Reynolds, T. J., Beaumont, A. J., Cheng, A. S. K., Delgado-Rannauro, S. A., and Spacek, L. A., (Aug. 1988), 'BRAVE - A Parallel Logic Language for Artificial Intelligence', *Future Generations Computer Systems*, Vol. 4, No. 1, pp. 69-75.

Ringwood, G. A., (Jan. 1988), 'PARLOG86 and the Dining Logicians', *Commun. ACM*, Vol. 31, No. 1, pp. 10-25.

Rizk, A. and Halsall, F., (June 1987), 'Design and Implementation of a C-based Language for Distributed Real-time Systems', *SIGPLAN Notices*, Vol. 22, No. 6, pp. 83-96.

Robinson, J. A., (Jan. 1965), 'A Machine-Oriented Logic Based on the Resolution Principle', *Journal of the ACM*, Vol. 12, No. 1, pp. 23-41.

Roman, G.-C., Cunningham, H. C., and Ehlers, M. E., (June 1988), 'A Shared Dataspace Language Supporting Large-scale Concurrency', *Proc. 8th Int. Conf. on Distributed Computing Systems*, pp. 265-72, San Jose, CA.

Roman, G.-C., Ehlers, M. E., Cunningham, H. C., and Lykins, R. H., (Sep. 1987), 'Toward Comprehensive Specification of Distributed Systems', *Proc. 7th Int. Conf. on Distributed Computing Systems*, pp. 282-9, Berlin.

Roper, T. J. and Barter, J., (Nov. 1981), 'A Communicating Sequential Process Language and Implementation', *Softw. Prac. Exper.*, Vol. 11, No. 11, pp. 1215-34.

Russell, R. M., (Jan. 1978), 'The CRAY-1 Computer System', *Commun. ACM*, Vol. 21, No. 1, pp. 63-72.

Safra, S. and Shapiro, E., (Sep. 1986), 'Meta Interpreters for Real', *Proc. IFIPS Congress 86*, pp. 271-78, Dublin, Ireland.

Saltzer, J. H., Reed, D. P., and Clark, D. D., (Nov. 1984), 'End-To-End Arguments in System Design', *ACM Trans. Comp. Syst.*, Vol. 2, No. 4, pp. 277-88.

Sato, M., (May 1987), 'Quty: A Concurrent Language Based on Logic and Function', *Proc. 4th Int. Conf. on Logic Programming*, pp. 1034-56, Melbourne, Australia.

Schaeffer, J., (Feb. 1989), 'Distributed Game-Tree Searching', *J. of Parallel and Distributed Computing*, Vol. 6, No. 1, pp. 90-114.

Schwartz, J. T., Dewar, R. B. K., Dubinsky, E., and Schonberg, E., (1986), 'Programming with Sets: an Introduction to SETL', Springer-Verlag, New York, NY.

Scott, M. L., (May 1985), 'Design and Implementation of a Distributed Systems Language', Report TR-596 (Ph. D. dissertation), University of Wisconsin at Madison.

Scott, M. L., (Aug. 1986), 'The Interface between Distributed Operating System and High-level Programming Language', *Proc. 1986 Int. Conf. Parallel Processing*, pp. 242-9, St. Charles, IL.

Scott, M. L., (Jan. 1987), 'Language Support for Loosely-Coupled Distributed Programs', *IEEE Trans. Softw. Eng.*, Vol. SE-13, No. 1, pp. 88-103.

Scott, M. L. and Cox, A. L., (Sep. 1987), 'An Empirical Study of Message-Passing Overhead', *Proc. 7th Int. Conf. on Distributed Computing Systems*, pp. 536-43, Berlin.

Seitz, C. L., (Jan. 1985), 'The Cosmic Cube', *Commun. ACM*, Vol. 28, No. 1, pp. 22-33.

Shapiro, E., (Feb. 1983), 'A Subset of Concurrent Prolog and its Interpreter', ICOT Report TR-003, Institute for New Generation Computer Technology, Tokyo.

Shapiro, E., (Nov. 1984), 'Systolic Programming: A Paradigm of Parallel Processing', *Proc. Int. Conf. on Fifth Generation Computer Systems 1984*, pp. 458-71, Tokyo.

Shapiro, E., (Aug. 1986), 'Concurrent Prolog: A Progress Report', *IEEE Computer*, Vol. 19, No. 8, pp. 44-58.

Shapiro, E., (1987), 'Concurrent Prolog: Collected Papers', MIT Press, Cambridge, MA.

Shapiro, E. and Mierowsky, C., (1984), 'Fair, Biased, and Self-Balancing Merge Operators: Their Specifications and Implementation in Concurrent Prolog', *J. of New Generation Computing*, Vol. 2, No. 3, pp. 221-40.

Shapiro, E. and Safra, S., (1986), 'Multiway Merge with Constant Delay in Concurrent Prolog', *J. of New Generation Computing*, Vol. 4, No. 3, pp. 211-216.

Shapiro, E. and Takeuchi, A., (1983), 'Object-Oriented Programming in Concurrent Prolog', *J. of New Generation Computing*, Vol. 1, No. 1, pp. 25-48.

Shulman, N. V., (June 1987), 'The Semantics of Shared Variables in Parallel Programming Languages', Ph.D. thesis, New York University, New York, NY.

Silberschatz, A., (Mar. 1984), 'Cell: A Distributed Computing Modularization Concept', *IEEE Trans. Softw. Eng.*, Vol. SE-10, No. 2, pp. 178-85.

Silverman, W., Hirsch, M., Houri, A., and Shapiro, E., (1986), 'The Logix System User Manual', Report CS86-21, The Weizmann Institute of Science, Rehovot, Israel.

Sloman, M. and Kramer, J., (1987), 'Distributed Systems and Computer Networks', Prentice-Hall, Englewood Cliffs, NJ.

Spector, A. Z., Bloch, J. J., Daniels, D. S., Draves, R. P., Duchamp, D., Eppinger, J. L., Menees, S. G., and Thompson, D. S., (Nov. 1986), 'The Camelot Project', Report CMU-CS-86-166, Carnegie-Mellon University, Pittsburgh, PA.

Stammers, R. A., (1985), 'Ada on Distributed Hardware', pp. 35-40, in *Concurrent Languages in Distributed Systems*, ed. G. L. Reijns and E. L. Dagless, Elsevier Science Publishers B.V. (North-Holland).

Staunstrup, J., (1982), 'Message Passing Communication Versus Procedure Call Communication', *Softw. Prac. Exper.*, Vol. 12, No. 3, pp. 223-34.

Stoer, J. and Bulirsch, R., (1983), 'Introduction to Numerical Analysis', Springer-Verlag, New York, NY.

Strom, R. E., (Oct. 1986), 'A Comparison of the Object-Oriented and Process Paradigms', *SIGPLAN Notices*, Vol. 21, No. 10, pp. 88-97.

Strom, R. E. and Yemini, S., (June 1983), 'NIL: An Integrated Language and System for Distributed Programming', *SIGPLAN Notices*, Vol. 18, No. 6, pp. 73-82.

Strom, R. E. and Yemini, S., (July 1984), 'The NIL Distributed Systems Programming Language: A Status Report', *Proc. NSF/SRC Seminar Semantics of Concurrency*, pp. 512-23, in *Lecture Notes in Computer Science 197*, Springer-Verlag, Berlin.

Strom, R. E. and Yemini, S., (1985a), 'Synthesizing Distributed and Parallel Programs through Optimistic Transformations', *Proc. 1985 Int. Conf. Parallel Processing*, pp. 632-41, St. Charles, IL.

Strom, R. E. and Yemini, S., (Aug. 1985b), 'Optimistic Recovery in Distributed Systems', *ACM Trans. Comp. Syst.*, Vol. 3, No. 3, pp. 204-26.

Strom, R. E. and Yemini, S., (Jan. 1986), 'Typestate: A Programming Language Concept for Enhancing Software Reliability', *IEEE Trans. Softw. Eng.*, Vol. SE-12, No. 1, pp. 157-71.

Strom, R. E., Yemini, S., and Wegner, P., (1985), 'Viewing Ada from a Process Model Perspective', *Proc. Conf. Ada in Use*, Paris.

Stroustrup, B., (1986), 'The C++ Programming Language', Addison-Wesley, Reading, MA.

Sugimoto, S., Agusa, K., Tabata, K., and Ohno, Y., (1983), 'A Multi-processor System for Concurrent Lisp', *Proc. 1983 Int. Conf. Parallel Processing*, pp. 135-43, Bellaire, MI.

Swinehart, D. C., Zellweger, P. T., and Hagmann, R. B., (July 1985), 'The Structure of Cedar', *SIGPLAN Notices (Proc. ACM SIGPLAN 85 Symp. Language Issues in Programming Environments)*, Vol. 20, No. 7, pp. 230-44, Seattle, WA.

Tai, K-C. and Carver, R. H., (Oct. 1988), 'Testing and Debugging of Concurrent Software by Deterministic Execution', North Carolina State University, Raleigh, NC.

Takeuchi, A. and Furukawa, K., (1985), 'Bounded Buffer Communication in Concurrent Prolog', *J. of New Generation Computing*, Vol. 3, No. 2, pp. 145-55.

Takeuchi, A. and Furukawa, K., (July 1986), 'Parallel Logic Programming Languages', *Proc. 3rd Int. Conf. on Logic Programming*, pp. 242-54, London.

Tanenbaum, A. S. and Mullender, S. J., (July 1981), 'An Overview of the Amoeba Distributed Operating System', *Oper. Syst. Rev.*, Vol. 15, No. 3, pp. 51-64.

Tanenbaum, A. S. and Van Renesse, R., (Dec. 1985), 'Distributed Operating Systems', *ACM Computing Surveys*, Vol. 17, No. 4, pp. 419-70.

Tanenbaum, A. S. and Van Renesse, R., (Apr. 1988), 'A Critique of the Remote Procedure Call Paradigm', *Proc. of the EUTECO 88 Conf.*, pp. 775-83, ed. R. Speth, North-Holland, Vienna, Austria.

Tanenbaum, A. S., Van Staveren, H., Keizer, E. G., and Stevenson, J. W., (Sep. 1983), 'A Practical Toolkit for Making Portable Compilers', *Commun. ACM*, Vol. 26, No. 9, pp. 654-60.

Tanenbaum, A. S., Van Staveren, H., and Stevenson, J. W., (Jan. 1982), 'Using Peephole Optimization on Intermediate Code', *ACM Trans. Program. Lang. Syst.*, Vol. 4, No. 1, pp. 21-36.

Taylor, S., Av-ron, E., and Shapiro, E., (1987a), 'A Layered Method for Process and Code Mapping', *J. of New Generation Computing*, Vol. 5, No. 2, pp. 185-205.

Taylor, S., Safra, S., and Shapiro, E., (1987b), 'A Parallel Implementation of Flat Concurrent Prolog', *Int. J. of Parallel Programming*, Vol. 15, No. 3, pp. 245-75.

Theimer, M., Lantz, K., and Cheriton, D. R., (Dec. 1985), 'Preemptable Remote Execution Facilities for the V-system', *Proc. 10th Symp. Operating Systems Principles*, pp. 2-12, ACM SIGOPS, Rosario Resort Orcas Island, WA.

Treleaven, P. C., Brownbridge, D. R., and Hopkins, R. P., (Mar. 1982), 'Data-Driven and Demand-Driven Computer Architectures', *ACM Computing Surveys*, Vol. 14, No. 1, pp. 93-143.

Tsujino, Y., Ando, M., Araki, T., and Tokura, N., (Nov. 1984), 'Concurrent C: A Programming Language for Distributed Systems', *Softw. Prac. Exper.*, Vol. 14, No. 11, pp. 1061-78.

Tucker, L. W. and Robertson, G. G., (Aug. 1988), 'Architecture and Applications of the Connection Machine', *IEEE Computer*, Vol. 21, No. 8, pp. 26-38.

US Department of Defense, (Jan. 1983), 'Reference Manual for the Ada Programming Language', ANSI/MIL-STD-1815A.

Ueda, K., (June 1985), 'Guarded Horn Clauses', ICOT Report TR-103, Institute for New Generation Computer Technology, Tokyo.

Van Katwijk, J., (Sep. 1987), 'The Ada- Compiler', Ph.D. dissertation, Delft University of Technology, Delft, The Netherlands.

Van Renesse, R. and Tanenbaum, A. S., (June 1988), 'Voting with Ghosts', *Proc. of the 8th Int. Conf. on Distributed Computing Systems*, pp. 456-62, San Jose, CA.

Van Renesse, R., Van Staveren, J. M., and Tanenbaum, A. S., (Oct. 1988), 'The Performance of the World's Fastest Distributed Operating System', *Oper. Syst. Rev.*, Vol. 22, No. 4, pp. 25-34.

Van Wijngaarden, A., Mailloux, B. J., Peck, J. E. L., Koster, C. H. A., Sintzoff, M., Lindsey, C. H., Meertens, L. G. L. T., and Fisker, R. G., (1975), 'Revised Report on the Algorithmic Language Algol 68', *Acta Informatica*, Vol. 5, pp. 1-236.

Vishnubhotia, P., (June 1988), 'Synchronization and Scheduling in ALPS Objects', *Proc. 8th Int. Conf. on Distributed Computing Systems*, pp. 256-64, San Jose, CA.

Wah, B. W., Li, G.-J., and Yu, C. F., (June 1985), 'Multiprocessing of Combinatorial Search Problems', *IEEE Computer*, Vol. 18, No. 6, pp. 93-108.

Wang, Y. and Morris, R. T. J., (Mar. 1985), 'Load Sharing in Distributed Computer Systems', *IEEE Trans. Computers*, Vol. C-34, No. 3, pp. 204-17.

Weihl, W. and Liskov, B., (Apr. 1985), 'Implementation of Resilient, Atomic Data Types', *ACM Trans. Program. Lang. Syst.*, Vol. 7, No. 2, pp. 244-69.

Welsh, J. and Bustard, D. W., (Nov. 1979), 'Pascal-Plus—Another Language for Modular Multiprogramming', *Softw. Prac. Exper.*, Vol. 9, No. 11, pp. 947-57.

Wichmann, B. A., (Feb. 1984), 'Is Ada Too Big? A Designer Answers the Critics', *Commun. ACM*, Vol. 27, No. 2, pp. 98-103.

Wilkes, C. T. and LeBlanc, R. J., (Oct. 1986), 'Rationale for the Design of Aeolus: A Systems Programming Language for an Action/Object System', *Proc. IEEE CS 1986 Int. Conf. on Computer Languages*, pp. 107-22, Miami, FL.

Wilkes, C. T. and LeBlanc, R. J., (Oct. 1988), 'Distributed Locking: A Mechanism for Constructing Highly Available Objects', *Proc. 7th Symp. Reliable Distributed Systems*, Columbus, OH.

Wirth, N., (1971), 'The Programming Language Pascal', *Acta Informatica*, Vol. 1, No. 1, pp. 35-63.

Wulf, W. A. and Shaw, M., (Feb. 1973), 'Global Variables Considered Harmful', *SIGPLAN Notices*, Vol. 8, No. 2, pp. 80-6.

Xu, A. S., (Aug. 1988), 'A Fault-tolerant Network Kernel for Linda', Report TR-424, MIT, Cambridge, MA.

Yang, R., (1987), 'P-Prolog: a Parallel Logic Programming Language', World Scientific Publishing Co., Singapore.

Yang, R. and Aiso, H., (July 1986), 'P-Prolog: a Parallel Logic Language based on Exclusive Relation', *Proc. 3rd Int. Conf. on Logic Programming*, pp. 255-69, London.

Yemini, S., (1982), 'On the Suitability of Ada Multitasking for Expressing Parallel Algorithms', *AdaTec Conf. on Ada*, pp. 91-7, Arlington, VA.

Yokote, Y. and Tokoro, M., (Nov. 1986), 'The Design and Implementation of ConcurrentSmalltalk', *SIGPLAN Notices (Proc. Object-Oriented Programming Systems, Languages and Applications 1986)*, Vol. 21, No. 11, pp. 331-40, Portland, OR.

Yokote, Y. and Tokoro, M., (1987a), 'Concurrent Programming in ConcurrentSmalltalk', pp. 129-58, in *Object-Oriented Concurrent Programming*, ed. A. Yonezawa and M. Tokoro, MIT Press, Cambridge, MA.

Yokote, Y. and Tokoro, M., (Dec. 1987b), 'Experience and Evolution of ConcurrentSmalltalk', *SIGPLAN Notices (Proc. Object-Oriented Programming Systems, Languages and Applications 1987)*, Vol. 22, No. 12, pp. 406-15, Orlando, FL.

Yonezawa, A., Briot, J-P., and Shibayama, F., (Nov. 1986), 'Object-Oriented Concurrent Programming in ABCL/1', *SIGPLAN Notices (Proc. Object-Oriented Programming Systems, Languages and Applications 1986)*, Vol. 21, No. 11, pp. 258-68, Portland, OR.

Zhongxiu, S. and Xining, L., (Apr. 1987), 'CSM: A Distributed Programming Language', *IEEE Trans. Softw. Eng.*, Vol. SE-13, No. 4, pp. 497-500.

Index